HARRY EMERSON FOSDICK

Harry Emerson Fosdick
Photo courtesy of Elinor Fosdick Downs

HARRY EMERSON FOSDICK

Persuasive Preacher

Halford R. Ryan

Great American Orators, Number 2

Bernard K. Duffy and Halford R. Ryan,
Series Advisers

Greenwood Press
New York • Westport, Connecticut • London

Library of Congress Cataloging-in-Publication Data

Ryan, Halford Ross.
  Harry Emerson Fosdick, persuasive preacher / Halford R. Ryan.
  p.   cm. — (Great American orators, ISSN 0898-8277 ; no. 2)
  Bibliography: p.
  Includes index.
  "Collected sermons and speeches": p.
  ISBN 0-313-25897-X (lib. bdg. : alk. paper)
  1. Preaching—United States—History—20th century. 2. Fosdick,
Harry Emerson, 1879-1969. 3. Sermons, American. 4. Baptists—
Sermons. I. Fosdick, Harry Emerson, 1879-1969. Selections.
1989. II. Title. III. Series.
BV4208.U6R93   1989
251'.0092'4—dc19   88-25101

British Library Cataloguing in Publication Data is available.

Library of Congress Catalog Card Number: 88-25101
ISBN: 0-313-25897-X
ISSN: 0898-8277

First published in 1989

Greenwood Press, Inc.
88 Post Road West, Westport, Connecticut 06881

Printed in the United States of America

The paper used in this book complies with the
Permanent Paper Standard issued by the National
Information Standards Organization (Z39.48-1984).

10 9 8 7 6 5 4 3 2 1

Copyright Acknowledgments

The author and publisher gratefully acknowledge the permission to reprint
material from letters, papers, sermons, sermon notes, and tapes included in
the Fosdick Papers, Burke Library, Union Theological Seminary, New York,
granted by Elinor Fosdick Downs.

Contents

Series Foreword

The idea for a series of books on great American orators grew out of the recognition that there is a paucity of book-length studies on individual orators and their speeches. Apart from a few notable exceptions, the study of American public address has been pursued in scores of articles published in professional journals. As helpful as these studies have been, none has or can provide a complete analysis of a speaker's rhetoric. Book-length studies, such as those in this series, will help fill the void that has existed in the study of American public address and its related disciplines of politics and history, theology and sociology, communication and law. In books, the critic can explicate a broader range of a speaker's persuasive discourse than reasonably could be treated in articles. The comprehensive research and sustained reflection that books require will undoubtedly yield many original and enduring insights concerning the nation's most important voices.

Public address has been a fertile ground for scholarly investigation. No matter how insightful their intellectual forebears, each generation of scholars must reexamine its universe of discourse, while expanding the compass of its researches and redefining its purpose and methods. To avoid intellectual torpor new scholars cannot be content simply to see through the eyes of those who have come before them. We hope that this series of books will stimulate important new understandings of the nature of persuasive discourse and provide additional opportunities for scholarship in the history and criticism of American public address.

This series examines the role of rhetoric in the United States. American speakers shaped the destiny of the colonies, the young republic, and the mature nation. During each stage of the intellectual, political, and religious development of the United States, great orators, standing at the rostrum, on the stump, and in the pulpit, used words and gestures to influence their audiences. Usually striving for the noble, sometimes achieving the base, they urged their fellow citizens toward a more perfect Union.   The books in this series chronicle and explain the accomplishments of representative American leaders as orators.

A series of book-length studies on American persuaders honors the role men and women have played in U.S. history. Previously, if one desired to assess the impact of a speaker or a speech upon history, the path was, at best, not well marked and, at worst, littered with obstacles. To be sure, one might turn to biographies and general histories to learn about an orator, but for the public address scholar these sources often prove unhelpful.   Rhetorical topics, such as speech invention, style, delivery, organizational strategies, and persuasive effect, are often treated in passing, if mentioned at all.   Authoritative speech texts are often difficult to locate and the problem of textual accuracy is frequently encountered. This is especially true for those figures who spoke one or two hundred years ago, or for those whose persuasive role, though significant, was secondary to other leading lights of the age.

Each book in this series is organized to meet the needs of scholars and students of the history and criticism of American public address. Part I is a critical analysis of the orator and his or her speeches. Within the format of a case study, one may expect considerable latitude. For instance, in a given chapter an author might explicate a single speech or a group of related speeches, or examine orations that comprise a genre of rhetoric such as forensic speaking. But the critic's focus remains on the rhetorical considerations of speaker, speech, occasion, and effect. Part II contains the texts of the important addresses that are discussed in the critical analysis that precedes it. To the extent possible, each author has endeavored to collect authoritative speech texts, which have often been found through original research in collections of primary source material. In a few instances, because of the extreme length of a speech, texts have been edited, but the authors have been careful to delete material that is least important to the speech, and these deletions have been held to a minimum.

In each book there is a chronology of major speeches that serves more purposes than may be apparent at first. Pragmatically, it lists all of the orator's known speeches and addresses. Places and dates of the speeches are also listed, although this is information that is sometimes difficult to determine precisely. But in a wider sense, the chronology attests to the scope of rhetoric in the United States. Certainly in quantity, if not always in quality, Americans are historically talkers and listeners.

Because of the disparate nature of the speakers examined in the series, there is some latitude in the nature of the bibliographical materials that have been included in each book. But in every instance, authors have carefully described original historical materials and collections and gathered critical studies, biographies and autobiographies, and a variety of secondary sources that bear on the speaker and the oratory. By combining in each book bibliographical materials, speech texts, and critical chapters, this series notes that text and research sources are interwoven in the act of rhetorical criticism.

May the books in this series serve to memorialize the nation's greatest orators.

Bernard K. Duffy
Halford R. Ryan

Foreword

Although the name Harry Emerson Fosdick does not ring today with the resonance that it did in the 1920s, the issues that Fosdick addressed are still very much alive: the Christian response to war, and the cogency of fundamentalism. Fosdick, a man much involved in the pressing issues of his time, argued for a set of ideals that has transcended his generation. Even if Fosdick had chosen themes that failed to engage public interest, the quality of his oratory would still appeal to today's critics of rhetoric, for his sermons are indisputably models of oral composition. The power of Fosdick's oratory derives, however, from the gravity of the issues he discussed as well as from his deft handling of them.

A distinguished preacher, Fosdick found himself embroiled in two controversies that made his preaching more memorable than that of his contemporaries. The sources of the controversies, war and fundamentalism, were the two great absolutes of his time and it is undoubtedly a mark of Fosdick's philosophical consistency that he could abide neither and felt the need to protest against both. Fosdick understood the Christian conscience to be political and social as well as personal. He believed that the individual's relationship with God has a great deal to do with his relationship with society. Like Soren Kierkegaard's discourses, Fosdick's orations presented sustained meditations and struggles of conscience that edified and uplifted his audiences. Like Kierkegaard, Fosdick was acutely concerned about the rectification of people in the throes of a modern scientific society and a religious faith that bore the trappings of the Middle Ages.

Fosdick's pulpit was Riverside Church in New York City, but his sermons reached a broader audience than the congregation in the neo-Gothic cathedral. His celebrated sermon "Shall the Fundamentalists Win?" received widespread attention and thrust him prominently upon the stage of the great national debate between modernism and that old-time religion. It incurred the wrath of the formidable stumper for fundamentalism, William Jennings Bryan, who indirectly forced Fosdick's resignation from the First Presbyterian Church in New York City.

Ten years later in 1935, Fosdick's valedictory on the subject of modernism, "The Church Must Go Beyond Modernism," seemed more conciliatory toward fundamentalism, and some fundamentalists wished to believe that Fosdick had recanted his earlier position. Like many a forceful but thoughtful advocate, Fosdick simply wanted to make his thinking clearer. There was, he argued, a danger in allowing religion to become too intellectual, for modernism should not wash away spirituality or the belief in God's reality.

The second theme for which Fosdick was well known was pacifism, which he preached in "A Christian Conscience About War," delivered before the representatives of the first countries to join the ill-fated League of Nations in the wake of World War I. In his elegiacal oration "The Unknown Soldier," Fosdick agonized over his role in strengthening the resolve of those who had entered the war to end all wars. His pacifism was born in a personal battle of conscience and in his deep sense of regret for promoting war. Fosdick's ethos is of the modern man struggling to understand rationally and spiritually the worst the twentieth century had brought: a total war requiring an unprecedented national resolve that had left little room for religious reflection.

His sermons and speeches represented in religion the practical rationality Fosdick's contemporary John Dewey had sought in his system of reflective problem-solving. Fosdick began with socially representative "felt difficulties," to use Dewey's term, and sought through a process of careful reflection to solve moral dilemmas of great immediacy. He was not concerned with theological questions for their own sake, but with matters that profoundly touched the lives of his parishioners.

It is appropriate that this book should have been written by Professor Halford Ryan, an experienced and perceptive rhetorical critic, whose own writing exhibits the careful reflection one finds in Fosdick's sermons. As a young student at Princeton Theological Seminary, Ryan found himself drawn more to the allied discipline of rhetoric, yet his understanding of the role of the clergy has enriched this study of a most significant preacher. Ryan's commitment to careful research and his use of archival collections will further enhance the value of this study.

In this, an era marked by political activism among fundamentalists, Fosdick's arguments speak eloquently to the question of the place of religion in the lives of individuals and in the life of the nation. Fosdick's poignant endorsement of pacifism stands as a testament to the importance of religion in resolving questions of ethics. On these and many other themes Fosdick presented gripping soliloquies that pricked the conscience of his generation.

Bernard K. Duffy

Preface

From Puritan times to the present, religious rhetoric has played an important role in the political and social life of the United States. Upon occasion, it has revealed the highest and lowest attainments of Americans.

Preaching had its roots in early Christianity, was practiced by the early apostles, especially St. Paul, and triumphed as the state religion in the Roman Empire under the Emperor Constantine in the fourth century. (*In hoc signo vinces*, in this sign you will conquer, which was emblazoned on Constantine's war flags, will play an important part in this book.) Under the banner of *sola scriptura*, great Protestant preachers, such as Martin Luther and John Calvin, re-emphasized the importance of the spoken word, as juxtaposed to a chanted liturgy, in the Reformation. Unfortunately, the Word of God was not always precise on all religious peccadilloes, so ardent reformers turned on their fellow human Christians, with an intolerance and ferocity that would make Beelzebub blush, over such matters as whether one should be baptized by sprinkling, dunking, or immersing, and whether Communion should be taken with fermented wine or unfermented grape juice. Not to be outdone by their Protestant counterparts, the Catholic Church mounted its own counter reformation that descended into the hell of the Inquisition. Never comfortable bedfellows, Protestants and Catholics could at least agree on their intolerance for Jews. And King Henry VIII founded the British state religion, among other considerations, over the divorce of Katherine of Aragon to marry Anne Boleyn.

When the Puritans landed in Massachusetts to work out their temporal and spiritual salvation, they brought to the New World propagations from the Old World: a spiritual seed and a worthless weed. They planted in the wilderness a reverence for the Word of God and a bigotry for any other way of preaching the Gospel. Although the Salem witch trials in the mid-seventeenth century witnessed the last excesses of European-style religious persecution in the colonies, intolerance lurked always at the edges of a well-manicured national religiosity: witness the anti-Catholicism of the mid-nineteenth century and the prejudice against presidential candidates Al Smith in 1928 and John Kennedy in 1960, and the anti-Mormonism that motivated Brigham Young to move to Deseret, to name a few examples. In times of spiritual drought, narrow-mindedness flourished as liberalism withered.

The late nineteenth and early twentieth century in the United States was such a time. Reeling from the onslaught of scientific discovery and the industrial revolution, Darwinian evolution and the robber barons, exclusionists who saw not the morning gilding the skies but the day dying in the west, retrenched to narrow valleys that usually comfort constricted minds. Believing that heavenly truth could be distilled into earthly truth, holding that the one God ordained only one way, preferring polarity to possibility, perceiving black and white rather than grey, not to mention God's rainbow, some religious figures decided to cope by relying on certain "fundamentals" that represented their Christianity. Reacting to the fossilized rocks they so feared, the fundamentalists countered with their version of Holy Writ written in granite, which, by Anglican Bishop Ussher's calculations, was only some six thousand years old. In the late nineteenth century, the Reverend Henry Ward Beecher raised his voice against the conservatives, but it fell to the Reverend Dr. Harry Emerson Fosdick to continue the persuasive work from the pulpit in the twentieth century.

Pastors and priests are not usually perceived as orators. As popularly conceived, persuasive prowess is usually associated with politicians and secular issues whereas the pulpit is reserved for ministerial matters. The richness of American oratory transcends such sterile roles.

Americans were electrified when William Jennings Bryan, the Great Commoner, delivered his "Cross of Gold" speech, with its obvious religious references, that won for him the Democratic presidential nomination in 1896. Fundamentalists welcomed Bryan when he transferred his secular oratorical training to a sacred role in the prosecution of John Scopes at Dayton, Tennessee, in 1925. Yet, just as Theodore Roosevelt made the presidency a bully pulpit and Republican presidents after World War I until the Depression preached a gospel of laissez faire economics, upon occasion men of the cloth seemed as well cut for the public platform as for the pulpit. Concerning this calling, Henry Ward Beecher immediately comes to mind as an exemplar in the nineteenth century: he seemed at home in his pulpit at Plymouth Church or on the Lyceum lecture circuit or on some secular rostrum; in the twentieth century, the Catholic church, generally not noted for generating great preachers because of its emphasis on liturgy, produced Father Charles Coughlin and Bishop Fulton J. Sheen, the one known for his mastery over the radio, the other for his commanding presence on television; the exigencies of black liberation called forth the voices of Father Divine, the Reverend Martin Luther King, Jr., and, most recently, the Reverend Jesse Jackson; Baptist polity has given the United States in the late twentieth century the Reverend Billy Graham and the Reverend Jerry Falwell; and assorted televangelists vie for Nielsen ratings as well as for souls. But the preacher who towers above them all, like the spire of his church on Riverside Drive that dominates the skyline of uptown New York City, is Harry Emerson Fosdick.

Such a man has not gone unnoticed. Taken separately, the parts of this book have been treated by other authors or editors. If this book were a biography of Fosdick, it would pale in comparison with Robert Moats Miller's impressive and definitive *Harry Emerson Fosdick: Preacher, Pastor, Prophet*. Neither could it stand as a collection of essays about Fosdick's preaching, because Lionel Crocker's *Harry Emerson Fosdick's Art of Preaching: An Anthology* accomplished that goal admirably well. Larry Moody assembled a fine bibliography of works by and about Fosdick, and Fosdick's sermons have been reprinted in his many books.

But taken together, the parts of this book give a synergism that has not obtained elsewhere. As a volume in the "Great American Orators" series, the work offers speech and sermon texts that figured prominently in the preacher's oratorical career, texts that are admittedly available but inconveniently scattered in Fosdick's books. A definitive alphabetical calendar of speeches and sermons and a chronology of sermons, which were not available heretofore, present in an orderly fashion Fosdick's oratorical pastorate. A bibliography details the works by and about Harry Emerson Fosdick. Most important, however, is the epicenter of the book around which the rest of these materials revolve.

The purpose of the book is to demonstrate that Fosdick was an orator. He cultivated the liberal seed among the conservative weed by means of the spoken word. Although his object of an inclusive church was completed by 1946 when he retired from the active pulpit, his husbandry of the cause has survived him in spirit if not in name. That the tenets of liberalism or modernism triumphed in the 1920s and remain more or less viable today is in no small measure accountable to the persuasive preaching of Harry Emerson Fosdick. He gave sermons and speeches that were spoken masterpieces, yet his critics have failed to appreciate the rhetorical techniques that innervated his persuasions and sustained his pastorates. Fosdick's success as a preacher and speaker attests to the fact that he knew what to do and how to do it. To review the persuasive choices he made at important junctures in his and the nation's life is to appreciate a craftsman at work with words. In fine, what the book sacrifices in breadth of biographical scope it hopefully requites in depth of rhetorical focus.

That his persuasive ministry was not totally successful, not in terms of his immediate congregation but in relationship to society at large, is witnessed by the resurgence of the so-called fundamentalist movement in the late twentieth century. This fact, which is not ascribable to Fosdick's lack of rhetorical talents, only confirms what gardeners and preachers know: that weeds are perennially hardy in almost any ground, and that the spoken word is sometimes sown successfully in fertile soil, may land in the fallow, and often falls flat.

Acknowledgments

This book exists in great measure due to the kindness of Dr. Elinor Fosdick Downs who graciously granted permission for the frontispiece, to quote extensively from her father's papers, and to reprint his sermons and voice recordings. Her permission does not imply an acceptance or rejection of my findings. Rather, I take it to bear witness to her belief that any rhetorical scholar who investigates the Reverend Harry Emerson Fosdick's speeches can not help affirming, concerning Fosdick's persuasive ministry, Matthew 25:21: "His master said to him, 'Well done, good and faithful servant.'"

My interest in Fosdick was sparked as an undergraduate student in speech at Wabash College, ignited in one year at Princeton Theological Seminary on a Rockefeller Theological Fellowship, fanned as a graduate student in speech communication at the University of Illinois, and brought to flame as an instructor at Washington and Lee University, where I began the circle anew with my own students. It is difficult to record precisely the interplay of ideas that followed from numerous lectures on and discussions about Fosdick's major sermons and speeches in American public address courses I have taught over the years, not to mention those courses in which I was a student. Suffice it to say that vestiges of those conversations inhere herein.

To the staff at Burke Library, Union Theological Seminary, New York City, and especially to archivist Seth Kasten who helped me immensely with the Fosdick papers, I express my sincere gratitude. Eleanor Godfrey at Union Theological Seminary, Richmond, Virginia, also provided me with valuable video and audio recordings of Fosdick's sermons. Peggy Hayes of the Washington and Lee University Library helped me with computerized bibliographical searches.

For the living of my days in research, I wish to thank John Elrod, Dean of the College, Washington and Lee University, for shepherding my request for a John W. Glenn Grant to conduct research in the two Unions. Without that subvention this book could not be. Karen Lyle, secretary of the department of religion, typed the speech texts. Ruth Floyd helped me immeasurably with the computer.

Marcus Loew, of the Loew chain of movie palaces that pampered their patrons in the 1920s and 1930s, is reputed to have remarked, "We sell tickets to theaters, not to movies." Without disparaging Fosdick's oratory, it may be safely ventured that few ministers had such an atmosphere as Riverside Church in which to preach. The Riverside Church is inspirational. By the hours of the great bourdon bell and in the shadow of its bell tower I began this book. In the Riverside tradition, organist Dr. John Walker kindly granted me permission to play the superb Aeolian-Skinner five manual pipe organ in the chancel.

Withal, I trust that my pleasant research period at Union has not unduly influenced my treatment of Fosdick's rhetoric. To that end, I wish to thank Bernard K. Duffy, my coeditor for two reference books on American oratory, who read the manuscript. He endeavored to make certain, with regard to diction, that *nihil obstat*. Therefore, any shortcomings are mine.

I
HARRY EMERSON FOSDICK

Introduction

The Reverend Dr. Harry Emerson Fosdick was a preeminent preacher from the 1920s to his retirement in 1946. He spoke from one of the famous pulpits in the country, the Riverside Church in New York City, and addressed his countrymen in the National Vespers radio program for twenty years. During this era, fraught with the concerns of the peace movement and the contest of liberalism versus fundamentalism, Fosdick not only contributed to the national discussion of these issues but also influenced a generation of preachers. He taught homiletics at Union Theological Seminary in New York City, and he reached other ministers through his numerous books and still others over the radio. Dr. Fosdick's persuasive practices continue to inform Christian suasory discourse.

This book is not about Fosdick's life and time, nor is it a history of religious issues between the two world wars or an explication of his doctrines and theology. However, these matters are within the scope of this study, as it focuses on Fosdick foremostly as a rhetorician, a practitioner of the art of persuasive discourse. The fact is that his oratory placed him in his prestigious pulpits, it innervated his career at critical junctures in his and the nation's religious life, and it kept his voice and views before an adoring, although sometimes antagonistic, audience. The subtitle of this book suggests the reason for Fosdick's fame and--in the view of the fundamentalists--his infamy. As a persuasive preacher, Fosdick crafted sermons to satisfy the spiritual needs of people in a secular context. He addressed everyday problems his audiences faced and counseled solutions his listeners could apply in their daily lives. This people-centered, rather than doctrine-centered, sermonizing was effective because Fosdick constructed his homilies for results by treating the here-and-now rather than the hereafter.

Fosdick was born a Baptist in 1878. His father was a professor of Greek and Latin, so young Harry had an affinity for Biblical studies. At

Colgate University (A.B., 1900), he rebelled against religion but returned in his senior year to a belief in God. At Union Theological Seminary (B.D., 1904), he pursued his progressive leanings that were reinforced by a liberal Presbyterian faculty. Upon graduation, he assumed the pastorate of the First Baptist Church of Montclair, New Jersey. He also returned to Union to teach and became in 1915 Morris K. Jessup Professor of Practical Theology. Because of Union's kinship with Presbyterian professors and contacts Fosdick had established while there, he was called as an associate pastor to the First Presbyterian Church of New York City in January 1919. He resigned that position in 1925 over the fundamentalist-modernist controversy, spent ten months abroad, and returned to the pulpit of the Park Avenue Baptist Church, New York City, in October 1926. In 1930, the congregation, accepting an interdenominational status at Fosdick's request, moved to the new neo-Gothic Riverside Church. He retired at age sixty-eight in 1946.

Chapter 1, "A Preacher Preaching," is a prolegomenon to a study of Fosdick's pastoral oratory. As a rhetorical technician, he developed a writing-sermonizing-publishing regimen that contributed to his varied ministries. His sermon preparation and organizational strategies were shaped by his collegiate training in speech. He was one of the first ministers to use the radio and his conversational delivery and style of language were well adapted to that medium. Fosdick's success in the pulpit was due in great measure to his firm foundation in the discipline of public speaking, a debt he freely acknowledged.

Chapter 2, "Fosdick vs. the Fundamentalists," is an exegesis of that critical debate. Two sermons are investigated: "Shall the Fundamentalists Win?" delivered in 1922, and because they did, his "Valedictory," delivered in 1925. Both of these homilies were preached at the First Presbyterian Church. The first one thrust him into the national debate on religious fundamentalism versus liberalism, coalesced the issues for public consumption, and eventually led to Baptist Fosdick's leaving his Presbyterian pulpit, from which he delivered his moving and widely disseminated apologia. This sequence of events led to his call to Park Avenue and then to Riverside, which John D. Rockefeller, Jr., built for about six million dollars in 1928-1930.

Chapter 3, "Quo Vadis: God of War or Peace," displays the disjunct that Fosdick consistently affirmed after his involvement in World War I. On secular platforms as well as in sacred pulpits, Fosdick cogently, if not convincingly, argued as World War II approached that one cannot reconcile Christianity with war. Two speeches exemplify his civic rhetoric: "A Christian Conscience About War," delivered in Geneva, Switzerland, in 1925, and "My Account with the Unknown Soldier," delivered at a peace rally in New York City in 1934. These addresses identified him with the pacifist movement of the 1920s and 1930s. A close analysis of these speeches, in conjunction with other ones he delivered even to the eve of the United States's entry into World War II, will demonstrate the timeliness of Fosdick's responses to war for his generation and the timelessness of his remarks to the tension between Mars and Christ. Even in his eighties, he lent his name to the anti-Vietnam War movement.

Chapter 4 is "Reforming the Reform: Going Beyond Modernism." As eloquently as Fosdick had advocated liberalism in his early days, he perceived that, as a molder of the modernist movement, he had strayed too far from the Gospel, had stressed humanity almost to the exclusion of the divinity. He rectified his error in another landmark sermon, "The Church Must Go Beyond Modernism," 1935. It was Fosdick's mea culpa. He did not please the complacent modernists because he advocated eschewing an easy romantic religion; he did not satisfy the fundamentalists because he refused to return to the fold by stressing doctrinal creeds. It was pure Fosdick: only Christ could help men and women to attain their full measure of personality.

Chapter 5 examines "Preaching at Riverside." Stellar speeches simply did not sustain Fosdick's Sunday-to-Sunday sermonic successes, so one representative homily will be discussed. "Handling Life's Second-Bests," first delivered in 1922 and redelivered in 1931, 1938, and 1944, is typical of the themes he preached on countless Sundays and illustrates many of the persuasive practices he used in his talks. This sermon is also an interesting case study to illustrate how he revised his thoughts. Based on a careful textual analysis of how the sermon evolved over a twenty-two year period, one can gauge the growth of Fosdick as a writer-speaker.

The back matter consists of several categories that are designed to help the researcher of Dr. Fosdick's rhetoric. First, one can find authoritative texts of the speeches and sermons discussed in the critical chapters. These speeches, often transcribed stenographically by Margaret Renton, Fosdick's secretary until 1939, were authenticated by research in the Fosdick Collection, Union Theological Serminary, New York City, and in Union Theological Seminary, Richmond, Virginia. Of particular significance is his "Shall the Fundamentalists Win?" which is printed with the alternate title and captioned heads that sensationalized this sermon to the national audience.

Second, one will find an alphabetical listing of Fosdick's sermons with the dates and places of delivery. Admittedly, a chronology of sermons could be helpful, but an alphabetical calendar was deemed more efficacious for the following reasons: (1) the sermons are better known by title than date; (2) his important sermons have been anthologized by name rather than date; and (3) Fosdick often delivered a revised sermon several times, and many sermons were often delivered on the National Vespers program weeks or even months later. Therefore, it is more instructive in Fosdick's case to find a sermon title with its dates of delivery than to search for a title throughout a chronology. The alphabetical calendar also indicates, where appropriate, publication data for sermons that were collected in Fosdick's own books.

Third, a chronology of speeches lists secular addresses organized by date. In all, some fifteen hundred addresses and sermons are thus described and listed.

Fourth, the bibliography details Fosdick's books, the forewords and introductions he wrote for other authors' books and editors' anthologies, his essays, and articles about him.

As Fosdick wrote his sermons and addresses for effect, so should this book have a purpose. The issues he addressed three generations ago--tolerance, liberalism and peace--have never triumphed completely, and are ironically being debated in the late twentieth century by the same kind of mentality that propelled attacks against Fosdick in the 1920s and 1930s. Fosdick's rhetoric prevailed in his day but, lacking a national spokesman in his mold, his views cannot be expected to quell the chorus of the video vicars. As for peace, his antiwar rhetoric was paradoxically similar to the militarism he decried. When a war came, critics have scored the U.S. for being well prepared to fight the previous war. Fosdick made a compelling stand on the peace issue after World War I, but his consistency blinded him to new and different arguments for U.S. intervention in World War II. Yet the honesty and integrity with which Fosdick addressed the peace debate is commendable, if for no other reason, because it compels Americans to pause before Armageddon.

The orator's craft is working with transient words that obtain permanency only on the printed page. On his deathbed, Daniel Webster is reputed to have said, "And yet I still live." Interpreters have taken that enigmatic statement to mean that Webster, a member of the triumvirate that held sway in the United States Senate during the golden age of American oratory, would endure through his speeches on the leading secular issues of his era. One seeks in vain Webster's voice in the old Senate chamber, yet he lives in his addresses. Likewise, one cannot find Fosdick at Riverside but one can feel his spiritual and intellectual presence there. Mindful of Sir Christopher Wren's famous inscription in St. Paul's Cathedral in London, *Si Monumentum Requiris, Circumspice* (If you require a monument, look around), one can read an appropriate tribute to Fosdick inscribed in the limestone walls of Riverside Church, but those walls ceased to echo his voice over forty years ago. If one requires a fitting memorial for Fosdick, it is surely to be found in the speeches and addresses through which he spoke and still speaks to the living of these days.

1
A Preacher Preaching

The nexus of Harry Emerson Fosdick's career was his ability to write for preaching and to preach in writing. "Translated by his pen and his voice," wrote Graham Hodges, "the foolishness of Christ has made sense to the cynics. Millions revolting from what now seems the incredible fundamentalism of the early 1900s drank from his fountains as thirsty men in a desert." In Fosdick, the twin but not always complementary talents of writing and speaking were admirably intertwined: "I do not see how a man can preach without writing. I have always thought with my pen in hand. My preaching naturally began to turn into books."[1]

The rhetorical habits that served Fosdick so well throughout his career were rooted in his education at Colgate University. With a firm foundation in the Bible, literature, and history, he possessed the intellectual materials to write well. He reported that as he wrote, he often consulted his two dictionaries for better expression. Moreover, he was thoroughly grounded in how to speak effectively. From courses in rhetoric and public speaking, he learned audience analysis, argumentation, organization, and delivery. He confessed that it was his undergraduate training in speech, which emphasized obtaining a response from the audience, that saved him in his first pastorate.[2]

A corollary of his education in speech was his ability to craft homilies in an oral style. At the level of craftsmanship, which Fosdick obtained, the writer-speaker composes for the ear. In two dictations, apparently in response to questions about his practices, he advised:

> The key to effectively written sermons lies, I think, in a vivid visualization of the audience. One can in imagination see his congregation while he writes, and can write as though he were speaking directly to them. Never write a sermon to be read; always write a sermon to be talked! In this way only can the discipline of writing be

combined with the freedom of direct address to a living
audience.

I have for all my ministry written every word of
every sermon that I preached. I do not see how anyone
can keep strength of thought and variety and facility of
language and illustration, if he does not discipline himself
to the severe task of writing everything he says. I have not
always delivered them as I have written them, but that
primary discipline, I think, is indispensable to preaching, if
it is going to grow and not slump as the years pass.

His rationale explains his phenomenal success as an orator-writer.
Relying on stenographic recordings of his words, Fosdick published two
early collections of sermons, *The Second Mile* and *The Manhood of the
Master* with the Association Press. This was his modus operandi for
subsequent anthologies of homilies.[3]

The Reverend Fosdick maintained a writing-for-speaking routine
throughout his professional ministry. Renting an unmarked room in
Montclair, New Jersey, he devoted three to four uninterrupted hours
every weekday to composing his sermons. He carried this practice
forward to the First Presbyterian Church, thence to the Park Avenue
Baptist Church, and finally to the Riverside Church. The care with which
he crafted his talks was doubly rewarded. After the successes of his early
books, he must have realized he could reach two audiences. With one
compositional effort, he concomitantly addressed the spiritual needs of
his immediate listeners and reached his reading public.

Although it is impossible to delineate the nature of Fosdick's
reading and radio audiences, the three congregations he served were
remarkably similar. One imagines that the socioeconomic distinctions
between his live and radio audiences were minimal. *Time* characterized
his first pastorate at Montclair and noted why the church called Fosdick:
"a prosperous to affluent suburb, which would have no youth but the
ablest." The First Presbyterian Church, the name of which speaks for
itself, ranked in the social cachet of New York City. So did the Park
Avenue Baptist Church, which numbered among its members John
Davison Rockefeller, Jr. Rockefeller helped attract Fosdick to the Park
Avenue pulpit with the understanding that the congregation, and the core
of what was to become the largest carillon in the world, would move to
a new location. Of the Riverside area, located at the academic acropolis
of New York City--comprised of Columbia University, Barnard College,
Union Theological Seminary, and Jewish Theological Seminary--*Time*
noted the nature of the audience that consisted of "professors and friends
of professors, thousands of educated people who live nearby and have
jobs of more or less importance 'down town.' And, besides these, just
people--one or two hundred thousand who live in tall medium-priced
apartment houses within walking distance."[4]

Before considering what he said to those people, it would be wise to explore how Fosdick composed his sermons. Handwritten materials in the Fosdick Collection are scant. Dorothy Noyes, his secretary, recalled that Fosdick burned his Montclair sermons; fortunately, typescript works, on which he made emendations, exist for the post-Montclair period.

Fosdick wrote cleanly. For instance, in writing a twenty-five line insert he added to a typed copy of "Lectures to the Missionaries in the Orient, I: Christianity and the Social Movement," 1921, he made only seven carat insertions and two deletions in diction. In redrafting "Handling Life's Second-Bests," a sermon to be discussed fully in Chapter 5, he made numerous changes, but these were surefooted because he took no second steps in revising his revisions; moreover, on an insert that consisted of eleven lines in his handwriting with characteristic purple ink, there were four deletions and one use of the carat. The point is, although he may have thought aloud before he wrote, he was a very efficient and accurate craftsman. This idea was affirmed by Eugene Exman, Fosdick's editor at Harper, which published eighteen of Fosdick's books. Upon receiving *The Hope of the World*, 1933, Exman had "a publisher's prayer," a book that was "written with a careful and experienced hand. No pretentious oratory, no embellished phrasings. No needless repetitions to be edited. What he had to say was in clean, clear prose. . . . The choice of a word, the pertinence of a phrase, and the cadence of a sentence have been carefully scrutinized before manuscript submission." [5]

Although it is afield to discuss Fosdick's theology in detail, rudiments of it must be known in order to appreciate what he said. He was primarily concerned with people, their personalities, the living of their lives. As an interdenominationalist he cared not for creeds but for Christian virtues and behaviors. As a liberal he wanted to free men and women from dogma so that they could experience religion. As a twentieth-century apologist for a post-Darwin Christianity, he did not ask believers to sacrifice their intelligence. "Yet," one critic observed, "his sermons were not so secularized as to be devoid of religious feelings and belief, for as adept as Fosdick was in the art of persuasion, his sermons still evinced a preacher calling man to man and, more important, man to God." [6]

Radio and Fosdick were inextricably linked. Although never given a sobriquet such as "The Radio Priest," as was Father Charles Coughlin, who began broadcasting in 1926, Fosdick was nevertheless intimately associated with the National Vespers, a pivotal part of his ministry. Fosdick could address twenty-five hundred people at Riverside compared with a national radio audience that numbered in the millions. The beginning was modest enough. His first broadcast, in 1925, was from the studio of WEAF in New York City. From October 1926 through the following May, he broadcasted live from the pulpit of the Park Avenue Church over station WJZ. The National Vespers program began on

October 2, 1927, and ran for twenty years until he retired at the end of the season in 1946. Altogether, he delivered 480 sermons on the program; however, many of these were rebroadcast under revised titles, and a few were redelivered two or more times.

The impact of his radio ministry can be gauged by statistics gathered in 1947. In its infancy, the National Broadcasting Company (NBC) had only sixteen stations to carry the program. But NBC grew and National Vespers eventually reached a peak in 1941 with 125 stations. At this time, his radio audience was estimated at twenty million, which included short wave transmission to England, Scotland, and New Zealand. Over 740,000 persons wrote for copies of his sermons, and after 1936 mimeographs were routinely supplied upon application. The largest number of requests for a single sermon was 8,248 letters for "A Time to Stress Unity," March 12, 1944. Understandably, the waning months of World War II witnessed the greatest volume of mail, some 135,000 pieces for the season of October 1944 to May 1945. Financially, Fosdick received no remuneration for his radio talks. (His salary in 1930 was five thousand dollars from Riverside plus an undisclosed amount from his professorship at Union.) NBC donated the air time on the assumption that appeals for donations would demean his message. Until the war, when everything that was broadcast was censored, Fosdick never submitted his sermons for review nor did NBC ask to see them. Initially, Fosdick had a committee that underwrote expenses such as music, secretarial assistance, postage, and so forth, but the committee ceased to function because listeners contributed free will offerings that subvented the ancillary costs.[7]

Only for the purposes of critical examination can the substance of what Fosdick said be separated from his style and manner of speaking. For when Fosdick preached or spoke, he combined all for effect. He wrote in *On Being Fit to Live With*: "A good sermon is direct personal address, individual consultation on a group scale, intended to achieve results." He thought the minister appealed to a jury for a decision: "in whatever way the sermon's theme may first be suggested, it must, early in the process, present to the preacher an object to be attained, a result to be worked for, a definite purpose to whose fulfillment everything he says will be directed. Aimless preaching, whether in exposition of texts or discussion of subjects, is the pulpit's curse. Whatever else a sermon has to start with, it should have an object, should be an appeal to the jury for a decision about something of momentous importance to life." This idea of appealing to the congregation as a jury he evidently learned at Union. According to Henry Sloane Coffin, Fosdick's speech professor, Francis Carmody, a Roman Catholic layman with legal training who taught at the seminary from 1903 to 1928, "kept reminding men that they 'preach for a verdict' and taught them to marshal their arguments and give their evidence tellingly."[8]

The form into which Fosdick cast his sermons was shaped by his purpose.   He had an organizational strategy for communicating his homilies. In his famous essay "What Is the Matter with Preaching?" he revealed his rationale for using the structure of the problem-solution format:

> Every sermon should have for its main business the solving of some problem--a vital, important problem, puzzling minds, burdening consciences, distracting lives. . . . There is nothing that people are so interested in as themselves. . . . That fact is basic. No preaching that neglects it can raise a ripple on a congregation. . . . and until that idea of it commands a preacher's mind and method, eloquence will avail him little and theology not at all.

The problem-solution pattern, wherein the orator states a problem and advocates a solution, aims at actuation. In *The Living of These Days*, he related why the pattern is efficacious for the pastor: "Here lies the difference between a sermon and a lecture.   A lecture is chiefly concerned with a *subject* to be elucidated; a sermon is chiefly concerned with an *object* to be achieved [his italics]." [9]

Fosdick's sermons were more sophisticated than a pedantic application of the problem-solution pattern.   He called his strategy "project preaching" or the "project method." He found a middle road between the doctrinal excesses of expository preaching, used in the United States since the time of the Puritans, and the overly secularized strategy of the topical preachers.   Twentieth-century topical homilists spoke on current subjects that interested them. Experientially, Fosdick found that people soon tired of recapitulations of issues they had read in their newspapers or heard on their radios. He also found the Puritan pattern limiting.   Expository preaching began with a Bbilical text, enunciated the doctrine it revealed, adduced reasons for the creed, and then ended with an application, which was an appeal to the congregation for belief.   What Fosdick really did in his so-called project preaching was to change the emphasis of the expository sermon without changing its essential form. Fosdick's sermons were based, although admittedly loosely at times, on Biblical texts. The doctrine, rather than a dry disquisition of some dogma, became the living problem he addressed and the Christian solution he advocated.   The reasons, rather than a compilation of Biblical proof texts, copious citations of other Biblical passages that proved the doctrine, became the persuasive analysis and appeals that made the problem and solution meaningful to his listeners. Lastly, Fosdisk's appeal-for-a-verdict was the application: "The preacher's business is . . . not merely to debate the meaning and possibility of Christian faith, but to produce Christian faith in the lives of his listeners. . . ." [10]

His training in speech and debate at Colgate, coupled with Carmody's legalistic approach to homilies, enabled Fosdick to practice adversative sermonizing.   He realized listeners would often make exceptions in their minds to his messages and he recognized how to reconcile their mental reservations. He knew a preacher must confront the congregation's doubts: "What objections to the truth involved in my theme are bound to be prevalent in the congregation? Too many preachers dodge this issue. The hearts of the hearers do not get their doubts and dismays completely recognized in the pulpit. It takes courage to face this question and to give it adequate attention." His technique was to offer compelling illustrations and telling examples to overcome objections. Correspondingly, he appreciated the rhetorical technique of repetition and restatement that reinforced a point for one's adherents and drove it home to one's doubters. His first sermon at Riverside illustrates the point. In response to his sermon title, "What Matters in Religion?" October 5, 1930, he repeated his answer of a "more abundant life" or "abundant living" twelve times. Fosdick knew a speech was not an essay on its hind legs. He often numbered his points in order to signpost orally the development of his messages. Enumeration in a literary product might not be appropriate, but Fosdick sensed its efficacy in sermonic discourse. That is why he cautioned readers of his sermons in *On Being Fit to Live With* that "sermons were not meant to be read, as essays are." In fact, Gilbert MacVaugh determined that Fosdick realized his congregation would tire of listening and that their mental awareness waned as the sermon waxed. Given a twenty- to thirty-minute sermon, Fosdick used long speech introductions to outline the problem when the audience's alertness was keen. As he moved through the body of the sermon, he devoted less verbiage to each mainhead. In fine, Fosdick used the essential form of the expository model by redirecting its emphasis from intellectual belief to effectual action. The success of Fosdick's addresses rested on his ability to incorporate rhetorical techniques into the expository pattern.[11]

Fosdick was a consummate stylist. Working about sixteen hours every week on a sermon that lasted about one-half hour, he was able to craft his communications with care: "Day by day he paid the price required; his persuasiveness did not just luckily turn up." In addition to utilizing the usual stylistic devices of alliteration, irony, and an occasional chiasmus in his sermons, Fosdick was a master of the metaphor. The following images illustrate his artistry in diction. In his "Charge to Rev. Jesse Lyons," he said, "there is personal uranium all through this congregation. Get out your Geiger counter. . . . We talk about the peaceful uses of atomic energy. Well, something like that you are charged with here"; and in *Lifetime Living Magazine*, he wrote: "Some may think of 65 as a period ending active life, whereas it can be a comma with the best of life's sentence coming after it." His style, seemingly literary upon cursory exmination, was the culmination of the writer-speaker at work. Getting things accomplished in the pulpit, Fosdick knew, involved persuading people with appealing language. *Time* remarked on his verbal virtuosity: "[he] said it with such eloquence, and such wealth of practical application, that his suburbanite parishioners were stunned and delighted," and the *Christian Century* praised his oral style: "that lightening by a surprising turn of phrase or an arresting homely illustration which formerly made Riverside sermons as effective when heard over the radio as within the setting of the stately church service." [12]

By design, Fosdick did not allow his delivery to dominate his message. He eschewed altogether old-time pulpit theatrics and the pulpit practices of preachers who warmed to their sermons with burning emotionalism and heated gesticulations. That is one of the reasons his spoken sermons could be read without forfeiting their impact. This was in clear juxtaposition to the "Radio Priest" whose addresses electrified audiences in person but lost voltage on the printed page. Having noted the subsidiary role Fosdick assigned delivery, that observation should not suggest that he was unmindful of it. Although he broadcasted his sermons from the studio and used a microphone to address the huge congregation at Riverside, he apparently never made any special adjustments to that technology. Just as he composed in an oral style, he managed in his delivery to communicate directly with people. He assured himself mentally that the microphone represented listeners, so he spoke conversationally on the radio as he did to his live congregation before him. Dr. Frederick W. Clampett, a speech critic for the San Francisco *Examiner*, captured the essence of Fosdick's delivery in 1927: "It was a powerful effect, and absolutely free from pyrotechnics. He seemed to forget the audience before him as he stood before the microphone. Dr. Fosdick, in my judgment, is the ablest preacher in the United States among the realm of Protestantism. His matter, not his manner, electrified his hearers. His delivery was slow, clear and even." William Hudnut, a student at Union under Fosdick, relayed his professor's admonition: "He advised us . . . to avoid the hushed voice and intimate manner that would only draw attention to ourselves." [13]

According to Edmund Holt Linn, Fosdick spoke in a conversational manner. He talked with, not at, his congregations. Although Linn believed that Fosdick spoke around 120 to 125 words per minute (wpm), a close examination of his sermonic rate revealed it was in the range of 90 to 100 wpm. This made Fosdick's speaking rate almost identical to President Franklin D. Roosevelt's unhurried pace. Their measured rate communicated an air of assurance and equanimity that appropriately befitted both orators' offices. Fosdick used the rhetorical pause for which FDR was famous. This technique made listeners anticipate important thoughts. Unlike FDR, Fosdick was not blessed with a rich baritone voice. Fosdick often said he did the best he could with what he had, which was a tenor voice without distinction. Yet Fosdick did modulate the pitch of his voice for emphasis and impact. He used the normal upward and downward vocal inflections one would associate with conversational speaking, but he went to neither extreme.

He stressed important ideas by increasing his volume or by using a staccato-like enunciation. In fact, the one aspect that recommended Fosdick's otherwise lackluster voice was his articulation. He pronounced his vowels and consonants clearly and precisely. This was an asset when addressing an audience the size of the Riverside Church, even though there was a public address system, and a distinct advantage for radio broadcasting for which the voice communicated the total and only impression.[14]

A few video materials exist that give a glimpse of what parishioners saw when Fosdick spoke from the pulpit. At Riverside, he was naturally constrained by the beautifully carved lecterns and the microphone (this was before the advent of the hand-held mike), so he did not move about the chancel, like some ministers do, as he talked. His body gestures were therefore limited to what was possible and tasteful in the circumstances: up-and-down head movements that punctuated his points, hand gestures that reinforced the fluidity of his train of thought, and an occasional grasping of his clerical robe.[15]

The astute reader may have inferred by now that Fosdick's delivery was not technically noteworthy. Then what accounted for his success? To be sure, a vital factor was his message, but there were other elements in his delivery that compensated for a mediocre technique. First, he readily conveyed earnestness and sincerity. No artifice came between him and his listeners. Second, he exuded liveliness. He was vividly aware of what he was saying as he said it. Third, he had an adequate amount of audience eye-contact. Although he first delivered his speeches from memory at Montclair, then experimented with topical outlines, and finally settled on reading the sermon from a manuscript at Riverside, this practice did not appreciably detract from his effectiveness. In fact, the careful work he invested in thoughtfully writing his sermons reaped benefits in the pulpit. No one seemed to notice he used a typed manuscript, because he wrote-to-speak: "As one can write a sermon to be talked, so one can read a sermon as though one were talking--talking naturally and freely, with all the irregularities, pauses, interpretative inflections, and direct address which should characterize any animated conversation."[16]

Harry Emerson Fosdick persuaded by sheer work. He learned rhetorical technique and applied it. He wrote sermons in an oral style. He left nothing to chance. Fosdick admired the Reverend Henry Ward Beecher and was, in many respects, Beecher's twentieth-century counterpart. Yet Fosdick recognized he did not possess Beecher's famous flair for impromptu speaking or extemporaneous address. Forever the craftsman with words, Fosdick revealed the verbal trap into which he never allowed himself to fall: "Experience indicates, however, that Beechers are few, and that without the discipline of writing most preachers fall into structural disorder, loose sentences, repetitious phrasing, monotonous vocabulary and general obscurity."[17]

2
Fosdick vs.
the Fundamentalists

The Reverend Harry Emerson Fosdick delivered "Shall the Fundamentalists Win?" on May 21, 1922. It was arguably the most famous sermon he ever preached.

The continental divide in Christianity is where one stands on the Bible. Unwilling to sacrifice his intellect nor ask his parishioners to do likewise, Fosdick stood with those ministers who read and preached the Bible for its spiritual insights, but not for its inerrant rules and creeds. The sermon did not spring anew from his mind. He had long been a liberal, had taught that creed at Union, and had preached an intellectual religion from the Montclair and First Presbyterian pulpits. Abreast of the higher criticism of the Holy Scriptures, scientific inquiry, form criticism, and the tenets of evolution, Fosdick believed the Bible *contained* the Word of God but that it was not *the* Word of God or infallible. In 1922 the Presbyterian watershed on Scripture was between the presbyteries of New York City and Philadelphia. Conservatives, led by the Reverend Clarence Macartney, a minister in Philadelphia who was soon to be elected moderator of the General Assembly of the Presbyterian Church, read the Bible narrowly and preached constrictingly. "Fundamentalism," according to the Reverend Karl Reiland, "is a state of mind. It is fixity against flexiblity, old tradition against new truth, literalism against liberalism, a static point of view rather than an active"; moroever, Reiland asserted, the fundamentalists' basic message to their liberal opponents was "Subscribe or get out." Indeed, William Merrill perceived that in the 1920s fundamentalists, although they would have vehemently denied it, were strikingly similar in theological mindset to the Romanists they abhorred, but that they could not match that church's derived doctrines nor inspired pageantry: "Such a Protestantism as the Fundamentalists would make is simply a shadow of Romanism, with its claims and pretensions, and none of its glamor and impressiveness." That

Baptist Fosdick's First Presbyterian Church did not mind his sermon on May 21, 1922, mattered very little to the fundamentalists, none of whom were present in the congregation that Sunday. They, like the Spanish inquisitors of the sixteenth century, could not abide heresy: "If a Presbyterian minister stood up and attacked 'adult immersion baptism' in a Baptist church, would people tolerate it?" The fundamentalists answered that rhetorical question with a resounding "No." But ironically, one of the conditions "Presbyterian" Fosdick made for his move to Riverside was that the Park Avenue Baptist congregation dispense with immersion baptism, a condition they met.[1]

This entire episode was in reality a series of accusations and apologies that sallied back and forth between contending parties. Although Fosdick emerged as the leading spokesman for the liberals in the 1920s, he was not the first to raise his voice against fundamentalism. For instance, the Reverend Henry Ward Beecher delivered a series of sermons from his Plymouth Church pulpit in the spring and summer of 1885 as an apologist for evolution. To make his case, Beecher accused the conservatives of enacting "the very feats of the monkey in an attempt to prove that the monkey was not their ancestor," and asserted that "faith that can be unsettled by the access of light and knowledge had better be unsettled." Forty years later, sermons on simians were no less in vogue. Not content to leave liberals on the other side of the aisle, the conservatives wanted to purge them from the church. Macartney and several leading fundamentalists, most notably William Jennings Bryan, a Presbyterian who figured prominently in Fosdick's ultimate dismissal from his pulpit, lent their voices and pens to the ongoing fray. Bryan, twice a Democratic candidate for the presidency and secretary of state under Woodrow Wilson, played his most famous or infamous role in the famous Scopes trial in 1925. Thomas Lessl demonstrated in the "Monkey" trial that the verbal combatants endeavored to portray themselves as apologists, as victims of the other's accusations: "Both sides in any sort of dispute will often simultaneously claim that they are merely defending their position, while their opponents are the ones making all the accusations." For their public audiences as well as their own constituents, Bryan and Clarence Darrow at Dayton, Tennessee, postured to accuse the other under the guise of apologetic discourse. Lessl's finding also incidentally illuminates the subtleties of Fosdick's rhetoric and reveals why the fundamentalists chose him as their devil figure. Fortunately for Fosdick, the fundamentalists had no better luck with him than Bryan had with Darrow, and they succeeded only in reaffirming, once again, Beecher's observation about simian speeches that enacted apish antics.[2]

APOLOGY AS ATTACK: "SHALL THE FUNDAMENTALISTS WIN?"

Fosdick meant to accuse the fundamentalists of certain doctrinal tenets that neither he nor his congregation believed. For his First Presbyterian audience, he was not persuading as much as he was reinforcing its liberal leanings. This rhetorical stance is quite obvious in Fosdick's introductory remarks wherein he identified with his congregation against the conservatives: "This morning we are to think of the Fundamentalist controversy which threatens to divide the American churches, as though already they were not sufficiently split and riven. . . . All of us must have heard about the people who call themselves the Fundamentalists. Their apparent intention is to drive out of the evangelical churches men and women of liberal opinions." While appearing to defend the liberals, Fosdick was in fact attacking his conservative opponents. They probably would not have been riled except for the efforts of Ivy Lee. A liberal member of old First and head of a nationwide publicity agency, Lee was so enthralled by the sermon that he renamed it and mailed it to his business clientele. Several critics, such as Allan Sager, Robert Clark, and Robert Miller, believed that part of the controversy was stirred by Lee's editorial work on the sermon's text. It is true, as they note, that Lee captioned the homily, but a perusal of the text as printed in "Collected Speeches and Sermons" will reveal that the headings were hardly inflammatory and were often paraphrases of Fosdick's language; it is true that Lee retitled the sermon to "The New Knowledge and the Christian Faith," which, it might be added, was a more conciliatory title than Fosdick's loaded rhetorical question, "Shall the Fundamentalists Win?"; and although it was true that Lee deleted some sentences in the sermon's introduction and conclusion, Fosdick's language was not as ameliorative as critics have imagined. Although he later termed the deleted parts "innocuous sentences of the homiletical introduction and conclusion," Fosdick's introductory narration, from the Book of Acts, about how Jewish leaders tried intolerantly to exclude Christians from the synagogue, subtly indicted the fundamentalists two millenia later; moreover, his concluding remarks polarized, rather than mollified, those on the other side of the aisle. The supposed lack of conciliation that critics perceived in Lee's deletions was in fact rhetorically conciliatory because Lee excised a theological sideswipe at the fundamentalists, and in their rush to exculpate Fosdick, critics have misread and conveniently overlooked Fosdick's actual language. (If anything, the advertising slip that Ivy Lee sent with the text of the sermon could be construed as provocative. Yet few critics have paid any attention to the slip. In reality, Lee's language was relatively inoffensive. Allowing that "A great chasm exists today between organized Christianity and a large part of the people," Lee opined that "One of the serious barriers is insistence by so many upon standards of orthodoxy to which a large number of men cannot subscribe." Lee went on to praise Fosdick as "The minister who is today attracting the largest congregations in New York City," and lauded his homily as a "landmark in the progress in religion that such a sermon should be preached in the old First

Presbyterian Church of New York." Lee acknowledged the sermon was
"slightly abridged," and gave his business address for those who wanted
to send him their comments.) Thus, Fosdick's motivation for delivering
the speech has been obscured. He clearly intended to attack the
fundamentalists. Lee's editorial effort publicized the sermon, but it did
not infuriate the fundamentalists. Fosdick did that. If he truly wanted
to be conciliatory, he need not have delivered the speech.[3]

Casting himself as an apologist for the liberals, Fosdick set about
attacking his opponents' doctrines. He took aim at the fundamentalists'
Five Points: the virgin birth of Jesus, the infallibility of Scripture, the
atonement, the bodily resurrection, and the second coming. In his
sermon, Fosdick skirmished in his introduction against the doctrine of
atonement, bypassed altogether the bodily resurrection, and trained his
rhetorical sights on the remaining three points in the body of his talk.
In a perfect chiasmus, he stated his rhetorical purpose: "We must be able
to think our modern life clear through in Christian terms and to do that
we also must be able to think our Christian life clear through in modern
terms." Typical of his organizational structure that was designed to help
the congregation understand his points, he signposted orally his first
contention: "We may as well begin with the vexed and mooted question
of the virgin birth of our Lord." He acknowledged the special quality of
Jesus that the doctrine of the virgin birth tried ineffably to express, but
he rejected belief in the "biological miracle," "the historical fact," that was
demanded by the fundamentalists. He summarized his first point by
juxtaposing the exclusiveness of the conservatives with the inclusiveness
of the liberals in a series of rhetorical questions: "Has intolerance any
contribution to make to this situation? Will it persuade anybody of
anything? Is not the Christian church large enough to hold within her
hospitable fellowship people who differ on points like this and agree to
differ until the fuller truth be manifested? The Fundamentalists say not.
They say that the liberals must go."

"Consider another matter," Fosdick continued in his second issue,
"on which there is a sincere difference of opinion between evangelical
Christians: the inspiration of the Bible." He argued his point with a
compelling analogy. He denigrated the Koran as "a millstone about the
neck of Mohammedanism" because its followers insisted on its textual
infallibility. Averring that many of the doctrines that Christians found
repelling in the Koran (polygamy, slavery, and the use of force on
unbelievers) could also be found in the Holy Scriptures, Fosdick let his
audience infer that the Bible cannot be taken literally lest the modern
believer fall into the same intellectual trap as Islamic believers. Fosdick
also ended this issue with a series of rhetorical questions that were
designed to decry the fundamentalists' views. "You cannot," Fosdick
declared, "fit the Lord Christ into that Fundamentalist mold."

Fosdick used the same structure in his third point on the second
coming of Jesus. He contrasted a traditional interpretation of "Christ is

coming!"--meaning that God was unfolding his will in human affairs--with the view that "Christ is literally coming, externally on the clouds of heaven, to set up his kingdom here." For the third time, he asked a series of questions that argued why fundamentalists should not "shut the door of Christian fellowship" on modern believers who interpreted "Christ is coming!" as spiritual progress and not as an arrival on the clouds.

Characteristic of his problem-solution format, Fosdick then assayed what attitude would bridge the theological divide he had described. In a kind of classical *partitio*, he first stated what was not the solution. He allowed that the fundamentalists' mindset could not span the gap but only widen it. As a liberal, he advocated two solutions. First, he urged Christian liberty. "When," he implored, "will the world learn that intolerance solves no problems?" Who, Fosdick asked, would capture the minds of the youth: those who invite youths to bring scientific reasoning to bear on their Christian religion, or those who would "feed . . . opinions from a spoon" to closed minds? To the old First congregation, the answer was obvious. To the conservatives, the answer must have been infuriating. Second, he chided the fundamentalists for "quarreling over little matters when the world is dying of great needs." When confronted with men and women who were wrestling with questions of life and death, Fosdick believed the "tiddledywinks and peccadillos of religion" obscured vital twentieth-century concerns. He castigated those who would "tithe mint and anise and cummin" while the world faced "weightier matters of the law, justice, and mercy, and faith." Exclaiming that "there is not a single thing at stake in the controversy on which depends the salvation of human souls. That is the trouble with this whole business. So much of it does not matter!," he stated the vital mission of ministers that did matter: "That men in their personal lives and in their social relationships should know Jesus Christ." Citing Turkish atrocities in Armenia, proclaiming as the ancient prohpets did that "The present world situation smells to heaven!," Fosdick characterized the fundamentalists' efforts to drive the liberals from the church as "immeasurable folly!"

APOLOGY AS ATTACK: FUNDAMENTALIST COUNTERCHARGES

Trying to picture themselves as apologists in responding to Fosdick's unwonted attack on the status quo, the fundamentalists decided that the best defense is a good offense. Spoiling for a good fight, Macartney opened on Fosdick with a sermon entitled "Shall Unbelief Win?" In a point-by-point refutation, Macartney denied many of Fosdick's findings and redefined those points that he thought his opponent had misanalyzed or misconstrued. He assured his congregation that he was not party to any conspiracy to remove Fosdick and his followers from the church, but disingenuously allowed that Fosdick and his fellowship were "already out of the Church" and that the Christian thing to do would be to pray them "back into the Church." With no self-professed lip service to Christian charity, the *Christian Scotsman* circulated a pamphlet entitled "The Spoilation of the First Presbyterian Church of New York, Through the Inane Fallacy in a Baptist Minister's Preaching." Exhibiting a flair for scathing sermonic titles, John Roach Straton, minister of the Calvary Baptist Church, New York City, preached a homily on September 24, 1922, that humorously turned the tables on Fosdick: "Shall the FunnyMonkeyists Win?" In that talk, Straton compared Fosdick to Robert Green Ingersoll, the "Great Agnostic," by complimenting Ingersoll for at least attacking the church from the outside whereas Fosdick insidiously undermined the church from within. And the Rev. G. E. Sihlhide was at pains to observe that Fosdick was the accuser: "This sad controversy was not made or caused by those who are known as fundamentalists, but by the so-called modernist-liberals, and by none other. It was they who threw the challenge and hurled the defiance."[4]

Macartney, speaking for the presbytery of Philadelphia, challenged Fosdick's heresy in New York City by sending the issue to the General Assembly that was to meet in Indianapolis in the spring of 1923. The presbytery of New York was in a delicate position, and the committee that was appointed to write a report did a credible job of straddling the fence. The constraints were to go far enough to mollify the conservatives throughout the church but not so far as to alienate Fosdick, the liberal camp, or his supporters in the congregation. The report began by applauding Fosdick's motive in delivering the sermon. However, the report allowed "that the title of the sermon was ill-chosen and provocative. It sounded more like a challenge to battle than a plea for harmony and peace." (This finding supports the contentions that Fosdick meant to force the issue and that Lee's rephrased title was actually more conciliatory.) Then, in a verbal obfuscation that was evidently designed to please readers on both sides of the aisle, the report criticized a straw issue: "The sermon itself seemed to us open to misunderstanding and criticism, for the reason, that while the preacher presented two extreme views on several points of Christian doctrine and did not clearly define his own position with regard to them, his hearers might not unreasonably infer that he was personally committed to all the advanced opinions for which he asked toleration." Giving the conservatives their due, the sermon's title and Fosdick's rhetorical treatment were straightforward statements of where he stood on the three, and not two, issues he discussed. Indeed, the Reverend J. Gresham Machen, a professor at Princeton Theological Seminary, whose book on New Testatment Greek was a staple for a generation of seminarians, criticized the committee's report for its sophistry: "Either Dr. Fosdick accepts the virgin birth and the other miracles of the New Testament; in that case, he will give joyful testimony to these things. Or else he disbelieves them (as of course he does disbelieve them); in that case it is highly objectionable to suggest, as the committee does, that he should be asked to conceal his disbeliefs as the committee does, that he should be asked to conceal his disbeliefs in the pulpit." Although the sermon supports a reading that Fosdick asked for toleration for his views, in truth its persuasive efficacy derived from Fosdick's clarion charge that intolerant fundamentalists were trying to drive the liberals from Christian fellowship. In a certain sense, then, the fundamentalists' complaint that Fosdick attacked their core beliefs in his sermon was well taken from their perspective. Writing in *Presbyterian*, noted for its polemical tone against Fosdick, the Reverend William W. McKinney could justifiably write: "It is very hard for the ordinary reader to understand why Dr. Fosdick is the center of controversy in the Presbyterian Church. But when you know Dr. Fosdick himself, and know the meaning he has placed on historic creeds . . . [you know why] the Presbyterians challenge his intellectual honesty."[5]

As at Dayton, Tennessee, three years later, the fundamentalists won the battle but lost the war. The denouement descended inexorably. At the hands of Macartney and Bryan, Fosdick was asked by the General Assembly either to regularize his ministry by becoming a Presbyterian, thus subjecting himself to church polity, or to leave his pulpit. This sophisticated strategy was designed by Bryan, the "Great Commoner," who stated that Fosdick "must either resign or enter the Presbyterian ministry." Although critics have taken at face value Fosdick's protestation that he had to resign rather than to accept a denominational "closed shop" that was so antithetical to his proclaimed interdenominationalist thinking, such a naive conclusion masks Fosdick's intelligence in church politics. Doubtless, he recognized the bait Bryan offered. Although pressed by the congregation at old First to remain, Fosdick realized that if he joined the Presbyterian church, then the conservative forces would have him where they wanted him. Under their jurisdiction, they could prosecute him as a heretic. As Queen Mary said of Archbishop Thomas Cranmer in the early sixteenth century, that she would have Cranmer a Catholic or no Cranmer at all, so would the fundamentalists have Fosdick a Presbyterian or no Fosdick at all. The difference was, of course, that Fosdick could not be burned at the stake as was Cranmer. Indeed, as long as Fosdick remained a Baptist, the Presbyterian church could not excommunicate him, and Fosdick wisely never gave his opponents their chance.[6]

As it played in the press, the fundamentalists clearly shot themselves in the foot. They obliged by enacting the very role Fosdick said they played. An editorializer in the *Christian Work* opined that when a clergyman professes ideas on economics, politics, and evolution, "he becomes a dangerous person to a very large section of Protestant clergy and laity." Fosdick underlined the following sentence, from the *Christian Century*, that seemed to capture the essence of the roles of the accuser-as-apologist and the apologist-as-accuser at which he rhetorically excelled: "The new preachers do not defend the gospel; they know that it is the gospel that defends us." Lastly, the *Continent* noted the nature of the self-inflicted wound: "When conservative theologians plan to promote schism, they merely plan to insure the triumph of liberalism."[7]

FOSDICK'S "FAREWELL"

"All my enemies have done to me," said Fosdick in the conclusion of his farewell sermon, March 1, 1925, "is to build a sounding board behind me so that my message reaches further than I ever dreamed it could." Fosdick preached his valedictory to his congregation at First Presbyterian Church without rancor. He realized the fundamentalists had dignified his attack on them, had given him valuable publicity, and had in truth come off rather badly in the persuasive exchange. Although not as stellar nor as widely anthologized, his Farewell sermon was better in many ways than his famous attack on the conservatives. He expounded a Biblical text that served as the basis for a homily and as an extended analogy for saying good-bye, he presented his usual concern for men and women's spiritual lives, and he developed his talk in his typical sermonic structure and style.[8]

Unlike "Shall the Fundamentalists Win?" which was preached without a Scriptural text, Fosdick chose for his Biblical passage the story of St. Paul, related in the eighteenth chapter of the Book of Acts. Paul finally took leave of his followers at Corinth after a fruitful but stormy ministry there. In the hands of a skilled exegete such as Fosdick, the ancient tale served two simultaneous functions for persuasive purposes. Defining the first fundamentalist controversy as whether the early Christians were to observe the old Jewish customs and law, Fosdick demonstrated that Paul, and by anology Fosdick himself, had stood "on the other side," had believed that nothing mattered except that the spirit of Christ lived in men and women. He admitted controversy had surrounded Paul, but gave the historical examples of John Greenleaf Whittier and Henry Ward Beecher to argue that heretics "grow respectable in retrospect." The inference Fosdick invited his audience to make was clear and, as history has proved, was valid. Having favorably compared himself to St. Paul by analogy, he then rehearsed in an apologetic manner his attacks once again. He, and his congregation, had stood for "*tolerance*," "*an inclusive church*," "*the right of people to think the abiding verities of Christianity through in modern terms*," "*the social application of the principles of Jesus*," and "*the abiding verities of experiences of the Gospel*" [his italics]. In terms of tolerance, Fosdick thought it was sufficient for people to center their lives around Jesus "and let them think as they will about the details of theology." Decrying the more than one hundred denominations of Protestantism in the United States, Fosdick framed a compelling rhetorical question: "They have the same Lord. They share a common purpose. Why cannot they do under one roof what they do under many?" As for a modern Christianity, he stated that science and evolution "are here to stay," and that his mission had been "to help young people to think through their religion in terms that will not do violence to their knowledge." In applying the social principles of Jesus, Fosdick reminded the audience of his commitment to square "our present economic system," "our international life," and "the cruelties of our modern industrialism" with Christianity, and for a theme that would be forever identified with his ministry, he vowed "I hate war and I never expect to bless another one." He concluded this portion of his sermon with a faith in the future, expressed in a fine anaphora: "We have lifted a standard that no one will put down. We have stated an issue that no man or denomination is strong enough to brush aside."

Moving to the application that was adapted from Puritan preaching, Fosdick recurred to the Biblical story of St. Paul to make it relevant to the spiritual needs of his listeners. For the uncommitted youth in the congregation, Fosdick used the example of two lakes on the Bernina Pass in Switzerland: one emptied eventually into the Adriatic, the other the Black Sea, yet they were separated by a distance of only a hundred feet. "Before I go," Fosdick said, "I am burdened about some of you. On which side of the watershed are you?" Observing that he always had another Sunday to ask his congregation to commit themselves to Christ, he poignantly acknowledged, "Now there isn't any next Sunday. I want you for Christ now."

Even in his moving conclusion, he analogously spoke as St. Paul must have when he left Corinth:

> And now, without enlarging on it, you know the burden on my heart as I go. I do not want to leave any personal partisans behind me. Leadership is not true leadership that draws people to the leader only. It must draw them past the leader to the cause. I do not want to leave any personal partisans behind me. . . . Never mind about me. Stand by the church.

The *Presbyterian*, which had railed against Fosdick since his sermon in 1922, could, in its perceived victory, magnanimously print a letter to the editor that must have summarized the reactions of those members of Fosdick's audience in 1925: "To have been at his farewell service I shall always count one of the most priceless privileges of my experience."[9]

The liberal press took delight in the spectacle that the fundamentalists forced Fosdick to enact. The *New Republic* observed that Fosdick's "ringing, confident, unpretending American voice" ignored the fundamentalists in his sermon and rather "spoke over their heads and beyond them." In an editorial, the *Nation* scored the conservative's cupidity for orthodoxy at any cost: "We are not aware that many preachers these days turn away hearers. That is what happens in the church where Dr. Fosdick preaches. A wise church, we think, would let such a man alone. . . ."[10]

CONCLUSION

In May of 1922, Harry Emerson Fosdick was a moderately well known minister in New York City. In December of 1924, *Current Opinion* compared Fosdick to Beecher as "a conspicuously successful preacher, occupying in the religious life of New York to-day something of the position that Henry Ward Beecher occupied in Brooklyn a generation ago." By March of 1925, *The Literary Digest*, in assaying "The 'Best' Protestant Preachers," ranked him fifth in the nation. Fosdick's religious rhetoric appealed to the future and met the spiritual needs of twentieth-century Americans who were emerging from a religious cocoon, in the making for nineteen hundred years, that consisted of creeds wrapped in dogmas encased in doctrines. The fundamentalists' speeches and writings turned to the past and appealed to those whose mindsets impelled them, by analogy, to repeat the tragedy of Galileo three centuries earlier. Without detracting from Fosdick's obvious talents as a persuader, it must be stated that he was helped immeasurably by the fundamentalists and their intolerant rhetoric. Winning a Pyrrhic victory, they unwittingly dignified his attack, inadvertently validated his charges, and succeeded in elevating Fosdick while sanctimoniously discrediting themselves before the national audience. Cleland McAfee noted the fix in which the fundamentalists found themselves: "In several instances they have fallen into the narrowest grooves of self-righteous opinion." In truth, Fosdick, as accuser, adroitly succeeded in portraying the fundamentalists as the accusers and himself as an apologist; as the true apologists in this religious debate, the fundamentalists succeeded admirably well in sacrificing the natural presumption for their Biblical argument by pressing their claims to absurd conclusions, thus allowing themselves to be conceived in the public's perception as the extremists. Fosdick's rhetorical victory was to goad the fundamentalists into inviting the American audience to view them as the accusers. The *Literary Digest* noted the paradox of accusation as apology and apology as accusation that was inherent in the verbal exchange of Fosdick vs. the fundamentalists: "the Rev. Harry Emerson Fosdick joins that distinguished company of heretics who have ridden roughshod over ecclesiastical decrees and won a hearing which no decree could suppress. And herein lies the grim irony of the situation . . . . [T]he effect of the decree of the Presbyterian General Assembly [is] to make the world his parish." With his newly created international pulpit, Fosdick proceeded to promulgate his views on yet another subject dear to his heart: pacifism.[11]

3
Quo Vadis:
God of War or Peace?

A major and recurring problem in Christianity is how one reconciles the gospel of love expounded in the New Testament and the sixth commandment given in the Old Testament with hate and killing. No American stated the issue more eloquently than did President Abraham Lincoln in his Second Inaugural Address. Presaging the theological problem on warfare that Harry Fosdick would address in the twentieth century, Lincoln observed of Unionists and Confederates on March 4, 1865: "Both read the same Bible and pray to the same God, and each invokes His aid against the other. . . . The prayers of both could not be answered." During World War I, Fosdick, in company with other patriotic pastors and priests, had cooperated with the government by blessing the war effort and by giving succor to the Allied troops. Doubtless, Fosdick realized that Germans and Americans prayed to the same God to give victory to Kaiser Wilhelm or President Wilson. Robert Miller and Robert Clark have thoroughly detailed the intellectual and theological transformations that Fosdick, along with many other Americans in secular and sacred callings, experienced against the war that was to have made the world safe for democracy, so there is no need to rehearse their findings here. Rather, Fosdick's speeches themselves may serve as indicators of his rhetoric at critical junctures in the nation's religious life. [1]

"Harry Emerson Fosdick . . . may have been mistaken, but the present writer, for one," opined Robert Miller, "is unwilling to pass judgment on men of this character and say they were wrong." Miller's observation is a departure point for explicating Fosdick's oratory on the tension in the Christian church between pacifism and belligerency. In Fosdick's favor it can be said that he delivered two of the most moving addresses on record against war, "A Christian Conscience About War," and "My Account with the Unknown Soldier." Adversely, one could allow that he applied derived truths from World War I, much as the fundamentalists used pre-Darwinian dogmas to appeal to twentieth-century Christians, to support a pacifism that was rhetorically unresponsive to a Germany ruled not by Huns in 1939-1941 but by Nazis.[2]

A CHRISTIAN CONSCIENCE ABOUT WAR

Fame smiled on Fosdick who had been found wanting by the fundamentalists. To be sure, having a brother, Raymond Fosdick, who was appointed by President Wilson as under secretary general of the League of Nations, probably facilitated Fosdick's obtaining an invitation to address the opening session of the League in 1925. But surely Fosdick's removal from the old First pulpit was not unrelated to his standing in the Protestant Cathedral of St. Peter, Geneva, Switzerland, to deliver a homily for peace. Presbyterian fundamentalists must have appreciated the irony in Baptist Fosdick's preaching in John Calvin's pulpit some two and one-half centuries later on September 13, 1925.

Before addressing "A Christian Conscience About War," it is worthwhile to assay briefly the contentions Fosdick made in an earlier sermon. Like his attack on the fundamentalists, the motivational antecedents to his pacifism predated the actual speech and, in this case, were grounded in his experiences as a pastor during World War I and in his subsequent reading of revelations about the war; unlike his sermon against the conservatives, his homily for peace had its inception in a prior sermon. On June 3, 1921, he preached "Shall We End War?" at the First Presbyterian Church in New York City. In terms of style, organization, and thematic argumentation, "Shall We End War?" precursed the speech in Geneva. His diction previewed his later speech, as in the following examples: "the irreconcilable conflict between war and the spirit of Jesus"; "[war] is brutal, organized butchery of human beings"; "If we are wise we will never again go down into hell expecting to come up with redeemed spirits"; and "For we can have war or civilization, but we cannot have both very long." He organized the problem part of his homily around six points, and he ended each with a compelling epistrophe [he constructed the epistrophes from the texts of his sermon, Isaiah 2:4 and Micah 4:3, "neither shall they learn war any more"]: "First of all, *there is nothing glorious about war any more*"; "In the second place, *war is not a school for virtue any more*"; "In the third place, *there is no limit to the methods of killing in war any more*"; "That leads me logically to my next point: *there are no limits to the cost of war anymore*"; his fifth point was, "and, now, *there is no possibility of sheltering any portion of the population from the direct effect of war any more*"; "Surely," he implored for his sixth point, "you are ready to accept my last proposition: *we cannot reconcile Christianity with war any more*" [his italics]. Averring that he was not a theoretical pacifist, that he did "not hold my ethics in a vacuum apart from the actualities," he applied his argumentation to the congregation in a conclusion that stressed how Christians could influence public opinion "to decide a great national issue" for peace. The logic of the speech was based on the method of residues. The method of residues is a rhetorical application of the disjunctive syllogism: either A, B, or C; not A, not B, therefore C. By systematically negating each of the disjuncts, which were positive values that previous generations had ascribed to warfare, Fosdick demonstrated the irreducible reasoning of the waste and futility of future wars.[3]

Whereas Fosdick preached "Shall the Fundamentalists Win?" without a text and chose two Old Testament texts for "Shall We End War?," he turned to the New Testament for a Scriptural warrant for his pacifism. The textual progression is interesting. Neither modernism nor fundamentalism are expounded in the Bible, so Fosdick had to rely on secular argumentation to demonstrate his holdings against the conservatives. When he preached the prophets Isaiah and Micah against war, he at least had a Biblical warrant for his sermon. In "A Christian Conscience About War," he took as his text Matthew 26:52, where Jesus said: "for all who take the sword will perish by the sword."

The speech was an intellectual and spiritual catharsis for Fosdick. As he had kept abreast of the higher criticism of the Bible, so he paid attention to the critics of war propaganda. Although compelling images during wartime, the Hun atrocity stories were fabrications; while dutiful citizens planted victory gardens, the war profiteers reaped gold; and after the last bands had played "Over There" and "You're a Grand Old Flag," the witching sounds of martial music gave way to wails welling from the grim statistics of wounded, maimed, and dead men and women. Nor was it particularly clear in the early 1920s, except for pieces of paper that said so, who won the war.

He expressed his thesis in a perfect chiasmus: "If mankind does not end war, war will end mankind." This time, two points, instead of six in "Shall We End War?," sufficed. First, he declared, "Indeed, there is modern war's futility to achieve any good purposes whatever." Tracing the history of warfare from ancient times to the present, he demonstrated the uselessness of war: "In the history of war we have one more example of a mode of social action possibly possessing at the beginning more of good than evil, which has outgrown its good, accentuated its evil, and become at last an intolerable thing." Fosdick usually used the well-turned phrase and the carefully constructed sentence to communicate his thoughts, and he normally eschewed appeals to facts and figures. However, the sobering statistics from World War I were staggering: "See how modern war protects the weak: 10,000,000 known dead soldiers; 3,000,000 presumed dead soldiers; 13,000,000 dead civilians; 20,000,000 wounded; 3,000,000 prisoners; 9,000,000 war orphans; 5,000,000 war widows; 10,000,000 refugees. What can we mean--modern war protecting the weak?" Running the argument to its logical conclusion, Fosdick forced the issue to a decision that demanded a commitment, one way or the other, from Christians:

> As for Christianity, the dilemma which it faces in all this seems unmistakable. The war system as a recognized method of international action is one thing; Christianity with all its purposes and hopes is another; and not all the dialectic of the apologists can make the two lie down in peace together. We may have one or we may have the other, but we cannot permanently have both.

The listener might not have appreciated Fosdick's organizational strategy thus far in the speech. After all, the method of residues can be a subtle form of argument, as he earlier applied it in his "Shall We End War?". But the method might have become apparent as the orator turned to his next subject.[4]

The brilliance of Fosdick's mind is reflected in his analysis of the relationship between Christianity and nationalism. This idea was not present in his earlier sermon, but was fully developed in this one. Playing the role of the ancient prophet, he blamed the Lord's people in his second point:

> Even our religion has been nationalized; with state churches or without them, the center of loyalty in the religious life of the people has increasingly become the nation. Let Protestantism acknowledge its large responsibility for this in Western Christendom! In our fight for liberty we broke up the inclusive mother church into national churches; we reorganized the worship of the people around nationalistic ideals; we helped to identify religion and patriotism. And so far has this identification gone that now, when war breaks, the one God of all humanity, whom Christ came to reveal, is split up into little tribal deities, and before these pagan idols even Christians pray for the blood of their enemies.

Claiming that internationalism was the new world order and that "it can never be crowded back again," Fosdick called for international cooperation.

In the statement of the problem, Fosdick had demonstrated that war and Christianity were irreconcilable and that religious nationalism could not harmonize with international cooperation. In the solution or application part of his talk, he again forced a choice: "On the one side a narrow patriotism saying, 'My country against yours,' on the other, a wider patriotism saying, 'My country with yours for the peace of mankind.' Is there any question where real Christianity must stand in that conflict?" Fosdick framed the crux of the problem, and hence its implicit solution, in unmistakable language:

> [M]ankind's realest conflict of interest is not between this nation and that, but between the forward-looking,

progressive, open-minded people of all nations, who have
caught a vision of humanity organized for peace, and the
backward-looking, reactionary, militaristic people of the
same nations. The deepest line of conflict does not run
vertically between the nations; it runs horizontally through
all the nations. The salvation of humanity from self-
destruction depends on which side of that conflict wins.

To actuate affirmation for the choice Fosdick hoped mankind would
make, he summarized this disjunct by reminding his audience at Geneva
that Christians could not worship "irreconcilable gods."

Fosdick used the conclusion of his speech to tread his points,
much as the soldier had tramped through the fields in France, into his
listeners' and readers' minds. To extend the military metaphor even
further, the speech was like an artillery barrage. He softened up the
audience with small-bore verbal projectiles in his introduction, deployed
his main artillery in the body of his speech, and fired parting shots in his
conclusion. He juxtaposed the early Christians, whom he described as
"the first peace society," with twentieth-century believers, and then
charged in powerfully emotive and descriptive language, "Since then the
Church has come down through history too often trying to carry the cross
of Jesus in one hand and a dripping sword in the other." His final salvo
was his central thesis: "We cannot reconcile Jesus Christ and war--that is
the essence of the matter." And giving a Scriptural and artistic unity to
his speech, he concluded, as he had begun, with the Master's admonition
that "All they that take the sword shall perish by the sword."

Fosdick had chosen his words effectively. His speech was received
with enthusiasm. Indeed, the *Literary Digest* noted that "The metropolitan
presses give ample space to Dr. Fosdick's sermon." The *New York Times*
reported that his address in Geneva was "courageous and brilliant" and
that his "voice reached to every corner of the great edifice"; in an
editorial the next day, it opined:

Calvin in his day was able to support the use of the sword
in defense of even a theological doctrine. How far a
foremost representative of Christianity has progressed from
Calvin's view is illustrated by Dr. Fosdick's standing in the
place of Calvin, in Geneva, with the challenging thesis: "We
cannot reconcile Jesus Christ and war."

The Reverend Dr. Cornelius Woelfkin, pastor of the Park Avenue Baptist
Church, who had resigned his position but was staying on until Fosdick
could assume the pulpit when he returned from his sabbatical leave from
Union Theological Seminary, lauded his soon-to-be successor's speech:
"With the boldness of a prophet of God he proclaimed a divorce between
the Spirit of Christ and war. That utterance will reign throughout the
world and adown the years."[5]

Given the assumed premise that Jesus's gospel did not support
any manner of warfare (Fosdick cavalierly overlooked theologies of the

"just war" that Christians had developed through the centuries to sanction hostilities), Fosdick marshalled his language so that the address marched ineluctably to its conclusion: Jesus and Mars are irreconcilable. Yet, ironically, he used human slavery as a supporting instance of social action that had finally become, like war, an intolerable thing; to complete the logic of his historical example, he should have pointed out that only an insufferable civil war in the United States could end another intolerable practice. Moreover, there is another interesting irony in Fosdick's rhetorical stance on pacifism. As he had charged the fundamentalists with intolerance for those who differed from their beliefs, Fosdick evidently never made allowances for those who might not ascribe to his ethics. It was one thing to preach against the horizontal line that ran between conservatives and liberals in the United States; it was an entirely different matter to adjust rhetorically that line between nations. To wit, his calling international Christians back to their pacifistic heritage naively overlooked the cleavage in these countries that he had so clearly delineated. In a sense, Fosdick addressed the choir at Geneva. To be sure, the League of Nations was conceived to keep international peace, but Fosdick openly acknowledged in his speech that he did not speak for his own country, which never joined the League. Although Fosdick cannot be faulted for his country's shortsightedness in spurning the League, neither can he be hailed for envisioning a practical modus operandi to facilitate his rhetoric. As the fundamentalists were wedded to a non-Biblical doctrine of Scriptural inerrancy, so was Fosdick committed to a modernist world view that elided evil.

MY ACCOUNT WITH THE UNKNOWN SOLDIER

If "Shall the Fundamentalists Win?" was Fosdick's foremost sacred speech, then surely "My Account with the Unknown Soldier" was his most significant secular speech. Unfortunately, the rhetorical critic confronts a problem of textual authenticity with this address that is not readily resolved.

The stirring speech he spoke at the Broadway Tabernacle, New York City, May 7, 1934, was preceded by the equally impassioned sermon he delivered at Riverside on November 12, 1933. The former speech, entitled "My Account with the Unknown Soldier," was delivered to an audience of three hundred ministers and laymen at a two-day Conference on War and Economic Injustice at the Tabernacle. The latter sermon, "The Unknown Soldier," was delivered to a much larger Riverside audience on the Sunday following Armistice Day. Of the two persuasive messages, the Riverside sermon contains the more robust rhetoric because Fosdick faced a congregation that did not totally share his convictions. The speech at the Broadway Tabernacle, although highly publicized in the media as an important statement in the peace movement, was derived from the Riverside sermon but lacked some of its persuasive techniques and appeals. This was because Fosdick addressed an audience at the Tabernacle that already agreed with his persuasive premises.

The sermon that Fosdick delivered in 1933, "The Unknown Soldier," was anthologized in *Riverside Sermons*. The *New York Times* reported his Tabernacle speech in 1934, but unfortunately it did not print everything Fosdick said and regrettably paraphrased substantial portions of the address. The *Christian Century* printed a text but identified it as the sermon Fosdick first delivered at Riverside and then at the Tabernacle. As well as can be determined, the sermon printed in the *Christian Century* is closer to what Fosdick said at the Tabernacle than at Riverside. Without a recording it is difficult to ascertain what he said in the Riverside sermon of November 12, 1933 (for instance, neither the *Christian Century* nor the *Riverside Sermons* version has Fosdick's allusion to General Sherman's famous "War is hell" aphorism or his "I'll see you in prison first" statement about not sanctioning war that the *New York Times* quoted). The text that is printed in "Collected Speeches and Sermons" in this volume is as nearly as can be determined the sermon he delivered on November 12, 1933, in Riverside Church.[6]

The focus in this section on the "Unknown Soldier" speech is not on what Fosdick said at the Tabernacle, because that is impossible to determine, but upon the nature of the appeals he employed in the two speeches. Whenever possible, the rhetorical criticism that follows will attempt to reconstruct what he said at the Broadway Tabernacle from the *New York Times*'s version. For in fact, Fosdick made rhetorical adjustments to two dissimilar publics. These adaptations, which are more illuminating than a futile attempt to determine exactly what he said, reveal Fosdick's sensitivity to language. He realized that appropriate appeals for the Riverside and Tabernacle audiences needed to be subtly different.

Although his Riverside sermon was the more eloquent of the two speeches, the Broadway Tabernacle speech received the greatest media attention. A two-day conference on the peace movement was more newsworthy than an ordinary sermon, however moving it might have been. The *Christian Century* noted that the Tabernacle speech "attracted international attention." Oswald Garrison Villard praised Fosdick's speech by noting that he had crossed the Rubicon: "he has burned his bridges behind him. He has taken the irrevocable step. Others might voice such sentiments and recant in wartime. Dr. Fosdick cannot and will not." (Villard was correct: Fosdick did not change for expediency in World War II.) However, the militarists decried Fosdick's kind of rhetoric. Referring to the recent peace parades on college campuses during a meeting of the Government Club in the Hotel Astor, New York City, Colonel H. P. Hobbs characterized them as "un-American" and a retired army major said the pacifists were "either too yellow to fight or wanted to grab-off something."[7]

Notwithstanding the persuasive stance he took on pacifism (and that will be criticized in due course), the two addresses, which were significantly more similar than different, excelled in four of the five classical canons of rhetoric. Cicero codified the canons in *De Inventione*: *inventio*, the creativity and inventiveness of the address; *dispositio*, the speech's organizational arrangement; *elocutio*, its style and diction; and *actio*, its delivery. The fifth canon, *memoria*, the commitment to memory of an address, was the most culturally bound canon of the ancient world. It has been increasingly ignored by speakers as paper-and-pencil technology improved, so much so, in fact, that by the twentieth-century, most orators had ceased to practice it at all; however, Fosdick's delivering the speech from a manuscript evidently had no appreciable negative effect on the reception of his address as gauged by his listening audience.[8]

Fosdick also used an organizational pattern, which suggested his indebtedness to classical rhetoric, that he probably learned in speech classes at Colgate. Credited to Korax, an ancient Greek rhetorician who lived in the fifth century B.C., the so-called "Classical" pattern aided the orator in the *dispositio* or arrangement of the address. Cicero also discussed the pattern in *De Inventione*. Korax and Cicero advised the orator to begin the speech with an *exordium*, or introduction, that was designed to make the listeners receptive to the speaker and the message. Next, the speaker used a *narratio*, or narration, to describe the thesis or problem in terms sympathetic to the orator's cause. The orator then used a *confirmatio*, or an arguments section, to marshal the reasoning and evidence that supported the main contentions. Cognizant that some members of the audience still might not be persuaded, Korax and Cicero advised the orator to adapt to those listeners in a section entitled the *refutatio*, or refutation. In this division, the speaker tried to refute objections or reservations that might reside in listeners' minds. To conclude the speech, the orator was advised to construct an *epilogus*, or a moving peroration, to bring belief and action.[9]

To arrest the attention of both audiences, Fosdick used irony in his introduction. Alluding to Armistice Day, he said it was "interesting" that Christians, committed to the worship of Christ, should partake in the military and patriotic pageantry that surrounded the unknown soldier, whom Fosdick characterized with alliteration as an "unrecognizable body of a soldier blown to bits on the battlefield." Claiming that the "war lords" chose the unknown soldier as the symbol of war, Fosdick, for argumentative purposes, accepted the symbol "from their hands."

Fosdick used the narration to frame his participation as a clergyman in World War I in an unfavorable perspective. Acknowledging that he had been sent by the government to address the troops in order "to strengthen their morale," he wondered if he had steeled the Unknown Soldier to go on a suicidal grenade mission, from which only half the company came back, or had admonished the Unknown Soldier to go on a patrol in No Man's Land. For the Riverside audience, but not for the Tabernacle listeners, Fosdick then made a remarkable statement. Using the rhetorical technique of affirmation-by-denial, wherein the orator affirms a point by appearing to deny it, he challenged his congregation to listen to his sermon by appearing indifferent to whether it did: "You here this morning may listen to the rest of this sermon or not, as you please. It makes much less difference to me than usual what you do or think. I have an account to settle in this pulpit today between my soul and the Unknown Soldier." Thusly challenged, even an opponent would be motivated to listen if for no other reason than to confute Fosdick's contentions.

At Riverside, he began the argument's division with a bitter irony. Reminding his audience that ancient gods and even Jehovah demanded the best animals for bloody sacrifice, Fosdick assured his audience that the Unknown Soldier was doubtlessly "sound of mind and body," that "The god of war still maintains the old demand." Scoring the uses toward which modern medicine and psychiatry were applied, he questioned whether "nations should pick out their best, use their scientific skill to make certain that they are the best, and then in one mighty holocaust offer ten million of them on the battlefields of one war?" This argument was not presented in the Tabernacle address probably because the partisan audience already believed it; however, for an audience that doubtlessly contained opponents, the irony was telling. Continuing in the vein that this was a personal sermon, he summarized the first argument with an emphasis on the pronoun *I*, with which a sympathetic listener could easily identify:

"I have an account to settle between my soul and the Unknown Soldier. I deceived him. I deceived myself first, unwittingly, and then I deceived him, assuring him that good consequences could come out of that. As a matter of hard-headed, biological fact, what good can come out of that? Mad civilization, you cannot sacrifice on bloody altars the best of your breed and expect anything to compensate for the loss.

Although these words passed as an apparent soliloquy, Fosdick cleverly invited the audience to acknowledge it had been duped, as he had been, by the implicit promise to make World War I the war to end all wars. (This passage was also in the Tabernacle address.)

The second argument in the Riverside sermon, but the first one for the peace conference, was an attack on conscription. Decrying the tautology that the reason the United States had to have conscription was because it was necessary to win the war, Fosdick placed that patriotic pablum in an undesirable perspective: "We cannot get soldiers--not enough of them, not the right kind of them--without forcing them. When a nation goes to war now, the entire nation must go. That means that the youth of the nation must be compelled, coerced, conscripted to fight."

Then to invoke sympathy with these young men, he used emotionally laden language to suggest how men loved girls rather than war, loved as young husbands or fathers rather than as fighters. To heighten the exigency, he predicted that in the next war women would be coerced as well as property, and eventually liberty would be lost. Giving an artistic unity to this argument, he again subtly invited his audience to join with him in soliloquizing to the Unknown Soldier: "If I blame anybody about this matter, it is men like myself who ought to have known better. We went out to the army and explained to these valiant men what a resplendent future they were preparing for their children by their heroic sacrifice. O Unknown Soldier, however can I make that right with you?" Amidst the Depression, with Hitlerism drawing nourishment from the miasmas of the aftermath of the Treaty of Versailles, Fosdick's proof was warranted.

At this point, the Riverside sermon diverged in persuasive intent, but not in language, from the Tabernacle address.   This apparent anomaly needs to be explained. For the Riverside listeners, Fosdick used a *refutatio* to confute objections in their minds (notwithstanding protestations in his introduction about not caring whether they listened, the refutation suggests that he was trying to persuade them). For the Tabernacle audience, the refutation did not serve a disputative purpose, given that the audience was initially pacifistic, but rather reinforced their pacifism.   That is, the same language that functioned in a refutation section for the mixed audience at Riverside served as additional reasons in a continued arguments section for the partisan audience at the peace conference.   Assuming assent from the audience at the Tabernacle, Fosdick could have sarcastically delivered the arguments that his committed audience already rejected.   But for the Riverside congregation, he would have tempered his tone of address and spoken straightforwardly.   How identical language can function differently for disparate audiences can be appreciated in his *refutatio*.

Fosdick framed the first objection. "Probably," he artfully allowed to his audience, "you say, the Unknown Soldier enjoyed soldiering and had a thrilling time in France. . . . Indeed, you say, how could martial music be so stirring and martial poetry so exultant if there were not at the heart of war a lyric glory?" His reply was a devastating rebuttal to his opponents but a reinforcing argument for his adherents:

> The trouble with much familiar talk about the lyric glory
> of war is that it comes from people who never saw any
> soldiers. . . . You ought to have seen the hardening-up
> camps of the armies which had been at the business since
> 1914. Did you ever see them? Did you look, as I have
> looked, into the faces of young men who had been over the
> top, wounded, hospitalized, hardened-up--over the top,
> wounded, hospitalized, hardened-up--over the top, wounded,
> hospitalized, hardened-up--four times, five times, six times?

Never talk to a man who has seen that about the lyric glory
of war.

Given that the Tabernacle audience would agree with Fosdick's
assessment, he deleted from his address additional refutation that was
contained in the Riverside sermon. For that audience, he offered more
analysis to sustain his rebuttal. After quoting famous poems that extolled
warfare, he claimed that the poets Sir Walter Scott, Thomas Macaulay,
and Alfred, Lord Tennyson, never saw war. Turning to those who did
know war firsthand, he quoted George Washington, who said war is "a
plague to mankind." Then, in one of the most damning passages in the
sermon, he condemned easy patriotism:

The glory of war comes from poets, preachers, orators, the
writers of martial music, statesmen preparing flowery
proclamations for the people, who dress up war for other
men to fight. They do not go to the trenches. They do not
go over the top again and again and again.

He dared his congregation, but not the audience at the peace conference,
to go down to Arlington and tell the Unknown Soldier about the lyric
glory of war "*now*" [his italics].

His second refutation concerned the supposed idealism
surrounding war. He began by enunciating the soldierly characteristics
associated with idealism: loyalty, courage, venturesomeness, care for the
downtrodden, and capacity for self-sacrifice. In juxtaposition, he quoted
eyewitnesses about the real horrors of battle. He dramatically used the
vocative to address a personified War, whom he accused of using men to
make, rather than "a heaven on earth," a "hell on earth instead." Having
stirred the emotions of his hearers, he concluded with a logical appeal:
"fifteen years after the Armistice we cannot be sure who won the war, so
sunk in the same disaster are victors and vanquished alike."

His third refutation for the Riverside audience, or additional
reinforcement for his Tabernacle hearers, was to suppose the Unknown
Soldier was a Christian. He noted that religion was a force and, when
supplemented by Christian devotion, it became a source "of confidence
and power." "No wonder," he exclaimed, "the war departments wanted
the churches behind them!" He then cited the case of an American
general who ordered his troops to kill everyone over the age of ten on
the island of Samar in the Philippines during the Spanish-American war.
Rather than condemning the general, Fosdick averred that he was
tempted to state the general's case for him. Using the rhetorical
technique of turning-the-tables, wherein the orator takes an opponent's
position and turns it to the opponent's disadvantage, Fosdick rhetorically
asked why not kill everyone over ten: "Cannot boys and girls of eleven
fire a gun?" Fosdick doubtless realized the cold logic of his question was
repulsive, yet he pressed the point to its revolting conclusion: "That is
war, past, present, and future."

Before turning to Fosdick's moving *exordium*, a slight respite is in order. If verbiage is any indication of persuasive intent, then the relative allotment between the argument and refutation divisions in the Riverside sermon is instructive. Fosdick developed two major arguments and three refutative points. But in terms of words, about 15 percent of the sermon was *confirmatio* whereas he devoted about 50 percent of it to the *refutatio*. This is additional evidence that he wanted to persuade neutrals and opponents in his congregation. However, the speech at the Tabernacle was composed almost totally of argumentation targeted to believers. What was one audience's refutation was another audience's reinforcement.

In his powerful peroration, Fosdick reiterated the thesis of his "Shall We End War?" sermon and his "A Christian Conscience About War" speech: "We can have this monstrous thing or we can have Christ, but we cannot have both." Puissant with pathos, Fosdick used the vocative, much as George Whitefield did during the Great Awakening, to portray the voice crying in the wilderness: "O my country, stay out of war! . . . O church of Christ, stay out of war! . . . And O my soul, stay out of war!" The stylistic device of epistrophe, the ending of clauses or sentences with the same or similar words, lent an elegance to his pleas.

Hopeful yet cognizant that his words might not have persuaded everyone at Riverside, he personalized the sermon by settling his account with the Unknown Soldier. In a series of declaratory sentences that began with the anaphora of "I renounce war," he listed the practices he reviled, including "the dictatorships it [war] puts in the place of democracy." His final words were an intimate expiation: "I renounce war and never again, directly or indirectly, will I sanction or support another! O Unknown Soldier, in penitent reparation I make you that pledge." This conclusion functioned differently for the Tabernacle audience. In settling his account with the Unknown Soldier, Fosdick cleverly asked his audience to settle vicariously their accounts by validating his renouncing of war. (This psychological principle would have worked for Fosdick's partisans in the Riverside congregation, would have perhaps lured some neutrals into his fold, and would have perhaps made his opponents take pause.)[10]

From 1925 to 1933-1934, Fosdick made an important step as an orator. Whereas the "Shall We End War?" and "A Christian Conscience About War" talks had developed the problem, they were short on any viable solutions. Although the "Unknown Soldier" speeches were not archetypal problem-solution persuasions, he did at least call for the United States to join the League of Nations and World Court and for Americans to "contend undiscourageably for disarmament." Fosdick fulfilled the letter, if not the spirit, of the oratorical obligation to present an audience with a solution to satisfy an exigency.

Having established himself as a leading advocate for pacificism, Fosdick from time to time was called to deliver speeches for and to lend his name to the peace movement. For instance, he delivered a speech in New York City for the Emergency Peace Campaign, of which he was chairman, on January 10, 1937, and the speech was printed in the *Congressional Record*. He espoused his usual position on pacificism, but one argument bears special examination. In an interesting application of the saw that old men declare wars and young men fight them, Fosdick sardonically proposed that if an administration failed to keep the United States out of war, then ten senators, ten representatives, and ten cabinet members, all chosen by lot, should be the first to die in the front lines. On April 6, 1937, he delivered a speech in Washington, D.C., to the Emergency Peace Campaign. He told the audience "We know that in the last war we were unmercifully gypped; that nothing we went into the war to do for democracy was really done." [11]

The lasting effect of Fosdick's "Unknown Soldier" speeches has been aptly summarized by Robert Clark:

> With his instinct for the dramatic, Fosdick placed himself
> at the head of the pacifists and, unwittingly, in the vanguard
> of the isolationists. He had excited a dream for a world of
> peace which the people who heard him could never forget,
> but it was a dream which took little account of the realities
> of the international scene.

Clark correctly summarized the effects of Fosdick's rhetorics but was overly harsh on the preacher with regard to the reality of 1933-1934, which was not that of 1939-1941. Robert Miller rendered a more sympathetic, yet balanced, judgment of Fosdick's pacifism between the Riverside/Tabernacle speeches and his nationally broadcast persuasion on the Selective Service Act in 1940. [12]

KEEPING HIS WORD IN WORLD WAR II

War came to Europe on September 1, 1939. Powerless to act in the crisis, President Franklin D. Roosevelt took to the airwaves in his Fireside Chat on War, September 3, 1939, to pledge the United States to neutrality. However, FDR allowed that citizens did not have to be neutral in their thoughts: "This nation will remain a neutral nation, but I cannot ask that every American remain neutral in thought as well. . . . Even a neutral cannot be asked to close his mind or his conscience." Fosdick was vacationing in Maine, but reporters reached him there and quoted him as saying that he "rejoiced" over the president's pledge to keep the United States neutral. [13]

Fosdick's first rhetorical response to World War II was a sermon he preached at Riverside on October 1, 1939. In "The Christian Church's Message to America Today," reprinted in the *Congressional Record*, Fosdick proclaimed himself an ambassador of Christ. As such, and following Roosevelt's lead, Fosdick allowed that even neutrals or pacifists could express "That's bad" when Nazi armies were victorious and "That's better" when the allies won a victory. But that was as far as Fosdick was prepared to go in currying favor with his listeners.[14]

First, he pledged his congregation that as an ambassador of Christ, he would not rehearse the "repercussions of war's hatred" in his pulpit. Second, he straightforwardly told his listeners that the culpability for the war was shared by the allies as well:

> Granted that Hitler, backed by Stalin, is immediately responsible for this war. Granted that France and Britain did not want it and that Hitler forced it. Still, never forget who it was that made Hitler possible. We all did. . . . The European democracies easily could have saved democracy in Germany if they had cared half as much about democracy as now they say they do, and they refused. As for us in America, we would not so much as join an international organization to help. Hitler made this war, but we all helped to make Hitler. Not hatred of any people but humility becomes us now.

Third, to the argument that World War II would rid the world of Hitler, Fosdick gave an interesting response. He allowed that the previous war had rid the world of the Kaiser and that hopefully the present war would remove Hitler; however, drawing on the outcome of World War I, Fosdick doubted a second peace would be much different:

> War can defeat a Hitler, but by its very nature it creates Hitlerism and sows dragon's teeth from which a crop of other Hitlers springs. Be sure of this--however little you wish to be sure of it--this war will create more problems than it solves. A futile conflict a generation ago issued in an evil peace that, after 20 years of power politics, has issued in an evil war.[15]

Without the advantage of prescience, Fosdick's argument was reasonably based on historical precedent that he knew firsthand. If fault is to be found in his logic, it is that he did not calculate how new leaders could react differently to a peace than those of his generation did in World War I. But to require that Fosdick make that kind of political leap of faith, in terms of what he knew at the time, is perhaps too much to ask of a man who did not have the advantage of historical hindsight. Of course, President Roosevelt determined not to repeat the mistakes of the past by championing the United Nations, but, to Fosdick's credit, FDR was not saying that in 1939-1940 nor did he broach the subject of a United Nations peace-keeping force to maintain the peace after the war until the 1944 campaign, and then only obliquely. Ironically, President Harry Truman used a logic similar to Fosdick's in seeking support for the Korean War. In a speech to the nation in 1951, Truman reiterated Fosdick's indictment against the democracies, that they could have acted to prevent World War II, in order to support the ongoing but unpopular war in Korea: "If they [the peace-loving nations] had followed the right policies in the 1930's--if the free countries had acted together, to crush the aggression of the dictators, and if they had acted in the beginning, when the aggression was small--there probably would have been no World War II."[16]

On the other side of the argument, however, it must be stated that when the democracies could have acted, Fosdick and the pacifists urged positions that were inimical to interventionism and beliefs that inculcated isolationism. The dictators reacted to the mood in the United States that was, in part, informed by pacifist rhetoric. Fosdick's saying that the western democracies had a hand in creating Hitler was true enough, but, except for lukewarmly advocating the League of Nations, his rhetoric helped create the very situation he decried.

Before Pearl Harbor, Americans were ambivalent toward the war in Europe. Although the opinion polls during 1940 indicated that about 60-70 percent of the American people favored aid-short-of-war to England, less than 10 percent believed the United States should declare war. Even after the fall of France in June 1940, only about 20 percent of the people thought the United States should fight, whereas around 80 percent believed the United States should stay out, and these figures remained fairly constant until November 1941. President Roosevelt read the same opinion polls that the isolationists, noninterventionists, pacifists, and Hitler did, but Roosevelt determined that the United States must prepare for war. Therefore, FDR decided to make small incremental steps toward intervention. Lend-Lease and the destroyer deal were parts of his strategy, but the issue of conscription coalesced forces on both sides of the debate.[17]

Fosdick was a well known cleric and had committed himself to pacifism in highly publicized orations, but was not perceived as a partisan figure. It was entirely appropriate from a persuasive perspective that Senator Burton K. Wheeler (D-Montana) enlisted Fosdick's rhetorical talents in the Senator's skirmishes with the Roosevelt administration over the Selective Service Act. During the summer of 1940, the Congress held hearings on the Burke-Wadsworth bill and it was ready to act in August. Sensitive to rhetorical timing, Senator Burton sought and received from the Columbia Broadcasting System a slot on its "Public Affairs" program for Fosdick's broadcast. On Wednesday evening, August 7, 1940, Fosdick addressed the nation, and he probably reached as many or more listeners as he did on the National Vespers radio program. *Vital Speeches of the Day* titled his talk "The Crisis Confronting the Nation."[18]

In this speech, Fosdick demonstrated his mastery over rhetorical technique. He targeted one set of appeals to neutrals or uncommitted listeners who might be persuaded to support his position and a slightly different set of appeals to his partisans who could be reinforced by his rhetoric. The rhetorical tightrope he walked was well constructed.

In his introduction, he characterized the situation as "a real crisis," decried that "we are being rushed pell-mell into military conscription as a settled national policy," and demanded that "this hysterical haste be stopped." Partisans would have applauded that. But for the neutrals in his national audience, he subtly shifted the focus away from pacifism to basic democratic values and procedures. Concerning conscription, he wisely framed two issues that were hard to quibble with: "The people . . . have a right to demand at least two things: first, adequate evidence that it is necessary, and second, decent time for careful consideration."

To refute the administration's argument that conscription was necessary, Fosdick quoted Hanson W. Baldwin, noted writer and military analyst for the *New York Times*, who stated that the numbers of men that would be produced by conscription were not needed for hemispheric defense. Fosdick let the listener infer that if not for this hemisphere, then the conscripts must be meant for the European war; since few favored U.S. involvement in a European war, then they should logically be against conscription because it was clearly intended for that purpose. He used a transitional device, "I ask you, then, to consider briefly three aspects of this matter," to move the audience to his following points. Although the language of his transition was vintage Fosdick, the close reader would observe that he had already advanced refutative language against the question of whether conscription was necessary; therefore, the speech really consisted of four mainheads rather than the three that Fosdick identified.

"First [actually his second point]," Fosdick said, "we are told that conscription is the democratic way in which to meet our crisis." Reminiscent of Abraham Lincoln's famous words at Freeport, Illinois, in the debate with Stephen Douglas--that you can fool all of the people some of the time, and some of the people all of the time, but not all the people all of the time--Fosdick exclaimed that the government was "fooling the American people . . . [by] telling them that conscription is democratic." Rather, Fosdick asserted, conscription is the essence of militaristic autocracy, and "never can be called *democratic* [his italics]." Fosdick's claim lacked a warrant. He tried to use guilt-by-association-- because totalitarian states conscript soldiers the act must be undemocratic--to confuse the argument. By definition, any act passed by the Congress and signed by the President is democratic unless overturned by the Supreme Court. He also tried to argue *reductio ad absurdum*: if the government can conscript men, then why not wealth, industry, factories, labor, and so forth? The fallacy in his trying to reduce to absurdity the premise of conscription is that the government was not seeking seizure of property or wealth nor would the American people permit it to do so. Although partisans might have given assent to his first argument, it does not reasonably substantiate his point.

Fosdick fared much better in his second refutation. Proponents for conscription argued that voluntary enlistment had not worked to meet the emergency, and conscription was therefore needed to fulfill the demand. Fosdick denied the argument and wisely pointed out that voluntary methods "have not yet been adequately attempted or even explored." He suggested, for instance, that enlistments be encouraged for one year rather than three years under the status quo, or that the registration part of the present legislation be extended so that the manpower resources would be known but not necessarily conscripted. Perhaps knowing that his personal ethos might be gainsaid, he again cited a notable authority. This time, Fosdick chose Harry Woodring. Woodring was eased out of his position of secretary of war by Roosevelt so that he could appoint Henry Stimson to the cabinet (Stimson was an interventionist and a Republican, two admirable traits that aided FDR as he faced a third term election). Fosdick quoted Woodring to his audience:

> How any fair-minded member of Congress could say that
> we have given the voluntary system of enlistment for the
> United States Army a fair trial and that it has broken
> down, and therefore we need compulsory service, is beyond
> my understanding.

Listeners who realized Woodring was an isolationist might have questioned his bias, but the accuracy of his observation was nevertheless correct.

In a hatchet attack on the pacifists and isolationists to discredit them, the proponents of the conscription bill had characterized them as citizens who believed that democracy had rights but no duties. It was a clever device to malign their patriotism because they opposed the conscription bill. But Fosdick was keen to the attack. He wisely destroyed the image the proponents of conscription had affirmed. In four sentences that began with the anaphora of "Of course," he acknowledged that citizens had duties and that he was patriotic. However, he logically demonstrated that being a patriot did not require "cheering for this Conscription Bill," and held that such a requirement was a "*non sequitur.*" He applied *reductio ad absurdum* by showing that although manufacturers, businessmen, and educators had a duty to support democracy, that duty did not necessarily imply the need for their being drafted. Although Fosdick could have mentioned it, these classes of individuals were exempted from conscription by the proposed legislation in order to make it more palatable to the people. He then called upon Major General James Parsons, who favored conscription in a modified form, to testify that if the government wanted to extend the Monroe Doctrine to China and South America the army would need millions of men; however, if the goal were to defend the United States, a smaller but well-trained army would suffice. Whereas Fosdick let his audience infer in the beginning of his speech that the draftees would be used in Europe rather than for the purported purpose of defending the United States, this time he baldly stated the implication: "What is this conscript army for? A conscript army is needed only if we are going to send an expeditionary force to conquer, let us say, Europe or Asia. . . . [T]his hectic haste to force conscription on us is the policy of the belligerent interventionists." Fosdick obviously reinforced the beliefs of his partisan audience, but he very carefully chose his language for uncommitted persons so they would plainly see the real rationale behind the bill. Although its proponents dressed it up as a domestic defense bill, in reality, as Fosdick cogently explained, the measure was intended for intervention in Europe. Thus, he wisely appealed to Americans' fear, amply recorded in the opinion polls, of being forced into a foreign war.

"Mark this," Fosdick said as he concluded his speech. He reminded the people that neither the Republicans nor the Democrats inserted a plank for conscription in their convention platforms. Rather, Congress returned to Washington and stampeded the conscription bill "without adequate thought, without a fair chance even for the people to realize what is going on." In a direct radio appeal for the people to assert their democratic rights, Fosdick asked them to contact their elected officials. In line with his two-pronged persuasions, Fosdick's entreaty could be interpreted by partisans to pressure their elected representatives in Washington to vote against the Burke-Wadsworth bill, or it could be taken as a plea to uncommitted listeners to press for deliberate speed on such important legislation. In either case, Congress would notice that the American people would not be fooled quickly or easily.

Having secured a slot for Fosdick on CBS, Senator Wheeler addressed the nation over the National Broadcasting Company's radio airwaves on August 15, 1940. "Marching Down the Road to War," the title of his address, said it all. As a matter of fact, Wheeler plainly described what Fosdick had only hinted at. The senator complained that the act purposefully drafted the ignorant, poor, unemployed, and unskilled while leaving desirable categories untouched. The class bias of the legislation, as exposed by Wheeler, was painfully obvious. Nevertheless, Congress passed the selective service act in September 1940 and Roosevelt signed it into law.[19]

CONCLUSION

The difficulty one encounters in pronouncing a verdict on Fosdick's pacifist rhetoric is similar to the onerous task that confronts professing Christians. Christ's way is not altogether easy or rational. Although there are cogent arguments for the just war and national self-defense, Fosdick constructed a sound theological and persuasive position for Christian ministers on war: Mars and Christ are irreconcilable. (Under Fosdick's direction, and to his credit, the Riverside Church throughout World War II aided servicemen at home and abroad in an extensive and meaningful outreach program.) Even in his eighties, Fosdick played what role he could in the anti-Vietnam War movement.[20]

On the other hand, as humans who miss the mark (the original meaning of the Greek verb *harmotano* that was used for *sin* in the New Testament), Christians killed, and still continue to do so, fellow believers.

The enormity of Nazism, which easily can be gleaned from newspapers of the day even before the war began and most certainly after the war commenced, demanded an evil response. To Fosdick's acclaim, he did not make sin patriotic: the Father was greater for Fosdick than the fatherland. Whatever difficulty one might have in accepting a pragmatic application of Fosdick's rhetoric to his era or to contemporary times, he at least bore witness to the standards to which humans strive but cannot obtain.

4
Reforming the Reform: Going Beyond Modernism

On November 3, 1935, in the pulpit of the Riverside Church, Harry Emerson Fosdick delivered his last landmark sermon. "The Church Must Go Beyond Modernism" was his response to certain exigencies that he perceived in contemporary Christianity's relationship to twentieth-century life. Specifically, he believed that in the church's attempt to adapt to the new knowledge and to transcend the fundamentalist's reaction to scientific inquiry, it had developed a response that stressed an intellectual approach to religion at the expense of man's spiritual needs. Daniel Ross Chandler noted this watered-down religion:

> Jesus as Suffering Servant became supplanted by a nice-guy Jesus neatly tailored in his grey flannel suit, telling children simple stories with a well-toned Virginia accent. No longer was a crude cross a symbol of sacrificial love; instead a golden lapel pin in the shape of a cross became emblematic of cloistered membership within a Sunday morning donut-dunking fellowship.

The operative word in the title of Fosdick's sermon was the preposition "beyond" because he did not envision a backward movement to conservatism but apparently a religion that arched over modernism.[1]

"The Church Must Go Beyond Modernism" was Fosdick's repudiation of the nineteenth- and early twentieth-century deification of man and especially of his intellect. At the basis of his attack on the fundamentalists was his belief that man's mental advances, particularly in the form of scientific discovery and Biblical scholarship, demanded that thinking Christians should give assent to a modern religion that was adjusted to the times. So, too, did he believe that a faith in reason, when confronted with the incredible human and material losses from World War I, would persuade people and leaders of all nations to ban war as an outmoded method of settling international conflicts and disputes. But the era of faith in man's spiritual and intellectual progress, sorely tested during and in the aftermath of World War I, had turned sour in a world of Depression, Mussolini, and Hitler by the 1930s.

Rhetorically, Fosdick had already supported and then gone beyond modernism in his important sermons. He helped assure the victory of modernism over fundamentalism in "Shall the Fundamentalists Win?" In truth, he eschewed the compromising tendencies in modernism when he threw down the theological gauntlet in "A Christian Conscience About War" in 1925. He enacted his pacifist rhetoric in "My Account with the Unknown Soldier" in 1934 by renouncing war. So, by 1935 Fosdick had personally and publically gone beyond modernism. True to his prophetic calling, he would now lead his congregation beyond modernism's twentieth-century reaction to fundamentalism, but to what "ism"?

The title of the sermon belied its intent. At first blush, Fosdick appeared to promise more than he delivered: he offered no new "ism." Although he uttered a clarion call for Christians to leave behind the modernist camp, he did not make it altogether clear in his talk where he intended the committed to march. (In this respect, the sermon was akin to "A Christian Conscience About War" wherein the problem was stated amply but a workable solution was notably lacking; although in that sermon he could not speak for his government or church, he implemented a solution a decade later when he crossed the Rubicon in his famous "Unknown Soldier" speech.) The modernist sermon was in truth an explication of a sacred and secular solution that Fosdick had already adopted personally. The next step was to urge the church to follow him. What has not been perceived before in this homily is Fosdick's integrity of rhetorical thought, even though not in tightly reasoned Scriptural exegesis, that informed his significant sermons on national spiritual issues.

The sermon was Fosdick's mea culpa, but to the degree that he spoke for the modernists, it was a nostra culpa. The modernist homily also shared similar ends with "Shall the Fundamentalists Win?" but these persuasive objectives were obtained by a directly opposite rhetorical stance. Ostensibly functioning as an attack on the modernist creed (whereas the fundamentalist homily was cleverly disguised as a defense of liberalism), the sermon really functioned as a personal apologia for Fosdick's modernism and a defense of his repudiation of certain of its tenets (as oppositionally Fosdick actually attacked the fundamentalists and their creeds). Moreover, by apologizing for his modernism, which he had tacitly done in his "Unknown Soldier" speech wherein he defined support for Mars as un-Christian, he subtly invited his congregation to eschew modernism, just as he had elusively enticed them to join the pacifist ranks in his earlier speech. Championing the moral position of the church, he challenged it and the modernists to renew the debate over the role of the Christian church in the mid-twentieth century.

Yet what Fosdick did not repudiate in modernism bears

examination. Although he decried modernism's cozy relationship with a faith in intellectual and spiritual attainment, he was not prepared to abandon the intellectual and spiritual advancements that modernism had given to modern Christians. Although he scored the concept of progress, it was doubtless his implied faith in progress that impelled him to move beyond modernism. Although he abhorred the tendency in modernism toward adjustment, Fosdick veritably sought adaptation to exigencies in the world as he perceived them; thus, his quibble was not so much with the practice of adjustment as it was with the end toward which adjustment was applied. And although he revived, almost in passing, the idea of sin, which was generally lacking in his religious rhetoric, he did not develop how man missed the mark or even what God's target was.

In truth, the sermon did not go beyond modernism. Rather, it was as a modernist and in the spirit of modernism that Fosdick de-emphasized some of its excesses and tinkered with some of its tenets, thereby readjusting it to the 1930s. The rhetoric of going beyond modernism was in reality an attempt to save modernism.

It is generally conceded that Fosdick was not a great systematic theologian, a characterization he was never at pains to refute. However, if the fundamentalist, Christian conscience, and modernist sermons are conceived as doctrines and reasons that were preached in installments, and if the unknown soldier speech is conceived as an application in the Puritan sermonic sense, then Fosdick's pastoral persuasions have a logical completeness that compels respect. To Fosdick's credit, he practiced what he preached: he went beyond modernism, but only in the sense that he assumed the high moral ground that he occupied until his death on the Mars-versus-Jesus rhetoric, which from Fosdick's perspective preachers of modernism had abandoned.

THE CHURCH MUST GO BEYOND MODERNISM

In terms of organizational strategy, Fosdick wittingly or unknowingly patterned his sermon after Abraham Lincoln's famous "House Divided" speech, delivered in Springfield, Illinois, on June 16, 1858. In that address, senatorial candidate Lincoln reviewed the history of the slavery question with these words: "If we could first know where we are, and whither we are tending, we could better know what to do, and how to do it." In his sermon, Fosdick assayed where the church stood in the 1930s and whence it tended, and, as Lincoln had proposed his candidacy as a solution to what Republicans could do about slavery, Fosdick called on Christians to follow him in advancing to a higher ground. Nor did the similarities end there. As Lincoln outlined the advancement of the cause of slavery in the United States, Fosdick traced the historical development of theologies that devolved to the present time. Like Lincoln, he perceived that current tendencies needed to be checked, that in a certain sense "a house divided against itself cannot stand." Moreover, Fosdick, as prophet, cast his argumentation so that the church, like Lincoln and his Republican party, would stand apart from society in order to lead society to its moral and spiritual fulfillment.

Fosdick introduced his sermon with a compelling example of the effects of the tenets of hellfire and damnation. "Fifty years ago," he narrated, "a boy of seven years of age was crying himself to sleep at night in terror lest, dying, he should go to hell, and his solicitous mother, out of all patience with the fearful teachings which brought such apparitions to the mind, was trying in vain to comfort him." With a flair for the dramatic moment, he then poignantly revealed "That boy is preaching to you today." The rest of the sermon was autobiographical, but not so personally so as was his introduction.

The problem, as Fosdick conceived it, was that Western civilization turned "one of the most significant mental corners" in the 1880s and the church "was utterly unfitted for the appreciation of that view." Like Lincoln, he used the past to explain the present, but contended that the present, as the past had been, was unable to meet moral questions; therefore, a viable future must break with the past and present. To warrant his assertion, he argued that the great documents of protestantism, the Augsburg and Westminister Confessions, were pre-Newtonian documents. As a result, Fosdick claimed that young people such as himself were faced with "an appalling lag" between intellect and religion. Referring to the "new knowledge," the nomenclature Ivy Lee had used to retitle Fosdick's attack on the fundamentalists in 1922, he claimed people of his generation "refused to live bifurcated lives, our intellect in the late nineteenth century and our religion in the early sixteenth."

Having already marched forward, as in the Mars-vs-Jesus sermons, Fosdick called on Christians to join him: "The church thus had to go as far as modernism but now the church must go beyond it." It is essential to understand that Fosdick condemned modernism for different reasons than he did fundamentalism. Fundamentalism was at best a freezing of the status quo, at worst a backward, regressive religion. In reaction to fundamentalism, modernism had been forward looking, but as an intellectual response grounded in late nineteenth- and early twentieth-century exigencies, it had become dogma. Unless reformed, it could become ossified as was fundamentalism. And in fundamentalism, Fosdick perceived no saving graces. Although he was not prepared to eschew modernism, for at its core it implied spiritual growth and secular progress, Fosdick wanted to adjust certain of its tenets because he perceived they needed adapting to the immediate present and to the forseeable future.

With regard to the slavery issue, Lincoln accused the Democratic party of compromising with the South. Indeed, according to Fosdick, that was modernism's essential nature: "it is primarily an adaptation, an adjustment, an accommodation of Christian faith to contemporary scientific thinking." Like the pre-Civil War society that accepted slavery as a peculiar institution, so did Fosdick complain that modernism had served its purpose for its time, but that it is "no adequate religion to represent the Eternal and claim the allegiance of the soul. Let it be a modernist who says that to you!" Then, as Lincoln did, Fosdick used the body of his sermon to develop his points in greater historical detail.

"In the first place," as Fosdick typically orally signposted his points, "modernism has been excessively preoccupied with intellectualism." Notice that he did not attack the core of modernism, just its excesses. Then, as he sometimes did (a practice to be developed in chapter 5), Fosdick fleshed out supporting materials from his fundamentalist sermon of 1922. There, he used man's achievements in music, painting, and architecture to support his contention that development was the manner in which God worked out his will on earth. In the modernist sermon, he used the same three examples for the same persuasive point, but name dropped musicians such as Bach and Beethoven, added artistic appellations such as Raphael and Michelangelo, and compared the catacombs of Rome with the Gothic (a broad hint to Riverside with its "expanded spaces and aspiring altitudes"?) in order to make the examples more eloquent. If Fosdick succeeded in making his style more Asian (the Greeks classified a style "Asian" if it was ornate and embellished, and "Attic" if it was plain and unadorned), he also achieved new attainments in diction. For surely such words as "sackbuts," an early form of the trombone, and "ambit," compass or limits, which were used in his first mainhead, would send one to a dictionary. He summarized his first point with an appeal to reason and a Scriptural proof text. As for reason, he combined the best of the Asian and Attic style in an eminently quotable line: "Our modern world, as a whole, cries out not so much for souls intellectually adjusted to it as for souls morally maladjusted to it, not most of all for accommodators and adjusters but for intellectual and ethical challengers." More to the point, he used the example of St. Paul to substantiate his plea. In his first letter to the Corinthians, Paul allowed that he had become all things to all men so that they might be saved. But in his second letter, he exhorted Christians to "come ye out from them, and be ye separate." Decrying the present tendency to harmonize with a secular culture, Fosdick opined: "Only an independent standing-ground from which to challenge modern culture can save either it or you."

"In the second place," Fosdick said, modernism was "dangerously sentimental." Addressing the congregation as well as himself, he observed "that two whole generations were fairly bewitched into thinking that every day in every way man was growing better and better." As man's goodness waxed, the need for God's moral judgment waned. As a matter of fact, Fosdick charged, "Modernism, however, not content with eliminating the excrescences of a harsh theology, became softer yet and created the general impression that there is nothing here to fear at all."

Turning to the dictionary, one would find that "excrescence" is an abnormal outgrowth. Note that Fosdick did not score the modernist tendency to eschew a hellfire and damnation theology, but said that it went too far in the debunking process. Fosdick advocated the middle road:

> Because I know that I am speaking here to many minds powerfully affected by modernism, I say to you as to myself: Come out of these intellectual cubicles and sentimental retreats which we built by adapting Christian faith to an optimistic era. Underline this: Sin is real. Personal and social sin is as terribly real as our forefathers said it was, no matter how we change their way of saying so. And it leads men and nations to damnation as they said it did, no matter how we change their way of picturing it.

In diction, Fosdick's depiction of sin is about as close to Jonathan Edwards's famous sermon entitled "Sinners in the Hands of an Angry God" as Fosdick ever came. Instead of graphically portraying man as a spider held over the pit of hell by an avenging God who at any time could drop the loathsome insect into the fire, Fosdick used the palliating imagery of a painted picture to suggest the church should "shine, like a Rembrandt portrait, from the dark background of fearful apprehension; . . . it must stand out from the world and challenge it, not be harmonized with it."

"In the third place," Fosdick enumerated, "modernism has even watered down and thinned out the central message and distinctive truth of religion, the reality of God." He used *reductio ad absurdum* effectively when he allowed that modernism had "left souls standing, like the ancient Athenians, before an altar to an Unknown God" and admitted that "We have at times gotten so low down that we talked as though the highest compliment that could be paid Almighty God was that a few scientists believed in him."

"Finally," he signposted his last mainhead, "modernism has too commonly lost its ethical standing ground and its power of moral attack. . . . Harmonizing slips easily into compromising." In an elegant series of anaphora, "Christianity adapts itself to contemporary nationalism, contemporary imperialism, contemporary capitalism, contemporary racialism," he mentioned the kinds of issues modernism might address. Yet that was as much or as far as Fosdick went in this sermon on those pressing problems; indeed, his oral nod to those exigencies was akin to paying lip service to them.

Having communicated his doctrines and reasons that concomitantly functioned as the problem part of his sermon, he then turned to the application or solution of his homily. As one might expect, it dealt with the issue of war. He contrasted American churches with those in Hitler's country: "It is not in Germany alone that the church stands in danger of being enslaved by society. There the enslavement is outward, deliberate, explicit, organized. Here it is secret, quiet, pervasive, insidious." In Germany and the United States, he believed, both societies whispered: "Adjust yourself, adapt yourself, accommodate yourself!" (In this oft-quoted statement, Fosdick elegantly combined alliteration with epistrophe.) But Fosdick would not have the church compromise with contemporary culture. Announcing that the modernists had already won the battle with the fundamentalists, Fosdick allowed they were still around "but mostly in the backwaters," he proclaimed that the future of the church was in the hands of the modernists. Therefore, it was as a modernist that Fosdick challenged the church to "stand out from it [secular society] and challenge it!"

The effects of Fosdick's modernist sermon were probably realized in the religious world more than in secular society. Aside from the Riverside congregation, Fosdick's mediating audiences were the modernists, fundamentalists, and neo-Orthodox. These camps continually traded accusations and apologies about their respective preaching. In assessing these theological skirmishes, Harold Brack believed that "Estimates of the extent to which the issue affected the bulk of weekly preaching across the nation differ from 'significantly' to 'minimally.' Some suggest that the impact was restricted mainly to centers of theological education and their environs." The neo-Orthodox had charged modernism and Fosdick, as one of its leading spokesman, with misunderstanding sin, the perverse nature of man, and man's total alienation from God. Perhaps as a sop to the neo-Orthodox, Fosdick told his congregation to underline that sin is real, but that figurative language was as far as he expressed himself on the subject. However, as Robert Clark concluded, Fosdick "did not ally himself with the neo-Orthodox." And Fosdick dismissed outright the fundamentalists in the conclusion of his sermon.[2]

The liberals reacted most favorably to Fosdick's sermon because he reinforced their theological and social battles with the fundamentalists. As a matter of fact, the *Christian Century* helped Fosdick make his case, and on one major point, better than he himself had. In an editorial, it supported Fosdick's sermon but quibbled with only one of his points. The editors suggested that Fosdick's thesis that modernism had led the way in compromising with contemporary culture was misanalyzed. They argued that "Protestantism was born with the birth of modern culture. Capitalism, nationalism, and Protestantism are historically, if the expression may be allowed, triplets." Only because Fosdick was a modernist could he perceive the problem, but it was not of modernism's making:

> In reality, of course, it is modernism which has opened our
> eyes to the existence of this alliance of Christianity with the
> most unchristian elements of secular culture. Dr. Fosdick
> and all who share his view have come to their present
> position by way of modernism. No fundamentalists have

joined their circle. . . . It is only in liberal circles that
Fosdick's thesis . . . is comprehended!

In the next installment, in which the text of Fosdick's "Beyond
Modernism" was not included because it had not been received by press
time, the *Christian Century* reiterated the efficacy of modernism: "This
betrayal of Christianity into the hands of nationalism and capitalism was
made, it must be repeated, not by liberalism, but by historical orthodoxy.
It was liberalism which discovered the betrayal. Orthodoxy never would
have discovered it, and has not yet discovered it."[3]

Conclusion

The only substantive application Fosdick made in his modernist
sermon was to talk about the Christian church's relationship to
militarism. To be sure, that was an exigency that certainly needed
mediation. But, as noted earlier, it is also instructive to observe what
Fosdick did not talk about. Although the United States was well into the
sixth year of the Depression, Fosdick was practically oblivious to that fact
in this sermon. He challenged in famous sermons only a small segment
of evil in the 1930s. Fosdick has not been identified with stances on
pressing economic issues, as was Father Charles Coughlin with his Union
for Social Justice, which arguably was an overarching of modernism for
a church that had not even progressed to modernism; or with political
issues, such as the role of labor unions in helping the working man
against an entrenched capitalist system; or with racial issues, such as the
plight of blacks, who were doubly hit with the Depression. Actually,
Fosdick had an early affinity with unions as this was his subject for an
M.A. thesis for Columbia University in 1908; however, as he progressed
from Montclair to Park Avenue to Riverside Drive, the obvious evidently
occured.[4]

The rhetorical and exegetical problem with modernism, or with
fundamentalism, is that modernism is what the preacher says it is. To
the degree that the spoken word deviates from the Word, it ceases
correspondingly to be the Word. Perhaps Fosdick feared he would water
down the efficacy of his message if he applied it to a broad spectrum of
issues, and so he limited himself to modernism and militarism. Yet, it
may be argued that in a sermon addressed to Christians, Fosdick used
the term "Christ" only five times, alluded only once, in relationship to
militarism, to "where Christ intended his church to stand," and was more
comfortable in quoting authors and poems than he was Scripture. Nor
can it be gainsaid that testimony from the Gospels indicates that Jesus
talked considerably more about theological and social problems than
militarism. As a matter of fact, Fosdick asserted, without any Scriptural
warrant, that Christ wanted his church to stand where Fosdick thought it
ought to stand. Having discarded an imperfectly dictated and humanly
transcribed Word, modernists were left merely with the word.

5
Preaching at Riverside

Fosdick was a fecund preacher. He generally eschewed statistics but in the case of the Christian conscience sermon he marshalled them tellingly. Accordingly, some data about his oratory reveals his reach as a persuader. At Riverside Church, where he made his lasting mark on a generation of listeners and swayed sermonizing for several generations, he preached some 657 sermons. This compares to approximately 76 sermons at First Presbyterian Church, 92 homilies at Park Avenue Baptist Church, and 28 talks at Temple Beth-El, New York City, where the Park Avenue congregation worshipped, having sold and vacated their edifice, until the Riverside Church could be occupied. Thus, Fosdick spoke from the pulpit approximately 853 times (this figure excludes the sermons he delivered at Montclair, New Jersey, because he burned them).

He did not, however, have a new homily every time he spoke. Many of his sermons were repreached several times (the record appears to be the sermon entitled "Blessed Are the Meek," which was given six times over thirteen years). In some instances, he preached a sermon in the First Presbyterian Church, then in the Park Avenue Baptist Chruch, then in Temple Beth-El, and finally at Riverside. True enough, he revised many of these homilies, though sometimes this was only a title change, and rewrote partially or substantially many of them for redelivering. As close as can be determined, Fosdick actually wrote about 652 sermons.

He also spoke over the National Vespers. Early in his career, he usually redelivered a Sunday's sermon weeks or months later. Throughout these years, he often first delivered an Easter, Thanksgiving, Christmas, or other thematic sermon on the morning of his evening broadcast. Increasingly during World War II, he tended to deliver a sermon on Sunday and then give it again that evening on the National Vespers. Interestingly, of Fosdick's major persuasions, he only delivered

"The Church Must Go Beyond Modernism" on his radio ministry. Fosdick delivered approximately 510 sermons on the radio. After his retirement from Riverside in 1946, Fosdick was called back occasionally to its pulpit, but he did not make any further radio broadcasts over the National Vespers.

If not the first preacher to hold the distinction of broadcasting on television (Franklin Roosevelt was the first president to broadcast over television in opening the 1939 World's Fair in New York City), Fosdick surely numbered among the pioneers. He delivered "The Decisive Babies of the World" on December 28, 1941 (see Calendar of Sermons).

The liturgical seasons of the year demanded responses. Palm Sunday, Easter, Thanksgiving, and Christmas deserved special preparation.   In the late 1920s and well into the 1930s, Fosdick remembered Armistice Day on the Sunday closest to that national holiday. On the first Sunday in May, he delivered a Children's Sermon, but these were not so childlike that he felt uncomfortable in delivering many of them over the National Vespers. However, two genres of sermons were not broadcast. Usually in April, Fosdick preached a budget sermon (such appeals would have appeared unseemly over the national radio), and he also preached communion sermons that were too intimate for the general radio audience.

In addition to these pastoral duties, from 1919 to 1954 when Fosdick declined further speaking engagements, he made time for approximately 120 secular speeches, which were often delivered as college and university commencement addresses or as chapel talks.   These addresses were usually on sacred topics. For instance, Fosdick went on a speaking tour of prestigious eastern college campuses where he gave six commencement addresses in thirteen days, June 7, 1929, to June 20, 1929, which averaged a speech every two days. Ironically, the title of that speech, which was also delivered at Park Avenue and Riverside, was "Religion and Play." When added to the times he preached that topic as a sermon, "Religion and Play" holds the record of being delivered to eleven audiences.

Thus, Fosdick delivered approximately 973 speeches and sermons during his pastorate. When the number of homilies he delivered over the National Vespers is added to his secular and sacred persuasions, he addressed the American people almost 1500 times (1484, to be exact) from 1919 to 1954.

On a Sunday-to-Sunday basis, Fosdick did not deliver sermons that shook the nation, such as "Shall the Fundamentalists Win?" or invigorated the peace movement, such as "My Account with the Unknown Soldier" or debated the neo-Orthodox, such as "The Church Must Go Beyond Modernism." Rather, he discharged his duties as a pastor in delivering homilies that were designed not to capture the nation's headlines, but to help members of his congregation and his listening audience for the National Vespers radio program. Of course, many of these sermons eventually were published in his many books, and occasionally one of them appeared in the *Christian Century*. Indeed, it should be said that his crafting sermon after sermon probably honed his abilities to construct the occasional persuasions by which he was, and still is, remembered.

The purpose of this chapter is to examine Fosdick's management of language in a sermon entitled "Handling Life's Second-Bests." It was selected because (1) it spanned his career; (2) it was delivered six times (once at First Presbyterian, October 29, 1922; thrice at Riverside, January 18, 1931, November 2, 1938, and March 21, 1944; and twice over National Vespers, February 8, 1931, and April 30, 1944; (3) a recording of the sermon exists; and (4) Fosdick anthologized it in *The Hope of the World* and *Riverside Sermons*. A confluence of these factors presents an interesting and useful case study on Fosdick's invention, arrangement, style, and delivery of a significant speech. Although the critic cannot assume this sermon is either representative of his overall sermonic preparation or of his revisions for subsequent delivery on the National Vespers program or of his revision of a homily for another Sunday at a later date, it is indicative of his general methods.

Handling Life's Second-Bests (first edition)

In rhetorical conception and spiritual execution, Fosdick's "Handling Life's Second-Bests" as initially delivered at First Presbyterian Church on October 29, 1922, surpasses the subsequent editions of this sermon.[1]

First, he organized this speech on the modified Puritan sermonic form. Taking as his text the sixteenth chapter of The Acts of the Apostles, Fosdick proposed to explain how "Paul handled one of the great disappointments of his life." The apostle had wanted to go to Bithynia in Asia Minor, but in a vision Paul ascertained that God wanted him to go to Macedonia. Thus, as Fosdick concluded, Christianity passed from Asia into Europe: "I am sure that Paul at first must have thought it lamentable. I picture him arriving on the shores of the Aegean saying, 'I wanted to be in Bithynia and here I am in Troas.'" (For later purposes of comparison and contrast, it is worthwhile to note that Fosdick introduced his sermon in the context of explaining and applying a Biblical passage and was at pains to ground his message in a Scriptural context throughout his address.)

The doctrine was not an intellectual exegesis of religious history or an explication of some arcane Biblical truth, but a living lesson that members of the congregation could use in their everyday situations. The problem people faced in the twentieth century, as Paul did in the first, was to capitalize on disappointments. "Wanting Bithynia and getting Troas," Fosdick assayed, "how familiar an experience it is! But to take Troas, the second-best, the broken plan, the remainders of a disappointed expectation, and to make out of it the best thing you ever did in all your life--how much less familiar!"

Fosdick amplified the doctrine or problem area by using three examples. First, he relayed the story of Phillips Brooks, who wanted to be a professor at Harvard University but ended in the pulpit of Trinity Church in Boston. "He wanted Bithynia," Fosdick reminded his audience, "and he got Troas." Sir Walter Scott served as Fosdick's second example. Wanting to be a poet, Scott bowed to Byron in poety but made his everlasting fame as a novelist: "He wanted Bithynia; he got Troas; and lo! through Troas the open door to the best work he ever did." The third example was drawn from the congregation. "Is there anybody here who has not wanted Bithynia and gotten Troas? Is there anybody here who has not dealt with the problem of handling life's second-bests? . . . What will they do when they strike Troas?"

The solution part of the sermon was developed with reasons, as a Puritan preacher would have done, except that Fosdick was more intent on guiding the living than explicating the dead. "In the first place," as Fosdick typically developed his transitions, "Paul's religion entered in." Fosdick claimed that God had a purpose, although not always clearly revealed nor as one might want it to be revealed, for his people. In support of his assertion, he offered as evidence the Hudson River tunnel that was then being started as an example of purpose and planning; the case of a missionary named Adoniram Judson who wanted to be a missionary in India and ended up in Burma; and the example of Joseph from the Old Testament that illustrated Joseph's rise from slavery to prominence under the Pharoah. Fosdick internally summarized his first reason by drawing together the two points he made about religious experiences and God's purpose in them: "My friends, this morning in whatever Troas you may be, let your religion enter in! God never leads anybody into any situation where all the doors are shut. We too can live our way into the conviction that our lives are in the guiding companionship of God."

The second solution or reason that Fosdick developed concerned handling frustration. "The trouble with most folks when they miss Bithynia and come to Troas is that they begin pitying themselves," Fosdick wisely observed. But again Paul served as the model for another approach. Instead of pitying himself and turning inward and accomplishing nothing, he threw himself into helping other people to know Christ in Greece. Fosdick also narrated the success story of one William Duncan, who had been a missionary in Alaska for forty years.

Having posited the doctrine and supporting reasons, Fosdick then moved to the application. "My friends," he claimed in language that Franklin D. Roosevelt would later use to introduce many of his presidential speeches and Fireside Chats, "there is nothing in that attitude and its results which we cannot carry over into our lives." Utilizing homey examples, such as the child who needs help from an adult in an accident or the mother who nurses a youngster back to health or the older person who suddenly comes alive after being mentally on death's door for many years or young persons who were faced with rebuilding their lives after World War I, Fosdick invited listeners who could identify with those or similar situations to conceive challenges and hardships as opportunities for growth and development. Indeed, he used the metaphor of the pearl to illustrate superbly his point. Noting that the oyster at first tries to expel an irritating piece of sand from its body, Fosdick spoke anthopomorphically for the oyster when he opined that it finally reconciles itself and "makes of it one of the most beautiful things in the world."

Still in the application part of the sermon, Fosdick clearly summarized his homily. "This, then, is the conclusion of the whole matter," he stated, "because Paul had these two elements [faith in God's purpose and love for mankind] in his life, when he got to Troas his imagination was filled, not with defeat, but with victory." Using the example of a thirty-foot plank on the ground, on which anybody could walk, versus the same plank at the height of a cathedral tower, on which very few would walk, Fosdick used the ironical humor inherent in that case to shame the listeners. Then he applied the irony:

So the trouble with most of us, when we strike Troas, is that we picture ourselves defeated. We wanted Bithynia--we got Troas. We think we are beaten. We say we *are* beaten. We imagine ourselves beaten. And we are beaten [Fosdick's italics]. But just as soon as Paul got to Troas his imagination pictured victory.

The final and compelling case was an application of one of Aristotle's common topics (*koinoi topoi*) of more and less: as Jesus had made the best of his Troas, namely Calvary, could not members of the congregation do likewise? Challenged Fosdick:

He took a very hard thing and he made a pearl ideed!
And do you mean that in our smaller Troas there is not divine grace enough to see us through, so that it shall be not failure, but victory; not catastrophe, but one of the best chances of usefulness we ever had in all our lives!

Second, the speech excelled in rhetorical execution. The relationship between Paul's Biblical experiences and the congregation's contemporary lives, the dichotomy between defeat and victory, despair and hope, and the spiritual theme that God's purpose was often revealed in unexpected ways and times, was communicated by repetition and restatement. At least sixteen times in the course of the sermon, Fosdick mentioned Bithynia and Troas. His linguistically reiterating Bithynia and Troas achieved the status of rhetorical metaphor. Although still grounded in Biblical geography, Fosdick made Bithynia and Troas transcend time and place to serve as a twentieth-century model for how to handle life's second-bests. As a matter of fact, through Fosdick's exuberance in juxtaposing Troas with Bithynia, one might even infer that a human's perception of second-bests was in fact God's definition of a first-best. Moreover, Fosdick's use of repetition and restatement throughout his address achieved artistic completeness. He thematically unified his introduction, body, and conclusion.

In addition to quoting from two hymns and from three poems, which lent a literary air to his sermon, Fosdick also used the rhetorical technique of epistrophe in his conclusion. When he spoke about people being beaten, as quoted above, he effectively ended four successive sentences with the word "beaten." This showed the audience how a pessimistic thought could become a negative reality. Conversely, Fosdick did not need to ask his audience to think affirmatively: he clearly implied the point with the epistrophe without belaboring it, and the congregation could easily infer that by thinking positively, a Troas could be a Bithynia in disguise. Thus, Fosdick placed a Biblical message in the context of modern society and urged creative solutions to everday problems that the congregation, like Paul, faced in life.

Handling Life's Second-Bests (second edition)

Fosdick delivered this sermon for the second time in Riverside Church on January 18, 1931. Although the second edition clearly evolved from the first, it is unclear how Fosdick produced the second sermon. Most likely, he took a typed text of the first edition and emended it, and then an entirely new sermon text was typed. That he probably worked that way, at least some of the time, is suggested by the following texts that do exist.

The next time Fosdick preached the second edition was on Church Night, November 2, 1938. He took a typed copy of his January 18, 1931, sermon and made a few emendations on it. Although this sermon will not be treated in detail because it varies only slightly from the 1931 version under investigation, it is worthwhile to note in passing some of the changes Fosdick made. He deleted "today," which was appropriate for the Sunday morning service, and inserted "tonight" for Church Night. He also excised the Sir Walter Scott example, the Biblical example of Joseph, and a paragraph that dealt with one of Edwin Markham's poems. These minor changes did not appreciably alter the message of the sermon, but were probably made to reduce its length. The fact is that Fosdick pulled on old sermon out of the files, made a few emendations on it, and delivered it again seven years later.

While this point is being made, Fosdick used the same approach to produce his Riverside sermon and National Vesper broadcast in March and April of 1944. He took a carbon copy of the 1931 sermon and made substantial emendations on it. Since these talks are significantly different from the 1931 and ever-so-slightly-emended 1938 sermons, they will be discussed fully in the next section.

Whereas in the first edition Fosdick had begun his homily with a direct reference to Paul, in the second edition he introduced his sermon with the observation "that very few persons have a chance to live their lives on the basis of their first choice." He then added the example of James Whistler, who, having failed chemistry at West Point, claimed that if silicon had been a gas, he would have been a major general rather than an artist. Fosdick then basically re-used the same language from the first edition about Paul, Bithynia, and Troas.

If the primacy effect had any rhetorical efficacy in this speech, then the manner in which Fosdick began the sermon could well have changed its emphasis. The primacy effect holds that the opening language in a speech determines the audience's perception of the speaker, the initial reaction to the message, and how the audience will tend to receive the rest of the speech. By beginning this sermon with a reference to personal problems, and then reinforcing the thesis with the Whistler example, and finally turning to the example of Paul in the later part of the introduction, Fosdick directed the audience's concentration in this sermon toward an intellectual handling of individual problems while detracting attention from Paul as the central theological or spiritual symbol. Whereas in the first edition Paul's story was central to handling life's second-bests, in this sermon it played an important but supporting role. This tendency to de-emphasize Paul is also discernible in Fosdick's development of his reasons. In the second edition, he enlarged considerably the example of Phillips Brooks. He quoted several sentences from Brooks about his failures with Harvard undergraduate students and quoted from Brooks's father to illustrate his despair with teaching. These emendations made the Brooks example more interesting and probably illustrated more concretely Fosdick's point. But to the extent Fosdick achieved that end, audience attention was focused more on Brooks as a central figure and less on Paul.

Perhaps Fosdick realized that fact, because he corrected his course in the solution part of the sermon. The Holland Tunnel example in the first edition was historically dated, so Fosdick introduced new language. If the sermon had veered too far to starboard in discussing notable personalities, as in the Brooks and Sir Walter Scott examples, then he tacked to port:

> What is impressive about Paul is that whenever he did get in a disappointing Troas, and he got into a good many of them, he did so effectually love God that he made all things work together for good.
>
> That is a fact about life which we cannot get around. His religion meant to him a positive faith about life and a positive attitude toward life so effective that watching his career is again and again like watching the Battle of Marengo--in the morning an obvious defeat, in the afternoon a resounding victory [in 1800, Bonaparte snatched victory from a superior Austrian army in Italy].

This emendation was vastly superior to Fosdick's language in the first edition because it stated clearly his central thesis and it also revitalized Paul's part as a spiritual role model, a function the Brooks and Scott examples only tangentially fulfilled.

Except for a few minor changes, the rest of the sermon proceeded on course until the conclusion. There, Fosdick deleted Aristotle's topic of the more and less and succeeded in diluting the recency effect. The recency effect holds that the audience tends to remember, is most affected by, what is communicated most recently in the speech, and particularly so in the conclusion. Carrying over the metaphor of the oyster and the pearl from the first edition, Fosdick concluded this sermon with a sentence that summarized Jesus and his Troas: "He took a very hard thing and he made of it a pearl." By shortening this conclusion, Fosdick sacrificed some of its exhortative effect. He invited contemplation but not action. Gone was the spiritual challenge to the congregation that if Christ could make Calvary a Bithynia, then surely listeners could turn their smaller Troas into a Bithynia.

To be sure, most of Fosdick's rhetorical techniques were still in the revised sermon. The repetition and restatement of Troas and Bithynia numbered twelve times, down slightly from sixteen in the first edition. He maintained the epistrophe of "beaten." And although he deleted the oral signpost of "In the first place" to mark his reasons, relying instead on "For one thing" in the second edition, he inserted an "In the second place" for the second reason whereas the first edition did not have that clear transitional phrase.

Still, the religious message was altered. (Doubtless, Fosdick intended to change the sermon: that is why he rewrote parts of it. Not all emendations, however, are necessarily preferable. The point of this exegesis is to suggest how, at least in this instance, Fosdick moved from admonition in the First Presbyterian Church edition to instruction in the Riverside edition.) How Christians ought to profit spiritually and analogously from Paul's handling of second-bests was transformed into an intellectual appreciation of the principle in the lives of leading figures. A listener might be motivated to adopt the concept in his or her life, but Fosdick did not challenge members of the audience to enact change. Troas and Bithynia remained as an artistic image but something less than a compelling rhetorical-religious metaphor; they were grounded less in sacred Scripture and more in a secular substratum.

Handling Life's Second-Bests (third edition)

On Sunday, April 30, 1944, from 2:30 to 3:00 P.M., Eastern War Time, Fosdick broadcast over radio station WJZ his National Vespers program on the Blue Network Company. He had previously delivered the third edition of "Handling Life's Second-Bests" at Riverside on March 12, 1944. The two sermons were virtually the same [for a transcript of the sermon as delivered at Riverside, with additions and deletions for the National Vespers broadcast, see "Collected Sermons and Speeches" in this volume].[2]

As already indicated, Fosdick took a carbon of the 1931 edition of the sermon and rewrote major portions of the 1944 edition. This draft of the Riverside sermon, in Fosdick's handwriting, affords an opportunity to gauge his management of language, and it bears witness to how far Fosdick had progressed since the 1922 edition in spiritual and secular matters.

Unlike the first and second editions, which were relatively timeless, Fosdick made the third edition correspond to the exigencies of World War II. "Even in ordinary times," he began in his own handwriting, "few persons have a chance to live their lives on the basis of their first choice." To a war-weary public, the allusion was obvious. Fosdick amplified with the well-worn Whistler example, but then composed a new insert of introductory material that reinforced his opening theme (in the following quotation his deletions are bracketed and additions italicized):

> Even in ordinary time life is full of this problem--having to do the best we can with [life's] second and third choices-- but in these days who escapes it? [None of us asked for it] *This ghastly war* [This] is no first choice *of ours* as an age to live in, and as for our individual fortunes, think of the millions of these boys whose first choices have been scrapped and whose task now is and will be somehow to make something out of their second and third [choices] *bests*.

Upon reflection, Fosdick evidently believed it was inappropriate, or too strong a statement, to state that no one asked for World War II, so he softened the sentence. Still, the introduction was clearly cast in the waning years of World War II. The primacy effect raised expectations that the rest of the homily might be aimed to the war audience.

The doctrine of Paul wanting Bithynia but getting Troas remained the same. Fosdick made several changes, but most of these achieved brevity. It is worthwhile to note, however, that he deleted two Scriptural passages from The Acts that had functioned as proof texts in the previous two editions of the sermon. He maintained the expanded example of Phillips Brooks that was carried over from the second edition (for the National Vespers broadcast he deleted a sentence dealing with a letter from a tailor to Brooks), but as he did for the 1938 Church Night service, Fosdick deleted for brevity the Sir Walter Scott example in the third edition.

In the previous editions, Fosdick had made reference to people in the congregation who, like Phillips and Whistler (and Scott until he was deleted), would face their Troas. This language served as a transitional device to move from the doctrine to the reasons or the solution part of

the sermon. For the third edition, he penned a new transition that again
thematically anchored the speech in World War II, and reinforced his
introductory remarks:

> Who here has not faced or does not face now the need for
> that kind of spiritual victory? Who here has not upon his
> heart some young man or woman in whose life everything
> depends on the ability to make something out of Troas?
> So, we ask now what it was in Paul that enabled him to
> turn his disappointment into such notable achievement.

Fosdick answered his question in the manner he did in the
previous editions: Paul's religion entered in. The supporting examples
were the same, save one interesting interpolation. When discussing the
work of Judson and the presence of Seagrave in Burma, Fosdick ad-
libbed over the radio, but not at Riverside, an aside that was anchored
in the war: "and will be there after this war is over." The second
mainhead remained the same, but, again, Fosdick added a sentence that
mentioned the war. When referring to the work of William Duncan in
Alaska, Fosdick penned this line in homey language: "One thinks of that
neck of the woods now because some of our sons are there." Fosdick
implied that the Duncan example came to mind because of U.S. military
presence in Alaska. Actually, the example had been in the first and
second editions. Fosdick merely capitalized on the example by fitting it
to new ends. Unless one could remember what he said in 1922 and 1931
and 1938, no one in the congregation or in the radio audience was the
wiser.

The last substantial emendation that Fosdick made again
grounded the sermon in the war. This was in the application section, and
it was Scripturally and thematically related to the thesis of making a
Bithynia from a Troas:

> Many of us hate this Troas of a bloody generation we are
> in, but we are awake too to the dangers of our civilization,
> to the possibility of losing it, to the critical need of a new
> world order if this is to be a decent earth for human
> children to be born in. That is our strength, our man from
> Macedonia, crying, Come over and help us.

With regard to diction, it is interesting to note how Fosdick inverted
Hitler's concept of a "new world order" to mean the opposite of the
Fuhrer's intentions.

In the conclusion of the Riverside and National Vesper talks,
Fosdick deleted the metaphor of the pearl and how Jesus made a pearl
from Calvary. He completed the rhetorical stance of contemplation,
versus exhortation, by asking his congregation and listeners to gaze upon
the Cross: "Take a good look, my friends, at what our Lord did with his
Troas:

> 'All the light of sacred story
> Gathers round its head sublime'"

CONCLUSION

The first and last editions of Fosdick's "Handling Life's Second-Bests" were the most preferable. As an exegesis of how Paul handled the Bithynia-Troas problem and how modern Christians could benefit from his religious role model, the 1922 sermon excelled. Rhetorically, the parts of the sermon reinforced one another for a persuasive and thematic completeness. By the 1944 edition, the Scriptural emphasis had changed in the homily, but it was nevertheless efficacious for different reasons. Although Paul now shared top billing with other leading lights, Fosdick did make the sermon responsive to the exigencies of World War II. Doubtless his subtle references to loved ones in the war would have been appreciated by listeners at Riverside and in homes across the nation. Nor did Fosdick have to go far afield to fetch his subtle applications because they were thematically related to the persuasive end of the sermon. However, he remained true to his pledge not to bless war. Phrases such as "This ghastly era," "this war is over," and "bloody generation" made his position abundantly clear. But he did play a pastoral role in verbally comforting those whose friends or relatives were fighting in Europe or the Far East.

This sermon also illustrated other factors in Fosdick's practices in the pulpit. For one thing, he did ad-lib. Like his famous counterpart, President Franklin Roosevelt, Fosdick made adjustments as he spoke, but like FDR, none of these ad libitum remarks were earth shaking. However, three in this sermon merit some attention.

First, he ad-libbed the following sentence: "My soul! as a matter of theory I'd like to see a man who could prove that to me." What Fosdick wanted proven had an interesting history. In the 1931 edition, Fosdick had remarked that Paul's statement from Romans 8:28, "all things work together for good to them that love God," was a "proposition [that] is extraordinarily difficult to prove." In rewriting the sermon for the 1944 edition, Fosdick penned an addition, which is italicized: ". . . to prove--*as it is*." When he delivered the speech, he inserted the "My soul" exclamation quoted above. This was evidently meaningful to Fosdick, especially since World War II refuted the veracity of Paul's observation, because he delivered the line with great excitement: he raised the pitch of his voice, increased the rate of speaking, and spoke the words louder than he usually did. He almost dared the congregation, as it were, to challenge him on the point.

The second verbal interpolation concerned Paul. In recounting Paul's spiritual sensitivity, Fosdick rehearsed how Paul saw the man from Macedonia: "That was the kind of person Paul was. He would see the man from Macedonia." In delivering the line, Fosdick orally stressed "would" rather than "see." As he delivered it, "would" had the sense of capacity or capability and not its normal futuristic meaning. In case the point were missed, he inserted in a forceful voice, "Most of us wouldn't, he would."

The last verbal emendation was ad-libbed as an exhortation. After the transition that introduced his application--"My friends, that spirit and its consequence can be transferred to our lives"--he raised the pitch of his voice and increased his loudness as he exclaimed: "It had better be."

The remaining parameters of Fosdick's oral delivery need to be established. Throughout the entire sermon, Fosdick pronounced exactly all vowels and consonants. In fact, the actor Vincent Price's precise articulation best parallels Fosdick's oral style. Fosdick's pronunciation was standard American, except that he enunciated a long "a" (he pronounced "task," "ask," and "after" as in "calm" whereas most Americans say the short "a" as in "cab"). The sermon lasted thirty-five minutes, and he delivered it at about 90 wpm. Lastly, the man's humanity lives in the sermon. He was vividly aware of what he said as he said it. Twice he uttered a subvocalized sound that stressed the sense of his words: when he allowed that Paul would have had a triumph in bringing Christianity to Bithynia and when he read Brooks's letter about his disagreeable students, Fosdick gave a giggle-like sound that demonstrated his appreciation of Paul's personality and Brooks's predicament.[3]

Conclusion

In 1924 *Current Opinion* observed that the Reverend Harry Emerson Fosdick was "a conspicuously successful preacher, occupying in the religious life of New York to-day something of the position that Henry Ward Beecher occupied in Brooklyn a generation ago." In 1935 *Time* magazine characterized Fosdick as the "most famed U.S. pulpit orator in this generation," and in 1939 it termed him "The nation's most famed Protestant preacher." None of these assessments was hyperbole.[1]

In many respects, the oratorical careers of Beecher and Fosdick interfaced remarkably well. Beecher moved from Indianapolis, Indiana, to the Brooklyn pastorate and thence to a national and international pulpit. Although Fosdick traversed less geographical distance from Park Avenue to Riverside, the move uptown propelled him to national prominence. New York City was *the* place to preach as theology, high finance, and oratory moved from Boston to New York in the late 1800s. Fosdick took up the modernist burden that Beecher had preached particularly well toward the later part of his career. As Beecher had been an apologist for Darwinism and a Victorian God that valued progress, and was therefore applauded or vilified by a polarized U.S. audience that consisted of a thinking mentality versus a grassroots mind, so did Fosdick make his mark in scoring the fundamentalist's intolerance in the twentieth century. Both men attained their national prominence as much for their oratorical abilities as for the theologies they preached.

In the application of their respective religions they differed substantially. Beecher, never one to mince words when it came to militarism as a means to end slavery, was identified with a larger spectrum of issues that seemed to overarch modernism. Of course, temperance and especially the woman's right to vote were no longer viable issues by Fosdick's era, but Beecher lent his voice to a wider range of reforms: prison, politics, and educational reform, to name some of the more important ones. Fosdick drew a smaller compass that emphasized pacificism. Yet as practitioners of the art of persuasive preaching, each was without peer in his era.

As an orator/preacher, Fosdick was blessed with a medium that was denied Beecher. Whereas Beecher had to rely on newspapers to print his rhetoric and subscriptions to his *Independent* and *Christian Union* to propagate his views, Fosdick was able, like his contemporary President Franklin Roosevelt, to project himself into the living rooms of the nation via the radio. Of the National Vespers and other broadcasts that even entered the early age of television, Norman Furniss observed: "whereas once the common folk had been taught by their ministers to consider Fosdick the supreme heretic, with the radio they could hear the man and discover that his doctrines were not, after all, the instruments of Satan."[2]   And to his everlasting credit, Fosdick never prostituted his radio ministry by soliciting money under the guise of fighting Satan.

Fosdick and rhetoric were a potent combination for religious change. The man, occasion, and *kairos* met on May 21, 1922, when he preached "Shall the Fundamentalists Win?" Although Beecher preached more famous sermons and delivered more significant speeches than Fosdick did, no single oratorical effort of Beecher's had the signal effect Fosdick's sermon had. George Marsden described the sermon (and note the very un-Fosdick-like militaristic metaphor) as the "shot heard around the nation in the modernist-fundamentalist wars. . . . Twenty-five years later, American public policy seemed to be proving correct Fosdick's resounding no to fundamentalism." In an earlier book, Marsden used a more powerful metaphor in describing the sermon as a "bombshell" that hit the Presbyterian church. The point here is that Fosdick's rhetoric had an immediate effect and also a far-reaching impact on U.S. society and religion that transcended the immediate era.[3]

"Heave an egg out of a Pullman window," satirist H. L. Mencken sardonically opined, "and you will hit a Fundamentalist almost anywhere in the United States today."   That was particularly true on the Pennsylvania Railroad's mainline between New York City and Philadelphia, the epicenter of the struggle. Fosdick's attack on the conservatives was by no means *the* factor that contributed to their sparseness along the route of the "Broadway Limited"--John Roach Straton in New York, J. Gresham Machen at Princeton, and Clarence Macartney at Philadelphia--but it was a contributing factor. Ernest Sandeen observed that Fosdick "touched off the dispute of the twenties" and Fosdick's rhetorical ability to cast his opponents as the aggressors (when in fact he was the accuser) allowed him to triumph in the encounter. Allyn Russell noted that Fosdick "popularized the movement and its beliefs with remarkable success" and when the casualties were counted, "public sympathies remained with him."[4]

To be sure, much of Fosdick's success with the modernist-fundamentalist controversy was the kind of liberal theology that he preached to early twentieth-century Americans who were receptive to his message. Yet withal, he was an orator who practiced a high art. Furniss credited much of Fosdick's success to "his great rhetorical gift" and William Hutchison observed his oratorical flair: "Fosdick's outspoken eloquence, and his involvement in a notorious public controversy made him known to an especially wide circle of Americans." In that respect, Fosdick most resembled his predecessor, Henry Ward Beecher.[5]

Concerning the other great issue of Fosdick's era, Mars versus Christ, the verdict is much harder to assess. For instance, in 1928 he composed a piece for the *Christian Century* that was entitled "What the War Did to My Mind." Anticipating his "Unknown Soldier" speech by six years, he announced he "did not propose to bless war again, or support it, or expect from it any valuable thing." In that same article, he also indicated the link between militarism and liberalism that he brought to fruition in the modernist sermon in 1935. He charged that the "question of war with its implicit problems of nationalism, racial prejudice, and economic imperialism presents the most crucial collision with Christianity that we are facing today." To be sure, by 1935 if not before, he was associated in the public mind at the time as a pacifist. He lent his voice to peace conferences and he was deemed important enough by isolationist Senator Wheeler to be enlisted in the senator's battle with President Franklin D. Roosevelt on the eve of World War II. Pragmatically, of course, Fosdick failed to persuade the American audience to remain pacifists, but President Roosevelt also failed to persuade the American people to be belligerants: only Pearl Harbor vindicated the president and mooted the preacher. But what of his effect in the long run?

On the one hand, Fosdick argued his pacifist thesis with a logic and an exegesis that were closer to a Scriptural based theology than was his modernist position. For his generation and all times, Fosdick grounded his words in the Word. But fifty years after Fosdick's foray with the fundamentalists, it is worthwhile to note that they, or at least the patriotic portion of their communion, have so overarched fundamentalism, if not modernism, that they have become comfortable bedfellows with right-wing militarists.

On the other hand, it may be that late twentieth-century contemporary society has so adjusted, accommodated, and adapted to the military-industrial complex in the United States that Fosdick's position on pacifism seems silly if not ridiculous. To that, Harry Emerson Fosdick has already responded in a hymn that he wrote for Riverside Church:

> God of grace and God of glory,
> On thy people pour thy power. . . .
> Grant us wisdom, grant us courage,
> For the living of these days.[6]

Notes

Chapter 1: A Preacher Preaching

1. Graham Hodges, "Fosdick at 90," *Christian Century*, May 22, 1968, p. 684; Harry Emerson Fosdick, *The Living of These Days: An Autobiography* (New York: Harper and Brothers, 1956), p. 89.

2. See "Harry Emerson Fosdick," file copy, Dorothy Noyes papers, Harry Emerson Fosdick Collection, Union Theological Seminary, New York City, Box 1 [hereafter given as Noyes-HEFC]; Robert D. Clark, "Harry Emerson Fosdick," in *History and Criticism of American Public Address*, ed. Marie Kathryn Hochmuth (New York: Russell and Russell, 1955), pp. 415-20; Fosdick, *The Living of These Days*, p. 83.

3. Harry Emerson Fosdick, "Methods of Sermon Preparation," Noyes-HEFC, Box 1, pp. 3-4; Harry Emerson Fosdick, "On Preaching," Noyes-HEFC, Box 1, p. 1.

4. "Riverside Church," *Time*, October 6, 1930, pp. 72, 70.

5. Harry Emerson Fosdick, "Lectures to the Missionaries in the Orient, I: Christianity and the Social Movement," 1921, Noyes-HEFC, Box 3, p. 2; "Handling Life's Second-Bests," Riverside Church, January 18, 1931, Sermon Boxes of Harry Emerson Fosdick, HEFC, pp. 1-13; Eugene Exman, "Fosdick as Author," *Christian Century*, May 21, 1958, p. 618.

6. Halford R. Ryan, "Harry Emerson Fosdick," in *American Orators of the Twentieth Century: Critical Studies and Sources*, edited by Bernard K. Duffy and Halford R. Ryan (Westport: Greenwood Press, 1987), p. 148.

7. "Odd Items about Dr. Fosdick's Broadcasting, " Noyes-HEFC, Box 4, pp. 1-2.

8. Harry Emerson Fosdick, *On Being Fit to Live With* (New York: Harper and Brothers, 1946), p. viii; Fosdick, "Methods of Sermon Preparation," p. 1; Henry Sloane Coffin, *A Half Century of Union Theological Seminary: An Informal History* (New York: Charles Scribners, 1954), p. 72.

9. Harry Emerson Fosdick, "What Is the Matter with Preaching?" *Harper's Magazine*, July 1928, pp. 134, 138, 141; Fosdick, *The Living of These Days*, p. 99.

10. Fosdick, *The Living of These Days*, p. 99.

11. Fosdick, "Methods of Sermon Preparation, " p. 3; "Crowd Turned Away at Riverside Church," *New York Times*, October 6, 1930, p. 11; Fosdick, *On Being Fit to Live With*, p. vii.

12. William H. Hudnut, Jr., "Fosdick as Teacher," *Christian Century*, May 21, 1958, p. 616; Harry Emerson Fosdick, "Charge to Rev. Lyons," November 11, 1956, Riverside Chuirch, Noyes-HEFC, Box 1, p. 1; Harry Emerson Fosdick, "How to Handle Retirement with Zest," *Lifetime Living Magazine*, October 1953, p. 4; "Crowd Turned Away at Riverside," p. 11; "The Liberal," *Time*, May 25, 1953, p. 62; "New York's Riverside," *Christian Century*, November 28, 1951, p. 1371.

13. Dr. Frederick W. Clampett, "Radio Changes Style of Oratory," San Francisco *Examiner*, September 12, 1927, p. 16; Hudnut, "Fosdick as Teacher," p. 616.

14. Edmund Holt Linn, *Preaching as Counseling* (Valley Forge: The Judson Press, 1966), pp. 153, 151; I determined the wpm from the following representative sermons: "Christian Faith: Fantasy or Truth," July 27, 1941, F-748-3; "Handling Life's Second-Bests," March 12, 1944, F-748-5; "On Being Fit to Live With," February 27, 1946, F-748-11; "The Importance of Doubting Our Doubts," April 12, 1953, F-748-1; Audio-Visual Collection, Union Theological Seminary, Richmond, Virginia.

15. "What Christmas Means to Me," Movie 184; "People at Home: Harry Emerson Fosdick," Movie 112, Audio-Visual Collection, Union Theological Seminary, Richmond, Virginia.

16. Linn, *Preaching as Counseling*, pp. 145-46; Fosdick, "Methods of Sermon Preparation," p. 4.

17. Fosdick, "Methods of Sermon Preparation," p. 3.

Chapter 2: Fosdick versus the Fundamentalists

1. Karl Reiland, "The Gist of Modernism," *Religious Weekly Review*, February 9, 1924, p. 180; William Pierson Merrill, "Protestantism at the Crossroads," *Christian Century*, February 1924, p. 423; "The Presbyterian Attack on Dr. Fosdick," *Literary Digest*, November 18, 1922, p. 37.

2. Henry Ward Beecher, "The Two Revelations," in *American Public Address: 1740-1952*, ed. A. Craig Baird (New York: McGraw-Hill, 1956), pp. 160-68; Halford R. Ryan, "Henry Ward Beecher," in *American Orators Before 1900: Critical Studies and Sources*, ed. Bernard K. Duffy and Halford R. Ryan (Westport: Greenwood Press, 1987), pp. 35-46; Thomas M. Lessl, "'Darrow vs. Bryan' vs. 'Bryan vs. Darrow,'" in *Oratorical Encounters: Selected Studies and Sources of Twentieth Century Political Accusations and Apologies*, ed. Halford R. Ryan (Westport: Greenwood Press, 1988), pp. 17-27.

3. Harry Emerson Fosdick, "The New Knowledge and the Christian Faith" (pamphlet giving no publication details), Union Theological Seminary Library, Richmond, Virginia; Harry Emerson Fosdick, "Shall the Fundamentalists Win?," in *Sermons in American History*, ed. DeWitte Holland (Nashville: Abingdon Press, 1971), pp. 338-48; Allan Sager, "The Fundamentalist-Modernist Controversy, 1918-1930," in *Preaching in American History*, ed. DeWitte Holland (Nashville: Abingdon Press, 1969), pp. 265-66; Robert D. Clark, "Harry Emerson Fosdick," in *History and Criticism of American Public Address*, ed. Marie Kathryn Hochmuth (New York: Russell and Russell, 1955), p. 427; among Fosdick's critics, only Miller succeeded in revealing the true origin of Lee's pamphlet and Fosdick's involvement with it, see Robert Moats Miller, *Harry Emerson Fosdick: Preacher, Pastor, Prophet* (New York: Oxford University Press, 1985), pp. 116-17; Harry Emerson Fosdick, *The Living of These Days: An Autobiography* (New York: Harper and Brothers, 1956), p. 146.

4. Clarence E. Macartney, "Shall Unbelief Win?" in *Sermons in American History*, p. 363; for a discussion of Roach's rhetoric and McCartney's role in Fosdick's removal from his pulpit, see C. Allyn Russell, *Voices of American Fundamentalism: Seven Biographical Studies* (Philadelphia: The Westminster Press, 1976), pp. 47-78, 190-211; *The Christian Scotsman*, no. 6 (pamphlet with no publication details), HEFC, Newspaper Clippings, Box 1; John Roach Straton, "Shall the FunnyMonkeyists Win?" New York City, September 24, 1922 (pamphlet with no publication details), HEFC, Newspaper Clippings, Box 2; G. E. Sihlhide, "The Presbytery of New

York Not All Untrue to the Standards of Our Church," *Presbyterian*, April 3, 1924, p. 8.

5. Edgar Whitaker Work, chairman, "To the Committee of the Presbytery of New York," HEFC, Newspaper Clippings, Box 2; J. Gresham Machen, "The Parting of the Ways," (pamphlet with no publication details), HEFC, Newspaper Clippings, Box 2; for a discussion of Machen's battle with Fosdick, see Russell, *Voices of American Fundamentalism*, pp. 135-161; William W. McKinney, "The Center of the Controversy," *Presbyterian*, June 12, 1924, p. 6.

6. William Jennings Bryan, "The Fosdick Case," *Presbyterian Advance*, June 5, 1924, p. 5.

7. Editorial, *Christian Work*, January 20, 1923, p. 74; Joseph Fort Newton, "The New Preaching," *Christian Century*, December 21, 1922, p. 1590; editorial, *Continent*, November 30, 1922, p. 1518.

8. Harry Emerson Fosdick, "Farewell," *The Church Tower*, March 1925, pp. 3-6, 22-24.

9. Howard Duffield, letter to the editor, *Presbyterian*, April 2, 1925, p. 20.

10. "Dr. Fosdick's Farewell," *New Republic*, March 18, 1925, p. 91; editorial, *Nation*, November 1, 1922, p. 452.

11. "The 'Best' Protestant Preachers," *Literary Digest*, March 21, 1925, pp. 32-33; Cleland B. McAfee, "The Presbyterian Church Facing the Future," *Christian Century*, November 9, 1922, p. 1387; "Dr. Fosdick's Hail and Farewell," *Literary Digest*, March 21, 1925, pp. 31-32.

Chapter 3: Quo Vadis: God of War or Peace?

1. Robert Moats Miller, *American Protestantism and Social Issues 1919-1939* (Chapel Hill: University of North Carolina Press, 1958), pp. 331-44; Robert Moats Miller, *Harry Emerson Fosdick: Preacher, Pastor, Prophet* (New York: Oxford University Press, 1985), pp. 490-532; Robert D. Clark, "Harry Emerson Fosdick" in *History and Criticism of American Public Address*, ed. Marie Kathryn Hochmuth (New York: Russell and Russell, 1955), pp. 411-57.

2. Miller, *American Protestantism and Social Issues*, p. 344.

3. Harry Emerson Fosdick, "Shall We End War?" June 3, 1921, sermon pamphlet, HEF Papers, pp. 3-14; for a discussion of the rhetorical applications of the disjunctive syllogism, see Halford Ryan, "Individual Events Speaking: Two Organizational Patterns," *Speaker and Gavel* 18 (1981): 79-82.

4. For a standard text, in addition to the one printed in "Collected Speeches and Sermons" in this volume, see Harry Emerson Fosdick, "A Christian Conscience About War," in *American Public Addresses: 1740-1952*, ed. A. Craig Baird (New York: McGraw-Hill, 1956), pp. 274-82.

5. "Fosdick's Challenge for Peace," *Literary Digest*, October 3, 1925, p. 31; "Fosdick Summons Church to End War in Geneva Session," *New York Times*, September 14, 1925, p. 1; editorial, "In Calvin's Stead," *New York Times*, September 15, 1925, p. 24; "Dr. Woelfkin Hails Fosdick as Prophet," *New York Times*, September 21, 1925, p. 22.

6. See Harry Emerson Fosdick, *Riverside Sermons* (New York: Harper and Brothers, 1958), pp. 342-53; "Anti-War Pledge Given by Fosdick," *New York Times*, May 8, 1934, p. 1; Harry Emerson Fosdick, "My Account with the Unknown Soldier," *Christian Century*, June 6, 1934, pp. 754-56.

7. "Harry Emerson Fosdick," *Christian Century*, June 6, 1934, p. 746; Oswald Garrison Villard, "Dr. Fosdick Renounces War," *Nation*, May 23, 1934, p. 581; "Fight on Pacifism Asked," *New York Times*, May 8, 1934, p. 7.

8. See George Kennedy, *The Art of Persuasion in Greece* (Princeton: Princeton University Press, 1963), p. 266; Gary Cronkhite, *Persuasion: Speech and Behavioral Change* (Indianapolis: Bobbs-Merrill, 1969), pp. 22-23.

9. See Kathleen Freeman, *The Murder of Herodes* (New York: W. W. Norton, 1963), p. 31.

10. For a standard text, in addition to the one printed in "Collected Speeches and Sermons" in this volume, see Harry Emerson Fosdick, "The Unknown Soldier," *Riverside Sermons*, pp. 342-53.

11. Harry Emerson Fosdick, "Five Sectors of the Peace Movement," in *Congressional Record*, 75th Cong., 1st. sess., vol. 81, pt. 9, Appendix, p. 592.

12. Clark, "Harry Emerson Fosdick," p. 432; Miller, *Harry Emerson Fosdick*, pp. 490-532.

13. *Public Papers of Franklin D. Roosevelt, 1939*, ed. Samuel I. Rosenman (New York: Macmillan Company, 1941), p. 463; "Stay Neutral, Says Fosdick," *New York Times*, September 5, 1939, p. 14.

14. Harry Emerson Fosdick, "The Christian Church's Message to America Today," in *Congressional Record*, 76th Cong., 2nd sess., vol. 85, pt. 2, Appendix, p. 338.

15. Ibid., pp. 338-39.

16. For a discussion of FDR's rhetoric on the United Nation's issue, see Halford Ross Ryan, *Franklin D. Roosevelt's Rhetorical Presidency* (Westport: Greenwood Press, 1988), pp. 67-68. Harry S. Truman, "Far Eastern Policy," Washington, D.C., April 11, 1951, in *American Rhetoric from Roosevelt to Reagan: A Collection of Speeches and Critical Essays*, ed. Halford Ross Ryan (Prospect Heights: Waveland Press, 1983), p. 86-87.

17. For tables of opinion polls on aid-short-of-war and whether to fight, see Ryan, *Franklin D. Roosevelt's Rhetorical Presidency*, pp. 148-49, or *Public Opinion, 1935-1946*, ed. Hadley Cantril (Princeton: Princeton University Press, 1951), pp. 969-75. For an overview of this critical political period, see Wayne S. Cole, *Roosevelt and the Isolationists* (Lincoln: University of Nebraska Press, 1983), pp. 375-79.

18. "Dr. Fosdick Opposes Haste in Draft Bill; Radio Talk Suggests Alternative Plans," *New York Times*, August 8, 1940, p. 2; Harry Emerson Fosdick, "The Crisis Confronting the Nation," *Vital Speeches of the Day*, September 1, 1940, pp. 686-87.

19. Burton K. Wheeler, "Marching Down the Road to War," *Vital Speeches of the Day*, September 1, 1940, pp. 689-92.

20. "Clergymen Score U.S. Aid to Diem," *New York Times*, August 15, 1963, p. 3.

Chapter 4: Reforming the Reform: Going Beyond Modernism

1. Daniel Ross Chandler, "Harry Emerson Fosdick," *Harvard Divinity Review*, February 1979, p. 5.

2. Harold Brack, "Neo-Orthodoxy and the American Pulpit," in *Sermons in American History*, ed. DeWitte Holland (Nashville: Abingdon Press, 1971), p. 366; Robert D. Clark, "Harry Emerson Fosdick," in *History and*

Criticism of American Public Address, ed. Marie Kathryn Hochmuth (New York: Russell & Russell, 1955), p. 439; Halford R. Ryan, "Harry Emerson Fosdick," in *American Orators of the Twentieth Century: Critical Studies and Sources*, ed. by Bernard K. Duffy and Halford R. Ryan (Westport: Greenwood Press, 1987), p. 150.

3. Editorial, "Dr. Fosdick Shifts the Emphasis," *Christian Century*, November 20, 1935, pp. 1481-82; editorial, "Dr. Fosdick's Sermon," and "Beyond Modernism," *Christian Century*, December 4, 1935, pp. 1539-40, 1549-52.

4. For an analysis of Fosdick's M.A. thesis, see Robert Moats Miller, *Harry Emerson Fosdick: Preacher, Pastor, Prophet* (New York: Oxford University Press, 1985), pp. 64-67.

Chapter 5: Preaching at Riverside

1. Harry Emerson Fosdick, "Handling Life's Second-Bests," First Presbyterian Church, New York City, October 29, 1922, stenographically recorded by Margaret Renton, Sermon Boxes, HEFC, pp. 3-13.

2. Harry Emerson Fosdick, "Handling Life's Second-Bests," A Radio Address by Dr. Harry Emerson Fosdick, Riverside Church, Sunday, April 30, 1944, Sermon Boxes, HEFC, pp. 1-5.

3. Harry Emerson Fosdick, "Handling Life's Second-Bests," March 12, 1944, Reigner Recording Library, Union Seminary, Richmond, Virginia, F-748-5.

Conclusion

1. "Fosdick Versus the Fundamentalists," *Current Opinion*, December 1924, p. 756; "Hymns for 8,000,000," *Time*, October 14, 1935, p. 32; "For Finland," *Time*, December 25, 1939, p. 25.

2. Norman F. Furniss, *The Fundamentalist Controversy, 1918-1931* (New Haven: Yale University Press, 1954), p. 180.

3. George Marsden, *Reforming Fundamentalism: Fuller Seminary and the New Evangelicalism* (Grand Rapids: William B. Eerdmans Publishing Company, 1987), p. 14; George M. Marsden, *Fundamentalism and American Culture* (New York: Oxford University Press, 1980). p. 172.

4. Quoted in Marsden, *Reforming Fundamentalism*, p. vii; Ernest R. Sandeen, *The Roots of Fundamentalism: British and American Millenarianism 1800-1930* (Chicago: University of Chicago Press, 1970), p. 252; C. Allyn Russell, *Voices of American Fundamentalism* (Philadelphia: The Westminster Press, 1976), pp. 16, 151.

5. Furniss, *The Fundamentalist Controversy, 1918-1931*, p. 131; William R. Hutchison, *The Modernist Impulse in American Protestantism* (Cambridge: Harvard University Press, 1986), p. 275.

6. Harry Emerson Fosdick, hymn, "God of Grace and God of Glory," HEFC, p. 1.

II

COLLECTED SERMONS AND SPEECHES

"Shall the Fundamentalists Win?"

First Presbyterian Church, New York City, May 21, 1922

Note: The following apparatus needs to be explained. Ivy L. Lee retitled the sermon, emended it slightly, added headings, and mailed his pamphlet to ministers and laymen across the nation. Hitherto, Lee's introduction and editorial version of the sermon have not been published. Lee's note to the sermon is printed in italics.

Following Lee's introduction is the text of the sermon. Except as noted, the sermon is as Fosdick delivered it, and it was recorded stenographically by Margaret Renton. The captions Ivy Lee added to the sermon are printed in bold. Fosdick's language that Lee deleted is indicated with brackets. It is hoped that the minor inconvenience of having the sermon text divided and captioned in a way that Fosdick did not originally deliver it to his listeners can be recompensed by an appreciation of Lee's efforts that sensationalized this sermon to the national reading audience.

THE NEW KNOWLEDGE AND THE CHRISTIAN FAITH

NOTE
That there are forces at work within our civilization which threaten its destruction is suggested by the conflicts between labor and capital and the wars and disputes between nations.

The only safety of the world must lie in the establishment of the Christian religion in the lives of men.

The Church must be depended upon to accomplish this purpose.

*   *   *

A great chasm exists today between organized Christianity and a large part of the people.

And yet the hunger for the things of the spirit was never so great on the part of all men as it is today.

One of the serious barriers is insistence by so many upon standards of orthodoxy to which a large number of men cannot subscribe.

*   *   *

The minister who is today attracting the largest congregation in New York City is the Rev. Dr. Harry Emerson Fosdick, preacher at the First Presbyterian Church, and a professor in the Union Theological Seminary.

A few weeks ago Dr. Fosdick preached upon the topic: "Shall the Fundamentalists Win?" It set a landmark in the progress of religion that such a sermon should be preached in the old First Presbyterian Church of New York.

That sermon, slightly abridged, is herewith reprinted and distributed to those who it is believed will find it peculiarly moving and stimulating.

Your comments upon this sermon would be read with great interest and appreciation.

Ivy L. Lee
61 Broadway
New York, July 25, 1922

SHALL THE FUNDAMENTALISTS WIN?

This morning we are to think of the Fundamentalist controversy which threatens to divide the American churches, as though already they were not sufficiently split and riven. [A scene, suggestive for our thought, is depicted in the fifth chapter of the Book of the Acts, where the Jewish leaders hail before them Peter and others of the apostles because they had been preaching Jesus as the Messiah. Moreover, the Jewish leaders propose to slay them, when in opposition Gamaliel speaks: "Refrain from these men, and let them alone: for if this counsel or this work be of men, it will be overthrown: but if it is of God ye will not be able to overthrow them; lest haply ye be found even to be fighting against God."

One could easily let his imagination play over this scene and could wonder how history would have come out if Gamaliel's wise tolerance could have controlled the situation. For though the Jewish leaders seemed superficially to concur in Gamaliel's judgment, they nevertheless kept up their bitter antagonism and shut the Christians from the synagogue. We know now that they were mistaken. Christianity, starting within Judaism, was not an innovation to be dreaded; it was the finest flowering out that Judaism ever had. When the Master looked back across his racial heritage and said, "I came not to destroy, but to fulfill," he perfectly described the situation. The Christian ideas of God, the Christian principles of life, the Christian hopes for the future, were all rooted in the Old Testament and grew up out of it, and the Master himself, who called the Jewish temple his Father's house, rejoiced in the glorious heritage of his people's prophets. Only, he did believe in a living God. He did not think that God was dead, having finished his words and works with Malachi. He had not simply a historic, but a contemporary God, speaking now, working now, leading his people now, from partial into fuller truth. Jesus believed in the progressiveness of revelation and these Jewish leaders did not understand that. Was this new gospel a real development which they might welcome or was it an enemy to be cast out? And they called it an enemy and excluded it. One does wonder what might have happened had Gamaliel's wise tolerance been in control.

We, however, face today a situation too similar and too urgent and too much in need of Gamaliel's attitude to spend any time making guesses at suppositious history. Already] all of us must have heard about the people who call themselves the Fundamentalists. Their apparent intention is to drive out of the evangelical churches men and women of liberal opinions. I speak of them the more freely because there are no two denominations more affected by them than the Baptists and the Presbyterians. We should not identify the Fundamentalists with conservatives. All Fundamentalists are conservatives, but not all conservatives are Fundamentalists. The best conservatives can often give lessons to the liberals in true liberality of spirit, but the Fundamentalist program is essentially illiberal and intolerant. The Fundamentalists see, and they see truly, that in this last generation there have been strange new movements in Christian thought. **The New Knowledge** A great mass of new knowledge has come into man's possession: new knowledge about the physical universe, its origin, its forces, its laws; new knowledge about human history and in particular about the ways in which the ancient peoples used to think in matters of religion and the methods by which they phrased and explained their spiritual experiences; and new knowledge, also, about other religions and the strangely similar ways in which men's faiths and religious practices have developed everywhere.

Now, there are multitudes of reverent Christians who have been unable to keep this new knowledge in one compartment of their minds and the Christian faith in another. They have been sure that all truth comes from the one God and is his revelation. Not, therefore, from irreverence or caprice or destructive zeal, but for the sake of intellectual and spiritual integrity, that they might really love the Lord their God not only with all their heart and soul and strength, but with all their mind, they have been trying to see this new knowledge in terms of the Christian faith and to see the Christian faith in terms of this new knowledge. Doubtless they have made many mistakes. Doubtless there have been among them reckless radicals gifted with intellectual ingenuity but lacking spiritual depth. Yet the enterprise itself seems to them indispensable to the Christian Church. The new knowledge and the old faith cannot be left antagonistic or even disparate, as though a man on Saturday could use one set of regulative ideas for his life and on Sunday could change gear to another altogether. We must be able to think our modern life clear through in Christian terms and to do that we also must be able to think our Christian life clear through in modern terms.

New Knowledge in Former Times There is nothing new about the situation. It has happened again and again in history, as, for example, when the stationary earth suddenly began to move and the universe that had been center in this planet was centered in the sun around which the planets whirled. Whenever such a situation has arisen, there has been only one way out: the new knowledge and the old faith had to be blended in a new combination. Now, the people in this generation who are trying to do this are the liberals, and the Fundamentalists are out on a campaign to shut against them the doors of the Christian fellowship. Shall they be allowed to succeed?

It is interesting to note where the Fundamentalists are driving in their stakes to mark out the deadline of doctrine around the church, across which no one is to pass except on terms of agreement. **What the Fundamentalists Demand** They insist that we must all believe in the historicity of certain special miracles, preeminently the virgin birth of our Lord; that we must believe in a special theory of inspiration—that the original documents of the scripture, which of course we no longer possess, were inerrantly dictated to men a good deal as a man might dictate to a stenographer; that we must believe in a special theory of the atonement—that the blood of our Lord, shed in a substitutionary death, placates an alienated deity and makes possible welcome for the returning sinner; and that we must believe in the second coming of our Lord upon the clouds of heaven to set up a millennium here, as the only way in which God may bring history to a worthy denouement. Such are some of the stakes which are being driven, to mark a deadline of doctrine around the church.

If a man is a genuine liberal, his primary protest is not against holding these opinions, although he may well protest against their being considered the fundamentals of Christianity. This is a free country and anybody has a right to hold these opinions or any others, if he is sincerely convinced of them. **Shall the Christian Name Be Denied to Those Who Differ** The question is: Has anybody a right to deny the Christian name to those who differ with him on such points and to shut against them the doors of the Christian fellowship? The Fundamentalists say that this must be done. In this country and on the foreign field they are trying to do it. They have actually endeavored to put on the statute books of a whole state binding laws against teaching modern biology. If they had their way, within the church they would set up in Protestantism a doctrinal tribunal more rigid than the pope's. In such an hour, delicate and dangerous, where feelings are bound to run high, I plead this morning the cause of magnanimity and liberality and tolerance of spirit. I would, if I could reach their ears, say to the Fundamentalists about the liberals what Gamaliel said to the Jews, "Refrain from these men, and let them alone: for if this counsel or this work be of men, it will be overthrown: but if it is of God ye will not be able to overthrow them; lest haply ye be found even to be fighting against God."

That we may be entirely candid and concrete and may not lose ourselves in any fog of generalities, let us this morning take two or three of these Fundamentalist items and see with reference to them what the situation is in the Christian churches. Too often we preachers have failed to talk frankly enough about the differences of opinion which exist among evangelical Christians, although everybody knows that they are there. Let us face this morning some of the differences of opinion with which somehow we must deal.

THE VIRGIN BIRTH OF CHRIST We may as well begin with the vexed and mooted question of the virgin birth of our Lord. I know people in the Christian churches, ministers, missionaries, laymen, devoted lovers of the Lord and servants of the gospel, who, alike as they are in their personal devotion to the Master, hold quite different points of view about a matter like the virgin birth. **One Point of View—the Fundamentalist's** Here, for example, is one point of view: that the virgin birth is to be accepted as historical fact; it actually happened; there was no other way for a personality like the Master to come into this world except by a special biological miracle. That is one point of view, and many are the gracious and beautiful souls who hold it. But, side by side with them in the evangelical churches is a group of equally loyal and reverent people who would say that the virgin birth is not to be accepted as a historic fact.

To believe in virgin birth as an explanation of great personality is one of the familiar ways in which the ancient world was accustomed to account for unusual superiority. Many people suppose that only once in history do we run across a record of supernatural birth. Upon the contrary, stories of miraculous generation are among the commonest traditions of antiquity. Especially is this true about the founders of great religions. **Supernatural Births In Other Faiths** According to the records of their faiths, Buddha and Zoroaster and Lao-Tse and Mahavira were all supernaturally born. Moses, Confucius and Mohammed are the only great founders of religion in history to whom miraculous birth is not attributed. That is to say, when a personality arose so high that men adored him, the ancient world attributed his superiority to some special divine influence in his generation, and they commonly phrased their faith in terms of miraculous birth. So Pythagoras was called virgin born, and Plato, and Augustus Caesar, and many more. **Another Point of View—the Liberal's** Knowing this, there are within the evangelical churches large groups of people whose opinion about our Lord's coming would run as follows: those first disciples adored Jesus—as we do; when they thought about his coming they were sure that he came specially from God—as we are; this adoration and conviction they associated with God's special influence and intention in his birth—as we do; but they phrased it in terms of a biological miracle that our modern minds cannot use. So far from thinking that they have given up anything vital in the New Testament's attitude towards Jesus, these Christians remember that the two men who contributed most to the church's thought of the divine meaning of the Christ were Paul and John, who never even distantly allude to the virgin birth.

What Has Intolerance To Offer? Here in the Christian churches are these two groups of people and the question which the Fundamentalists raise is this: Shall one of them throw the other out? Has intolerance any contribution to make to this situation? Will it persuade anybody of anything? Is not the Christian church large enough to hold within her hospitable fellowship people who differ on points like this and agree to differ until the fuller truth be manifested? The Fundamentalists say not. They say that the liberals must go. Well, if the Fundamentalists should succeed, then out of the Christian church would go some of the best Christian life and consecration of this generation— multitudes of men and women, devout and reverent Christians, who need the church and whom the church needs.

THE LITERAL INSPIRATION OF THE BIBLE Consider another matter on which there is a sincere difference of opinion between evangelical Christians: the inspiration of the Bible. **One Point of View—the Fundamentalist's** One point of view is that the original documents of the scripture were inerrantly dictated by God to men. Whether we deal with the story of creation or the list of the dukes of Edom or the narratives of Solomon's reign or the Sermon on the Mount or the thirteenth chapter of first Corinthians, they all came in the same way and they all came as no other book ever came. They were inerrantly dictated; everything there— scientific opinions, medical theories, historical judgments, as well as spiritual insights—is infallible. That is one idea of the Bible's inspiration. **Another Point of View—the Liberal's** But side by side with those who hold it, lovers of the Book as much as they, are multitudes of people who never think about the Bible so. Indeed, that static and mechanical theory of inspiration seems to them a positive peril to the spiritual life. The Koran similarly has been regarded by Mohammedans as having been infallibly written in heaven before it came to earth. But the Koran enshrines the theological and ethical ideas of Arabia at the time when it was written. God an oriental monarch, fatalistic submission to his will as man's chief duty, the use of force on unbelievers, polygamy, slavery—they are all in the Koran. The Koran was ahead of the day when it was written, but, petrified by an artificial idea of inspiration, it has become a millstone about the neck of Mohammedanism.

When one turns from the Koran to the Bible, he finds this interesting situation. All of these ideas, which we dislike in the Koran, are somewhere in the Bible. Conceptions from which we now send missionaries to convert Mohammedans are to be found in the Book. **Revelation Is Progressive in the Bible** There one can find God thought of as an oriental monarch; there, too, are patriarchal polygamy, and slave systems, and the use of force on unbelievers. Only in the Bible these elements are not final; they are always being superseded; revelation is progressive. The thought of God moves out from oriental kingship to compassionate fatherhood; treatment of unbelievers moves out from the use of force to the appeals of love; polygamy gives way to monogamy; slavery, never explicitly condemned before the New Testament closes, is nevertheless being undermined by ideas that in the end, like dynamite, will blast its foundations to pieces. Repeatedly one runs on versus like this: "It was said to them of old time. . . . but I say unto you"; "God, having of old time spoken unto the fathers in the prophets by divers portions and in divers manners, hath at the end of these days spoken unto us in his Son"; "The times of ignorance therefore God overlooked; but now he commandeth men that they should all everywhere repent"; and over the doorway of the New Testament into the Christian world stand the words of Jesus: "When he, the spirit of truth is come, he shall guide you into all the truth." That is to say, finality in the Koran is behind; finality in the Bible is ahead. We have not reached it. We cannot yet compass all of it. God is leading us out toward it. There are multitudes of Christians, then, who think, and rejoice as they think, of the Bible as the record of the progressive unfolding of the character of God to his people from early primitive days until the great unveiling in Christ; to them the Book is more inspired and more inspiring than ever it was before; and to go back to a mechanical and static theory of inspiration would mean to them the loss of some of the most vital elements in their spiritual experience and in their appreciation of the Book.

Here in the Christian church today are these two groups, and the question which the Fundamentalists have raised is this: Shall one of them drive the other out? Do we think the cause of Jesus Christ will be furthered by that? If he should walk through the ranks of this congregation this morning, can we imagine him claiming as his own those who hold one idea of inspiration and sending from him into outer darkness those who hold another? You cannot fit the Lord Christ into that Fundamentalist mold. The church would better judge his judgment. For in the middle west the Fundamentalists have had their way in some communities and a Christian minister tells us the consequence. He says that all the educated people are looking for their religion outside the churches.

THE SECOND COMING OF OUR LORD Consider another matter upon which there is a sincere difference of opinion between evangelical Christians: the second coming of our Lord. The second coming was the early Christian phrasing of hope. No one in the ancient world had ever thought, as we do, of development, progress, gradual change, as God's way of working out his will in human life and institutions. They thought of human history as a series of ages succeeding one another with abrupt suddenness. The Graeco-Roman world gave the names of metals to the ages—gold, silver, bronze, iron. The Hebrews had their ages too—the original paradise in which man began, the cursed world in which man now lives, the blessed messianic kingdom some day suddenly to appear on the clouds of heaven. It was the Hebrew way of expressing hope for the victory of God and righteousness. When the Christians came they took over that phrasing of expectancy and the New Testament is aglow with it. The preaching of the apostles thrills with the glad announcement, "Christ is coming!"

In the evangelical churches today there are differing views of this matter. **One Point of View—the Fundamentalist's** One view is that Christ is literally coming, externally on the clouds of heaven, to set up his kingdom here. I never heard that teaching in my youth at all. It has always had a new resurrection when desperate circumstances came and man's only hope seemed to lie in divine intervention. It is not strange, then, that during these chaotic, catastrophic years there has been a fresh rebirth of this old phrasing of expectancy. "Christ is coming!" seems to many Christians the central message of the gospel. In the strength of it some of them are doing great service for the world. But unhappily, many so overemphasize it that they outdo anything the ancient Hebrews or the ancient Christians ever did. They sit still and do nothing and expect the world to grow worse and worse until he comes.

Another Point of View—the Liberal's Side by side with these to whom the second coming is a literal expectation, another group exists in the evangelical churches. They, too, say, "Christ is coming!" They say it with all their hearts; but they are not thinking of an external arrival on the clouds. They have assimilated as part of the divine revelation the exhilarating insight which these recent generations have given to us, that development is God's way of working out his will. They see that the most desirable elements in human life have come through the method of development. Man's music has developed from the rhythmic noise of beaten sticks until we have in melody and harmony possibilities once undreamed. Man's painting has developed from the crude outlines of the cavemen until in line and color we have achieved unforseen results and possess latent beauties yet unfolded. Man's architecture has developed from the crude huts of primitive men until our cathedrals and business buildings reveal alike an incalculable advance and an unimaginable future. Development does seem to be the way in which God works. And these Christians, when they say that Christ is coming, mean that, slowly it may be, but surely, his will and principles will be worked out by God's grace in human life and institutions, until "he shall see of the travail of his soul and shall be satisfied."

These two groups exist in the Christian churches and the question raised by the Fundamentalists is: Shall one of us drive the other out? Will that get us anywhere? **What of the Young Men and Women in Our Schools?** Multitudes of young men and women at this season of the year are graduating from our schools of learning, thousands of them Christians who may make us older ones ashamed by the sincerity of their devotion to God's will on earth. They are not thinking in ancient terms that leave ideas of progress out. They cannot think in those terms. There could be no greater tragedy than that the Fundamentalists should shut the door of the Christian fellowship against such.

I do not believe for one moment that the Fundamentalists are going to succeed. Nobody's intolerance can contribute anything to the solution of the situation which we have described. **The Solution Of The Problem** If, then, the Fundamentalists have no solution of the problem, where may we expect to find it? In two concluding comments let us consider our reply to that enquiry.

The first element that is necessary is a spirit of tolerance and Christian liberty. When will the world learn that intolerance solves no problems? This is not a lesson which the Fundamentalists alone need to learn; the liberals also need to learn it. Speaking, as I do, from the viewpoint of liberal opinions, let me say that if some young, fresh mind here this morning is holding new ideas, has fought his way through, it may be by intellectual and spiritual struggle to novel positions, and is tempted to be intolerant about old opinions, offensively to condescend to those who hold them and to be harsh in judgment on them, he may well remember that people who held those old opinions have given the world some of the noblest character and the most memorable service that it ever has been blessed with, and that we of the younger generation will prove our case best, not by controversial intolerance, but by producing, with our new opinions, something of the depth and strength, nobility and beauty of character that in other times were associated with other thoughts. It was a wise liberal, the most adventurous man of his day—Paul the apostle—who said, "Knowledge puffeth up, but love buildeth up."

Nevertheless, it is true that just now the Fundamentalists are giving us one of the worst exhibitions of bitter intolerance that the churches of this country have ever seen. As one watches them and listens to them, he remembers the remark of General Armstrong of Hampton Institute: "Cantankerousness is worse than heterodoxy." **Opinions May Be Mistaken; Love Never Is** There are many opinions in the field of modern controversy concerning which I am not sure whether they are right or wrong, but there is one thing I am sure of: courtesy and kindliness and tolerance and humility and fairness and right. Opinions may be mistaken; love never is.

As I plead thus for an intellectually hospitable, tolerant, liberty-loving church, I am of course thinking primarily about this new generation. We have boys and girls growing up in our homes and schools, and because we love them we may well wonder about the church which will be waiting to receive them. Now, the worst kind of church that can possibly be offered to the allegiance of the new generation is an intolerant church. Ministers often bewail the fact that young people turn from religion to science for the regulative ideas of their lives. But this is easily explicable. **How Science Treats a Young Man's Mind** Science treats a young man's mind as though it were really important. A scientist says to a young man: "Here is the universe challenging our investigation. Here are the truths which we have seen, so far. Come, study with us! See what we already have seen and then look further to see more, for science is an intellectual adventure for the truth." Can you imagine any man who is worth while turning from that call to the church, if the church seems to him to say: "Come and we will feed you opinions from a spoon. No thinking is allowed here except such as brings you to certain specified, predetermined conclusions. These prescribed opinions we will give you in advance of your thinking; now think, but only so as to reach these results." My friends, nothing in all the world is so much worth thinking of as God, Christ, the Bible, sin and salvation, the divine purposes for humankind, life everlasting. But you cannot challenge the dedicated thinking of this generation to these sublime themes upon any such terms as are laid down by an intolerant church.

What Are the Main Issues of Christianity?   The second element which is needed if we are to reach a happy solution of this problem is a clear insight into the main issues of modern Christianity and a sense of penitent shame that the Christian church should be quarreling over little matters when the world is dying of great needs. If, during the war, when the nations were wrestling upon the very brink of hell and at times all seemed lost, you chanced to hear two men in an altercation about some minor matter of sectarian denominationalism, could you restrain your indignation? You said, "What can you do with folks like this who, in the face of colossal issues, play with the tiddledywinks and peccadillos of religion?" So, now, when from the terrific questions of this generation one is called away by the noise of this Fundamentalist controversy, he thinks it almost unforgivable that men should tithe mint and anise and cummin, and quarrel over them, when the world is perishing for the lack of the weightier matters of the law, justice, and mercy, and faith.

These last weeks, in the minister's confessional, I have heard stories from the depths of human lives where men and women were wrestling with the elemental problems of misery and sin—stories that put upon a man's heart a burden of vicarious sorrow, even though he does but listen to them. Here was real human need crying out after the living God revealed in Christ. **Fruitless Controversy in the Face of Urgent Need** Consider all the multitudes of men who so need God, and then think of Christian churches making of themselves a cockpit of controversy when there is not a single thing at stake in the controversy on which depends the salvation of human souls. That is the trouble with this whole business. So much of it does not matter! And there is one thing that does matter—more than anything else in all the world—that men in their personal lives and in their social relationships should know Jesus Christ.

A Sick World Needs Christ and His Church Just a week ago I received a letter from a friend in Asia Minor. He says that they are killing the Armenians yet; that the Turkish deportations still are going on; that lately they crowded Christian men, women and children into a conventicle of worship and burned them together in the house where they had prayed to their Father and to ours. During the war, when it was good propaganda to stir up our bitter hatred against the enemy we heard of such atrocities, but not now! Two weeks ago, Great Britain, shocked and stirred by what is going on in Armenia, did ask the Government of the United States to join her in investigating the atrocities and trying to help! Our government said that it was not any of our business at all. The present world situation smells to heaven! And now, in the presence of colossal problems, which must be solved in Christ's name and for Christ's sake, the Fundamentalists propose to drive out from the Christian churches all the consecrated souls who do not agree with their theory of inspiration. What immeasurable folly!

[Well, they are not going to do it; certainly not in this vicinity. I do not even know in this congregation whether anybody has been tempted to be a Fundamentalist. Never in this church have I caught one accent of intolerance. God keep us always so and ever increasing areas of the Christian fellowship: intellectually hospitable, open-minded, liberty-loving, fair, tolerant, not with the tolerance of indifference as though we did not care about the faith, but because always our major emphasis is upon the weightier matters of the law.]

"A Christian Conscience About War"

Geneva, Switzerland, September 13, 1925

All they that take the sword shall perish with the sword.
Matthew 26:52

One ought to read with awe these words spoken nearly two thousand years ago and only now beginning to seem obviously true. Reliance on violence is suicidal, said Jesus. "All they that take the sword shall perish with the sword."

When the Master said that, it could not possibly have seemed to be true. Then it seemed evident that those who took the sword and knew how to use it could rule the world. Reliance on violence did not seem suicidal but necessary, salutary, and rich in its rewards. In these words of Jesus we have one of those surprising insights where, far ahead of the event, a seer perceives an obscure truth which only long afterward will emerge clear, unmistakable, imperative, so that all men must believe it.

Pythagoras in the sixth century B.C. had such a flare of insight when he guessed that the sun did not go about the earth but that the earth circled about a central fire. It was a surprising leap of intuition. No one believed it. Long centuries had to pass before Copernicus and Galileo came and people in general were convinced of what Pythagoras with his inner eye had seen. So when the Master said that the sword would destroy those who used it, that seemed incredible. War suicidal! The world did not even note this strange thing that He said, and ever since men have tried to explain it away or laugh it off as idealism too lofty for this earth. But today that insight of the Master comes to its own. Once more the seer is justified of his vision. Reliance on violence is self-defeating; war is suicidal; civilization itself cannot survive it. That fact has been written in fire across the world until not seers alone, but multitudes of plain people of every tongue, tribe, and nation under heaven are beginning to see the truth once so incredible—"If mankind does not end war, war will end mankind."

Today my plea is simple and direct Of all the people on earth who ought to take in earnest this unforeseeable confirmation of the Master's insight, Christians come first. This question of war and its denial of the method and spirit of Jesus is peculiarly their business. Speaking from this historic Christian pulpit to Christians of many races and nations gathered here, one finds himself inevitably concerned with that matter—addressing, as it were, the conscience of Christendom about war. The destinies of humankind depend upon the arousing of that conscience. Here in Geneva you once more are setting your minds to the high task of working out the technique of international cooperation. In this sanctuary we set ourselves this morning to consider the dynamic without which all the technique will fail—the conscience of Christians about war.

Doubtless we represent here many different kinds of Christianity. We belong to different Churches, hold various theories about ecclesiastical polity, subscribe to diverse creeds. But one thing does unite us all. We start with and include the Master Himself. To all of us He is the Lord and His way is the way of life. At the fountainhead of our Christianity is Jesus Christ. His life with the Father, His faith in the moral possibilities of man, His devotion to the Kingdom of Heaven on earth, His Good Samaritan, His Golden Rule, His Sermon on the Mount, His law of finding life by losing it, His insight into the self-defeating nature of violence, and His substitution of the way of love—all this is included in any special kind of Christianity we severally may profess. How, then, can any of us avoid the conviction that this colossal and ominous question of war, upon the answer to which the future of man depends, is in particular a crucial affair for Christianity? It has been said again and again that if another war befalls us and shakes civilization to its foundations, as it surely would, the Christians of the world will be to blame. Surely that is true. The continuance of war will advertise that the 576,000,000 professed Christians on earth have not had an earnest conscience about their Master's view of life; it will bear evidence that while they have called Him, "Lord, Lord," they have not been willing to do what He said.

Let us dwell, then, on some elements that ought to enter into the operation of the conscience of Christians about war.

For one thing, there is plainly the futility of war to achieve any of the purposes that Christianity is meant to serve. Indeed, there is modern war's futility to achieve any good purposes whatever. Once it was possible really to win a war. Once victors and vanquished stood in such opposite categories at a war's conclusion that there was no possibility of mistaking the prestige, prosperity, increased power and happiness of the one and the dismal annihilation of the other, but one shocking revelation of the last war was the indiscriminate ruin in which war plunged victor, vanquished, and neutrals alike, the ferocious and untamable way in which war, once let loose, tore at the garments of civilization as a whole so that, regardless of who won it, half the world found itself unclad and shivering when the storm was over.

In the history of war we have one more example of a mode of social action possibly possessing at the beginning more of good than evil, which has outgrown its good, accentuated its evil, and become at last an intolerable thing.

That was true of slavery. Men at first reduced to slavery those whom else they would have slaughtered after battle. Slavery was a substitute for massacre, profitable, doubtless, but also merciful. It was a forward step from brutal murder to enforced labor. But slavery did not retain its philanthropic good. In the end it outgrew all its benefits and become an intolerable curse. In an evolutionary world ethics and modes of social action evolve also.

So there may have been times when war could serve good ends, when armed conflict was a means of social progress. Of this war or that it may be claimed that the sword won benefactions lacking which mankind would be the poorer. At least, there is little use in arguing the contrary. For the conviction now growing strong in this generation's mind is that whatever may have been true about war in times past, modern war is futile to achieve any good or Christian thing.

To fight with the gigantic paraphernalia of modern science; to make war in our intimately inter-related and delicately balanced modern world, where our most indispensable means of existence already have become international; to fight, not with armies against armies as of old, but with entire populations massed against entire populations so that bombs rain indiscriminate destruction on whole cities and blockades mean indiscriminate starvation to millions of families; to make war now, when an average five hours of fighting, as in the last war, burns up the endowment of a great university; to fight, knowing that, agreements or no agreements to limit the weapons of war, demonic forces like gas and bacteria are certain to be used—that is obviously futile to achieve any good thing for which a Christian man might wish or pray.

The old appeals for war in the name of a good cause fall coldly now on the instructed ear and cease to carry conviction to thoughtful minds. "Would you not go to war to protect the weak?" men ask. The answer seems obvious. A modern war to protect the weak: 10,000,000 known dead soldiers; 3,000,000 presumed dead soldiers; 13,000,000 dead civilians; 20,000,000 wounded; 3,000,000 prisoners; 9,000,000 war orphans; 5,000,000 war widows; 10,000,000 refugees. What can we mean—modern war protecting the weak? The conviction grows clear in increasing multitudes of minds that modern war is no way to protect the weak.

A World Court would protect the weak. A League of Nations would protect the weak. An international mind, backed by a Christian conscience, that would stop the race for armaments, provide cooperative substitutes for violence, forbid the nations to resort to force, and finally outlaw war altogether—that would protect the weak. But this is clear: war will not do it. It is the weak by millions who perish in every modern war.

As for Christianity, the dilemma which it faces in all this seems unmistakable. The war system as a recognized method of international action is one thing; Christianity with all its purposes and hopes is another; and not all the dialectic of the apologists can make the two lie down in peace together. We may have one or we may have the other, but we cannot permanently have both.

Another stake which Christianity has in this task of overpassing war and providing international substitutes for it lies in the new and ominous developments of nationalism. In our modern world nationalism, with its attendant patriotic emotions and loyalties, has increasingly taken a form which threatens to be the chief rival of Christianity. To be sure, passionate love of country is nothing modern or new. Its roots are deep in man's instincts and man's history. We here today are patriots. We intend to be patriots. We should think less of each other if we were not patriots. Love of fatherland is one of the oldest, deepest, most instinctive and most noble sentiments of man.

But within the last four hundred years nationalism has taken a new and startling form in our Western world. With the England of Elizabeth, the France of Louis XI, the Russia of Peter the Great, the development began which more and more has nationalized both the inner and the outer life of all of us. Our politics has become nationalized until the aggrandizement of one's own country in the competitive struggle with other nationalities has been the supreme aim of statesmanship. Our economic life has become nationalized; the powerful financial interests of each nation have wielded so enormous an influence over its statecraft that government, with its army and navy to back it, has frequently been a docile instrument for the furtherance of the country's economic aims. Our education has become nationalized; our children have been taught from infancy history all out of perspective, with national egoism for its organizing center and with hatred of other nations masquerading as patriotic training of the young. Even our religion has been nationalized; with state churches or without them, the center of loyalty in the religious life of the people has increasingly become the nation. Let Protestantism acknowledge its large responsibility for this in Western Christendom! In our fight for liberty we broke up the inclusive mother church into national churches; we reorganized the worship of the people around nationalistic ideals; we helped to identify religion and patriotism. And so far has this identification gone that now, when war breaks, the one God of all humanity, whom Christ came to reveal, is split up into little tribal deities, and before these pagan idols even Christians pray for the blood of their enemies.

Never before has human life, its statecraft, its economics, its education, its religion, on so large a scale been organized on a nationalistic basis, and the issue is obvious. The supreme object of devotion for multitudes is the nation. In practical action they know no higher God. They really worship Caesar. That is the limit of their loyalty. What once was said of the king is said now of the nation: it can do no wrong. And such sheer paganism is sometimes openly flaunted, at least in my country, and I presume in yours, as "Our country! . . . may she always be in the right; but our country, right or wrong."

Nevertheless, at the same time that this nationalistic process has been going on, another movement has been gathering headway. The enlarging fellowship of human life upon this planet, which began with the clan and tribe and has moved out through ever widening circles of communication and contact, has now become explicitly and overwhelmingly international, and it never can be crowded back again. Moreover, within this unescapable internationalism of modern life, not yet adequately recognized in government, mankind has been learning one great lesson from his social experiments. In area after area he has succeeded in getting what he wanted, not by violence, but by overpassing violence and substituting cooperation. That is what social progress consists in. All social progress can be defined as carrying over one more realm of human life from the régime of force to the régime of cooperation. Wherever we have civilized any social group, the essential thing which has happened is that in that group, not force, but cooperation has become the arbiter.

That is true of the family. A household where men captured their wives, exposed their children in infancy, relied for obedience on the power of life and death over their offspring, would be recognizably uncivilized. A civilized family, with all its faults, enters into marriage by mutual consent, relies on reasonableness, not on force, for its coherence, and from the beginning welcomes children into the democracy of the household. At least we have learned that violence is no way to bring up a good family. The same path of progress we have traveled in education. Once violence ruled our schools. It was said of an old pedagogue, the Rev. James Boyer, that "it was lucky the cherubim who took him to heaven were nothing but wings and faces or he infallibly would have flogged them by the way." But now our schools at their best would be ashamed to rely on violence since reasonableness and cooperation so plainly offer, not only a more ideal, but a more effective substitute. In religion also, being civilized means traveling that road from violence to cooperation. Once force was used to compel faith. If a man wished to be a Christian he could be a Christian, but if he did not wish to be a Christian he had to be a Christian, and the centuries are sad with the horrors of religious persecution. But social progress has largely left all that behind and what compelled its supersession was not sentimentality but the insight that violence is self-defeating, that force is no way to get religion. so, too, has government been carried over from violence to cooperation. The process is lamentably incomplete, but, so far as it has gone, it has furnished the indispensable background for all the civilization we possess. Still upon our Western clothes we wear the buttons, now decorative only, on which once our fathers' swordbelts hung. How impossible it would have seemed to them that the time would ever come when the common carrying of private weapons would be unnecessary because cooperative and peaceful government had provided a substitute!

In one realm after another the Master's insight has proved true. Violence defeats itself. It is no way to achieve family life or education or religion or stable government. Those who rely on it as their mainstay and effective instrument are sure to miss what they are seeking to achieve. Always progress has consisted in carrying over human life from violence to cooperation.

And now we face the next great step, the momentous step in human history. Can we achieve a like result with our international relationships? Can we carry them over from brutality and organized slaughter to reasonableness and cooperation? How the best thinking and praying of our time center around that hope of superseding belligerent nationalism with cooperative international substitutes for war!

Here, then, we face one of the most crucial and dramatic conflicts of loyalty that men ever dealt with. On the one side, our life has been organized as never before in history on a nationalistic basis. On the other hand, the one hope of humanity today, if it is to escape devastating ruin, lies in rising above and beyond this nationalism and organizing the world for peace. On the one side a narrow patriotism saying, "My country against yours," on the other, a wider patriotism saying, "My country with yours for the peace of mankind." Is there any question where real Christianity must stand in that conflict? Is there any question that if she does not stand there she faces the most tragic and colossal moral failure of her history? One would like to cry so that all Christians should hear: Followers of Christ, so often straining out the gnat and swallowing the camel, tithing mint, anise, and cumin, and neglecting the weightier matters of the law, what do all the minutiae of creed and institution that distinguish us amount to in the presence of this gigantic problem in which one of the central meanings of Christ for the world is involved? A narrow belligerent nationalism is today the most explicit and thorough-going denial of Christianity, its thought of God and its love of man, that there is on earth.

How evident this central problem is when we try to discuss the real issues of the world today! Some still see those issues in terms of one nation against another. That is the level on which their thinking runs. America versus Japan or France versus Germany—so in a long list of nation against nation they see the world's affairs. How desperately real the problems are on that level no one needs to be told, but, after all, those are not the deepest issues. A clear conviction grows in the best thinking of today that mankind's realest conflict of interest is not between this nation and that, but between the forward-looking, progressive, open-minded people of all nations, who have caught a vision of humanity organized for peace, and the backward-looking, reactionary, militaristic people of the same nations. The deepest line of conflict does not run vertically between the nations; it runs horizontally through all the nations. The salvation of humanity from self-destruction depends on which side of that conflict wins.

What has happened thus to make a local, national patriotism, however sacred and beautiful in many of its forms, inadequate to meet our present need is clear. In unforgettable words the world has been told by a great patriot: "Patriotism is not enough." Why is it not enough? Well, patriotism once took men of little, local loyalties and expanded their outlook and allegiance. They had been citizens of a shire; patriotism made them citizens of a nation. Patriotism once called men to the widest imaginable out-reach of their devotion; it broke down local provincialisms; it stretched human horizons; it demanded unaccustomed breadth of vision and unselfishness of life. To be a patriot for the nation meant a large loyalty as against the meanness and parochialism of a local mind. But the world has moved. Life has expanded and become international. Now it is possible for patriotism to fall from its high estate. Instead of calling men to wider horizons, it can keep them within narrow ones. Once the issue was patriotism versus a small parochialism; now the question may become patriotism versus a large care for humanity. Once patriotism was the great enemy of provincialism; now it can be made to mean provincialism and to sanctify the narrow mind.

This conflict of loyalties creates your difficult problems here in Geneva. You know how tenacious the adhesions of nationalism are, how difficult to entwine the thoughts and affections of men around new ideals and new methods of world peace. But this struggle between two loyalties goes deeper than the realm of statesmanship; it runs far down into the souls of men where the destinies of religion lie. How can a man be a follower of Jesus Christ and still be a belligerent nationalist, when once this better hope of a world organized for peace has dawned upon his view? Whatever else Christianity may believe in, it must believe in God, Father of all men; it must believe in men of every tribe, tongue, people, and nation, as God's children; it must believe in the Kingdom of God on earth. The spirit of Christianity is not narrowly nationalistic, but universally inclusive. When the world, therefore, organizes itself on the basis of belligerent nationalism the very genius of the Christian Gospel is at stake. Once more we can have our old war systems with their appalling modern developments, or we can have Christianity, but we cannot permanently have both. They worship irreconcilable gods.

I need not, and I must not, press the analysis further. Two generations ago one of our great statesmen, Charles Sumner, said, "Not that I love country less, but Humanity more, do I now and here plead the cause of a higher and truer patriotism. I cannot forget that we are men by a more sacred bond than we are citizens—that we are children of a common Father more than we are Americans." Shall not each one of us here pray for his own country, as I pray earnestly for mine, that that spirit may come into the ascendancy? Christianity essentially involves it.

The first Christians saw this. "The early Christian Church," says a recent writer, "was the first peace society." Then came Christianity's growing power—the days when Christians, no longer outcast, were stronger than their adversaries, until at last the imperial household of Constantine himself accepted Christianity. Then Christianity, joined with the state, forgot its earlier attitudes, bowed to the necessities of imperial action, became sponsor for war, blesser of war, cause of war, fighter of war. Since then the Church has come down though history too often trying to carry the cross of Jesus in one hand and a dripping sword in the other, until now when Christians look out upon the consequence of it all, this abysmal disgrace of Christendom making mockery of the Gospel, the conviction rises that we would better go back to our traditions, our early purity, and see whether those first disciples of the Lord were not nearer right than we have been.

We cannot reconcile Jesus Christ and war—that is the essence of the matter. That is the challenge which today should stir the conscience of Christendom. War is the most colossal and ruinous social sin that afflicts mankind; it is utterly and irremediably unchristian; in its total method and effect it means everything that Jesus did not mean and it means nothing that He did mean; it is a more blatant denial of every Christian doctrine about God and man than all the theoretical atheists on earth ever could devise. It would be worth while, would it not, to see the Christian Church claim as her own this greatest moral issue of our time, to see her lift once more, as in our fathers' days, a clear standard against the paganism of this present world and, refusing to hold her conscience at the beck and call of belligerent states, put the Kingdom of God above nationalism and call the world to peace? That would not be the denial of patriotism but its apotheosis.

Here today, as an American, under this high and hospitable roof, I cannot speak for my government, but both as an American, and as a Christian I do speak for millions of my fellow citizens in wishing your great work, in which we believe, for which we pray, our absence from which we painfully regret, the eminent success which it desires. We work in many ways for the same end—a world organized for peace. Never was an end better worth working for. The alternative is the most appalling catastrophe mankind has ever faced. Like gravitation in the physical realm, the law of the Lord in the moral realm bends for no man and no nation: "All they that take the sword shall perish with the sword."

"The Unknown Soldier"

Riverside Church, New York City
November 12, 1933

It was an interesting idea to deposit the body of an unrecognized soldier in the national memorial of the Great War, and yet, when one stops to think of it, how strange it is! Yesterday, in Rome, Paris, London, Washington, and how many capitals beside, the most stirring military pageantry, decked with flags and exultant with music, centered about the bodies of unknown soldiers. That is strange. So this is the outcome of Western civilization, which for nearly two thousand years has worshipped Christ, and in which democracy and science have had their widest opportunity, that the whole nation pauses, its acclamations rise, its colorful pageantry centers, its patriotic oratory flourishes, around the unrecognizable body of a soldier blown to bits on the battlefield. That is strange.

It was the war lords themselves who picked him out as the symbol of war. So be it! As a symbol of war we accept him from their hands.

You may not say that I, being a Christian minister, did not know him. I knew him well. From the north of Scotland, where they planted the sea with mines, to the trenches of France, I lived with him and his fellows—British, Australian, New Zealand, French, American. The places where he fought, from Ypres through the Somme battlefield to the southern trenches, I saw while he still was there. I lived with him in his dugouts in the trenches, and on destroyers searching for submarines off the shores of France. Short of actual battle, from training camp to hospital, from the fleet to No Man's Land, I, a Christian minister, saw the war. Moreover, I, a Christian minister, participated in it. I too was persuaded that it was a war to end war. I too was a gullible fool and thought that modern war could somehow make the world safe for democracy. They sent men like me to explain to the army the high meaning of war and, by every argument we could command, to strengthen their morale. I wonder if I ever spoke to the Unknown Soldier.

One night, in a ruined barn behind the lines, I spoke at sunset to a company of hand-grenaders who were going out that night to raid the German trenches. They told me that on the average no more than half a company came back from such a raid, and I, a minister of Christ, tried to nerve them for their suicidal and murderous endeavor. I wonder if the Unknown Soldier was in that barn that night.

Once in a dugout which in other days had been a French wine cellar I bade Godspeed at two in the morning to a detail of men going out on patrol in No Man's Land. They were a fine company of American boys fresh from home. I recall that, huddled in the dark, underground chamber, they sang,

> Lead, kindly Light, amid th' encircling gloom,
> Lead thou me on.
> The night is dark, and I am far from home,—
> Lead thou me on.

Then, with my admonitions in their ears, they went down from the second- to the first-line trenches and so out to No Man's Land. I wonder if the Unknown Soldier was in that dugout.

You here this morning may listen to the rest of this sermon or not, as you please. It makes much less difference to me than usual what you do or think. I have an account to settle in this pulpit today between my soul and the Unknown Soldier.

He is not so utterly unknown as we sometimes think. Of one thing we can be certain: he was sound of mind and body. We made sure of that. All primitive gods who demanded bloody sacrifices on their altars insisted that the animals should be the best, without mar or hurt. Turn to the Old Testament and you find it written there: "Whether male or female, he shall offer it without blemish before Jehovah." The god of war still maintains the old demand. These men to be sacrificed upon his altars were sound and strong. Once there might have been guessing about that. Not now. Now we have medical science, which tests the prospective soldier's body. Now we have psychiatry, which tests his mind. We used them both to make sure that these sacrifices for the god of war were without blemish. Of all insane and suicidal procedures, can you imagine anything madder than this, that all the nations should pick out their best, use their scientific skill to make certain that they are the best, and then in one mighty holocaust offer ten million of them on the battlefields of one war?

I have an account to settle between my soul and the Unknown Soldier. I deceived him. I deceived myself first, unwittingly, and then

I deceived him, assuring him that good consequence could come out of that. As a matter of hard-headed, biological fact, what good can come out of that? Mad civilization, you cannot sacrifice on bloody altars the best of your breed and expect anything to compensate for the loss.

Of another thing we may be fairly sure concerning the Unknown Soldier—that he was a conscript. He may have been a volunteer but on an actuarial average he probably was a conscript. The long arm of the nation reached into his home, touched him on the shoulder, saying, You must go to France and fight. If some one asks why in this "land of the free" conscription was used, the answer is, of course, that it was necessary if we were to win the war. Certainly it was. And that reveals something terrific about modern war. We cannot get soldiers—not enough of them, not the right kind of them—without forcing them. When a nation goes to war now, the entire nation must go. That means that the youth of the nation must be compelled, coerced, conscripted to fight.

When you stand in Arlington before the tomb of the Unknown Soldier on some occasions, let us say, when the panoply of military glory decks it with music and color, are you thrilled? I am not—not any more. I see there the memorial of one of the saddest things in American history, from the continued repetition of which may God deliver us!—the conscripted boy.

He was a son, the hope of the family, and the nation coerced him. He was, perchance, a lover and the deepest emotion of his life was not desire for military glory or hatred of another country or any other idiotic thing like that, but love of a girl and hope of a home. He was, maybe, a husband and a father, and already, by that slow and beautiful graduation which all fathers know, he had felt the deep ambitions of his heart being transferred from himself to his children. And the nation coerced him. I am not blaming him; he was conscripted. I am not blaming the nation; it never could have won the war without conscription. I am simply saying that that is modern war, not by accident but by necessity, and with every repetition that will be more and more the attribute of war.

Last time they coerced our sons. Next time, of course, they will coerce our daughters, and in any future war they will conscript property. Old-fashioned Americans, born out of the long tradition of liberty, some of us have trouble with these new coercions used as short cuts to get things done, but nothing else compares with this inevitable, universal, national conscription in time of war. Repeated once or twice more, it will end everything in this nation that remotely approaches liberty.

If I blame anybody about this matter, it is men like myself who ought to have known better. We went out to the army and explained to these valiant men what a resplendent future they were preparing for their children by their heroic sacrifice. O Unknown Soldier, however can I make that right with you? For sometimes I think I hear you asking me about it:

Where is this great, new era that the war was to create? Where is it? They blew out my eyes in the Argonne. Is it because of that that now from Arlington I strain them vainly to see the great gains of the war? If I could see the prosperity, plenty, and peace of my children for which this mangled body was laid down!

My friends, sometimes I do not want to believe in immortality. Sometimes I hope that the Unknown Soldier will never know.

Many of you here knew these men better, you may think, than I knew them, and already you may be relieving my presentation of the case by another picture. Probably, you say, the Unknown Soldier enjoyed soldiering and had a thrilling time in France. The Great War, you say, was the most exciting episode of our time. Some of us found in it emotional release unknown before or since. We escaped from ourselves. We were carried out of ourselves. Multitudes were picked up from a dull routine, lifted out of the drudgery of common days with which they were infinitely bored, and plunged into an exciting adventure which they remember yet as the most thrilling episode of their careers.

Indeed, you say, how could martial music be so stirring and martial poetry so exultant if there were not at the heart of war a lyric glory? Even in the churches you sing,

Onward, Christian soldiers,
Marching as to war.

You, too, when you wish to express or arouse ardor and courage, use war's symbolism. The Unknown Soldier, sound in mind and body—yes! The Unknown Soldier a conscript—probably! But be fair and add that the Unknown Soldier had a thrilling time in France.

To be sure, he may have had. Listen to this from a wounded American after a battle. "We went over the parapet at five o'clock and I was not hit till nine. They were the greatest four hours of my life." Quite so! Only let me talk to you a moment about that. That was the first time he went over the parapet. Anything risky, dangerous, tried for the first time, well handled, and now escaped from, is thrilling to an excitable and courageous soul. What about the second time and the third time and the fourth? What about the dreadful times between, the long-drawn-out, monotonous, dreary, muddy barrenness of war, concerning which one who knew said, "Nine-tenths of War is Waiting"? The trouble with much familiar talk about the lyric glory of war is that it comes from people who never saw any soldiers except the American troops, fresh, resilient, who had time to go over the parapet about once. You ought to have seen the hardening-up camps of the armies which had been at the business since 1914. Did you ever see them? Did you look, as I have looked, into the faces of young men who had been over the top, wounded, hospitalized, hardened up—over the top, wounded, hospitalized, hardened up—over the top, wounded, hospitalized, hardened up—four times, five times, six times? Never talk to a man who has seen that about the lyric glory of war.

Where does all this talk about the glory of war come from, anyway?

"Charge, Chester, charge! On, Stanley, on!"
Were the last words of Marmion.

That is Sir Walter Scott. Did he ever see war? Never.

And how can man die better
    Than facing fearful odds,
For the ashes of his fathers,
    And the temples of his Gods?

That is Macaulay. Did he ever see war? He was never near one.

Storm'd at with shot and shell,
Boldly they rode and well,
Into the jaws of Death,
Into the mouth of Hell,
Rode the six hundred.

That is Tennyson. Did he ever see war? I should say not.

There is where the glory of war comes from. We have heard very little about it from the real soldiers of this last war. We have had from them the appalling opposite. They say what George Washington said: it is "a plague to mankind." The glory of war comes from poets, preachers, orators, the writers of martial music, statesmen preparing flowery proclamations for the people, who dress up war for other men to fight. They do not go to the trenches. They do not go over the top again and again and again.

Do you think that the Unknown Soldier would really believe in the lyric glory of war? I dare you; go to Arlington and tell him that now.

Nevertheless, some may say that while war is a grim and murderous business with no glory in it in the end, and while the Unknown Soldier doubtless knew that well, we have the right in our imagination to make him the symbol of whatever was most idealistic and courageous in the men who went out to fight. Of course we have. Now, let us do that! On the body of a French sergeant killed in battle was found a letter to his parents in which he said, "You know how I made the sacrifice of my life before leaving." So we think of our Unknown Soldier as an idealist, rising up in answer to a human call and making the sacrifice of his life before leaving. His country seemed to him like Christ himself, saying, "If any man would come after me, let him deny himself, and take up his cross daily, and follow me." Far from appealing to his worst, the war brought out his best—his loyalty, his courage, his venturesomeness, his care for the downtrodden, his capacity for self-sacrifice. The noblest qualities of his young manhood were aroused. He went out to France a flaming patriot and in secret quoted Rupert Brooke to his own soul:

If I should die, think only this of me:
    That there's some corner of a foreign field
That is for ever England.

There you say, is the Unknown Soldier.

Yes, indeed, did you suppose I never had met him? I talked with him many a time. When the words that I would speak about war are a blistering fury on my lips and the encouragement I gave to war is a deep self-condemnation in my heart, it is of that I think. For I watched war lay its hands on these strongest, loveliest things in men and use the noblest attributes of the human spirit for what ungodly deeds! Is there anything more infernal than this, to take the best that is in man and use it to do what war does? This is the ultimate description of war—it is the prostitution of the noblest powers of the human soul to the most dastardly deeds, the most abysmal cruelties of which our human nature is capable. That is war.

Granted, then, that the Unknown Soldier should be to us a symbol of everything most idealistic in a valiant warrior, I beg of you, be realistic and follow through what was made the Unknown Soldier do with his idealism. Here is one eye-witness speaking:

"Last night, at an officers' mess there was great laughter at the story of one of our men who had spent his last cartridge in defending an attack. 'Hand me down your spade, Mike,' he said; and as six Germans came one by one round the end of a traverse, he split each man's skull open with a deadly blow." The war made the Unknown Soldier do that with his idealism.

"I can remember," says one infantry officer, "a pair of hands (nationality unknown) which protruded from the soaked ashen soil like the roots of a tree turned upside down; one hand seemed to be pointing at the sky with an accusing gesture. . . . Floating on the surface of the flooded trench was the mask of a human face which had detached itself from the skull." War harnessed the idealism of the Unknown Soldier to that!

Do I not have an account to settle between my soul and him? They sent men like me into the camps to awaken his idealism, to touch those secret, holy springs within him so that with devotion, fidelity, loyalty, and self-sacrifice he might go out to war. O war, I hate you most of all for this, that you do lay your hands on the noblest elements in human character, with which we might make a heaven on earth, and you use them to make a hell on earth instead! You take even our science, the fruit of our dedicated intelligence, by means of which we might build here the City of God, and, using it, you fill the earth instead with new ways of slaughtering men. You take our loyalty, our unselfishness, with which we might make the earth beautiful, and, using these our finest qualities, you make death fall from the sky and burst up from the sea and hurtle from unseen ambuscades sixty miles away; you blast fathers in the trenches with gas while you are starving their children at home by blockades; and you so bedevil the world that fifteen years after the Armistice we cannot be sure who won the war, so sunk in the same disaster are victors and vanquished alike. If war were fought simply with evil things, like hate, it would be bad enough but, when one sees the deeds of war done with the loveliest faculties of the human spirit, he looks into the very pit of hell.

Suppose one thing more—that the Unknown Soldier was a Christian. Maybe he was not, but suppose he was, a Christian like Sergeant York, who at the beginning intended to take Jesus so seriously as to refuse to fight but afterward, otherwise persuaded, made a real soldier. For these Christians do make soldiers. Religion is a force. When religious faith supports war, when, as in the Crusades, the priests of Christ cry, "Deus Vult"—God wills it—and, confirming ordinary motives, the dynamic of Christian devotion is added, then an incalculable resource of confidence and power is released. No wonder the war departments wanted the churches behind them!

Suppose, then, that the Unknown Soldier was a Christian. I wonder what he thinks about war now. Practically all modern books about war emphasize the newness of it—new weapons, new horrors, new extensiveness. At times, however, it seems to me that still the worst things about war are the ancient elements. In the Bible we read terrible passages where the Hebrews thought they had command from Jehovah to slaughter the Amalekites, "both man and woman, infant and suckling, ox and sheep, camel and ass." Dreadful! we say, an ancient and appalling idea! Ancient? Appalling? Upon the contrary, that is war, and always will be. A military order, issued in our generation by an American general in the Philippines and publicly acknowledged by his counsel afterwards in a military court, commanded his soldiers to burn and kill, to exterminate all capable of bearing arms, and to make the island of Samar a howling wilderness. Moreover, his counsel acknowledged that he had specifically named the age of ten with instructions to kill every one over that. Far from launching into a denunciation of that American general, I am much more tempted to state his case for him. Why not? Cannot boys and girls of eleven fire a gun? Why not kill everything over ten? That is war, past, present, and future. All that our modern fashions have done is to make the necessity of slaughtering children not the comparatively simple and harmless matter of shooting some of them in Samar, one by one, but the wholesale destruction of children, starving them by millions, impoverishing them, spoiling the chances of unborn generations of them, as in the Great War.

My friends, I am not trying to make you sentimental about this. I want you to be hard-headed. We can have this monstrous thing or we can have Christ, but we cannot have both. O my country, stay out of war! Cooperate with the nations in every movement that has any hope for peace; enter the World Court, support the League of Nations, contend undiscourageably for disarmament, but set your face steadfastly and forever against being drawn into another war. O church of Christ, stay out of war! Withdraw from every alliance that maintains or encourages it. It was not a pacifist, it was Field-Marshal Earl Haig who

said, "It is the business of the churches to make my business impossible."
And O my soul, stay out of war!

At any rate, I will myself do the best I can to settle my account
with the Unknown Soldier. I renounce war. I renounce war because of
what it does to our own men. I have watched them coming gassed from
the front-line trenches. I have seen the long, long hospital trains filled
with their mutilated bodies. I have heard the cries of the crazed and the
prayers of those who wanted to die and could not, and I remember the
maimed and ruined men for whom the war is not yet over. I renounce
war because of what it compels us to do to our enemies, bombing their
mothers in villages, starving their children by blockades, laughing over
our coffee cups about every damnable thing we have been able to do to
them. I renounce war for its consequences, for the lies it lives on and
propagates, for the undying hatreds it arouses, for the dictatorships it puts
in the place of democracy, for the starvation that stalks after it. I
renounce war and never again, directly or indirectly, will I sanction or
support another! O Unknown Soldier, in penitent reparation I make you
that pledge.

"The Church Must Go Beyond Modernism"

Riverside Church, New York City, November 3, 1935

If we are successfully to maintain the thesis that the church must go beyond modernism, we must start by seeing that the church had to go as far as modernism. Fifty years ago, a boy seven years of age was crying himself to sleep at night in terror lest, dying, he should go to hell, and his solicitous mother, out of all patience with the fearful teaching which brought such apparitions to the mind, was trying in vain to comfort him. That boy is preaching to you today and you may be sure that to him the achievements of Christian modernism in the last half century seem not only important but indispensable.

Fifty years ago the intellectual portion of Western civilization had turned one of the most significant mental corners in history and was looking out on a new view of the world. The church, however, was utterly unfitted for the appreciation of that view. Protestant Christianity had been officially formulated in prescientific days. The Augsburg Confession was a notable statement but the men who drew it up, including Luther himself, did not even believe that the earth goes round the sun. The Westminster Confession, for the rigorous acceptance of which the Presbyterian rear-guard still contends, was a memorable document but it was written forty years before Newton published his work on the law of gravitation. Moreover, not only were the mental patterns of Protestant Christianity officially formulated in prescientific days but, as is always true of religion, those patterns were sacred to their believers and the changes forced by the new science seemed impious and sacrilegious.

Youths like myself, therefore, a half century ago faced an appalling lag between our generation's intellect on one side and its religion on the other, with religion asking us to believe incredible things. Behind his playfulness the author of *Through the Looking Glass* had this serious matter in mind when he represented the White Queen as saying to Alice, "I'm just one hundred and one, five months and a day." Said Alice, "I can't believe *that*!" Said the Queen pityingly, "Can't you? Try again: draw a long breath, and shut your eyes." So the church seemed to be speaking to us.

Modernism, therefore, came as a desperately needed way of thinking. It insisted that the deep and vital experience of the Christian soul with itself, with its fellows, with its God, could be carried over into this new world and understood in the light of the new knowledge. We refused to live bifurcated lives, our intellect in the late nineteenth century and our religion in the early sixteenth. God, we said, is a living God who has never uttered his final word on any subject; why, therefore, should prescientific frameworks of thought be so sacred that forever through them man must seek the Eternal and the Eternal seek man? So we said, and, thanks to modernism, it became true of many an anxious and troubled soul in our time that, as Sam Walter Foss expressed it,

He saw the boundless scheme dilate,
In star and blossom, sky and clod;
And as the universe grew great,
He dreamed for it a greater God.

The church thus had to go as far as modernism but now the church must go beyond it. For even this brief rehearsal of its history reveals modernism's essential nature; it is primarily an adaptation, an adjustment, an accommodation of Christian faith to contemporary scientific thinking. It started by taking the intellectual culture of a particular period as its criterion and then adjusted Christian teaching to that standard. Herein lies modernism's tendency toward shallowness and transiency; arising out of a temporary intellectual crisis, it took a special type of scientific thinking as standard and became an adaptation to, a harmonization with, the intellectual culture of a particular generation. That, however, is no adequate religion to represent the Eternal and claim the allegiance of the soul. Let it be a modernist who says that to you! Unless the church can go deeper and reach higher than that it will fail indeed.

In the first place, modernism has been excessively preoccupied with intellectualism. Its chosen problem has been somehow to adjust Christian faith to the modern intellect so that a man could be a Christian without throwing his reason away. Modernism's message to the church has been after this fashion: When, long ago, the new music came, far from clinging to old sackbuts and psalteries, you welcomed the full orchestra and such composers as Palestrina, Bach, Beethoven, to the glory of God; when the new art came you did not refuse it but welcomed Cimabue, Giotto, Raphael, and Michelangelo, to the enrichment of your faith; when the new architecture came, far from clinging to primitive catacombs or the old Romanesque, you greeted the Gothic with its expanded spaces and aspiring altitudes; so now, when the new science comes, take that in too, and, however painful the adaptations, adjust your faith to it and assimilate its truths into your Christian thinking.

Surely, that has been a necessary appeal but it centers attention on one problem only—intellectual adjustment to modern science. It approaches the vast field of man's experience and need head first, whereas the deepest experiences of man's soul, whether in religion or out of it, cannot be approached head first. List as you will the soul's deepest experiences and needs—friendship, the love that makes a home, the enjoyment of music, delight in nature, devotion to moral causes, the practice of the presence of God—it is obvious that, whereas, if we are wise, we use our heads on them, nevertheless we do not approach them mainly head first, but heart first, conscience first, imagination first. A man is vastly greater than his logic, and the sweep and ambit of his spiritual experience and need are incalculably wider than his rational processes. So modernism, as such, covers only a segment of the spiritual field and does not nearly compass the range of religion's meaning.

Indeed, the critical need of overpassing modernism is evident in the fact that our personal spiritual problems do not lie there any more. When I was a student in the seminary, the classrooms where the atmosphere grew tense with excitement concerned the higher criticism of the Bible and the harmonization of science and religion. That, however, is no longer the case. The classrooms in the seminary where the atmosphere grows tense today concern Christian ethics and the towering question whether Christ has a moral challenge that can shake this contemporary culture to its foundations and save us from our deadly personal and social sins. So the world has moved far to a place where mere Christian harmonizers, absorbed with the intellectual attempt to adapt faith to science and accommodate Christ to prevalent culture, seem trivial and out of date. Our modern world, as a whole, cries out not so much for souls intellectually adjusted to it as for souls morally maladjusted to it, not most of all for accommodators and adjusters but for intellectual and ethical challengers.

When Paul wrote his first letter to the Corinthians, he said that he had become a Jew to the Jews that he might win the Jews, and he intimated that he had become a Greek to the Greeks that he might win the Greeks. "I am become," he said, "all things to all men, that I may by all means save some." That is a modernistic passage of adjustment and accommodation. But that is not all Paul said. Had it been all, Paul would have sunk from sight in an indistinguishable blend with the Greco-Roman culture of his day and we should never have heard of him. When he wrote the second time to the Corinthians he said something else:

> Come ye out from among them, and be ye separate,
> saith the Lord,

And touch no unclean thing.
Church of Christ, take that to yourself now! Stop this endeavor to harmonize yourself with modern culture and customs as though they were a standard and criterion. Rather, come out from among them. Only an independent standing-ground from which to challenge modern culture can save either it or you.

In the second place, not only has modernism been thus predominantly intellectualistic and therefore partial, but, strange to say, at the same time it has been dangerously sentimental. The reason for this is easy to explain. One of the predominant elements in the intellectual culture of the late nineteenth and twentieth centuries, to which modernism adjusted itself, was illusory belief in inevitable progress. So many hopeful and promising things were afoot that two whole generations were fairly bewitched into thinking that every day in every way man was growing better and better. Scientific discovery, exploration and invention, the rising tide of economic welfare, the spread of democracy, the increase of humanitarianism, the doctrine of evolution itself, twisted to mean that automatically today has to be better than yesterday and tomorrow better than today—how many elements seduced us in those romantic days into thinking that all was right with the world!

In the intellectual culture to which modernistic Christianity adapted itself, such lush optimism was a powerful factor, and the consequences are everywhere present in the natural predispositions of our thought today. In the little village of Selborne, England, the visitor is shown some trees planted by a former minister near his dwelling, so that he might be spared the view of the village slaughter-house. Those trees are suggestive and symbolic of the sentimental illusions we plant to hide from our eyes the ugly facts of life. Especially we modernistic Christians, dealing, as we were, with thoughts of a kindly God by evolution lifting everything and everybody up, were deeply tempted to live in a fool's paradise behind our lovely trees.

For example, modernistic Christianity largely eliminated from its faith the God of moral judgment. To be sure, in the old theology, the God of moral judgment had been terribly presented so that little children did cry themselves to sleep at night for fear of him and of his hell. Modernism, however, not content with eliminating the excrescences of a harsh theology, became softer yet and created the general impression that there is nothing here to fear at all. One of the most characteristic religious movements of the nineteenth century heralded this summary of faith:

The Fatherhood of God.
The Brotherhood of Man.
The Leadership of Jesus.
Salvation by Character.
The Progress of Mankind—
        onward and upward forever.

Well, if that is the whole creed, this is a lovely world with nothing here to dread at all.

But there *are* things here to dread. Ask the physicians. They will tell us that in a law-abiding world are stern conditions whose fulfillment or non-fulfillment involve bodily destiny. Ask the novelists and dramatists, and at their best they are not lying to us as they reveal the inexorable fatality with which character and conduct work out their implied consequence. Ask the economists. They will tell us there are things to dread which lead to an inevitable economic hell. Ask even the historians and they will talk at times like old preachers about the God of moral judgment, as James Anthony Froude did when he said, "One lesson, and only one, history may be said to repeat with distinctness: that the world is built somehow on moral foundations; that, in the long run, it is well with the good; in the long run, it is ill with the wicked."

Indeed, cannot we use our own eyes to see that there are things here to fear? For this is no longer the late nineteenth and early twentieth centuries. This is the epoch after the first world war shook the earth to its foundations, and the God of judgment has spoken. My soul, what a world, which the gentle modernism of my younger ministry, with its kindly sentiments and limitless optimism, does not fit at all! We must go beyond that. Because I know that I am speaking here to many minds powerfully affected by modernism, I say to you as to myself: Come out of these intellectual cubicles and sentimental retreats which we built by adapting Christian faith to an optimistic era. Underline this: *Sin is real.* Personal and social sin is as terribly real as our forefathers said it was, no matter how we change their way of saying so. And it leads men and nations to damnation as they said it did, no matter how we change their way of picturing it. For these are times, real times, of the kind out of which man's great exploits have commonly been won, in which, if a man is to have a real faith he must gain it from the very teeth of dismay; if he is to have real hope, it must shine, like a Rembrandt portrait, from the dark background of fearful apprehension; if he is to have real character, he must achieve it against the terrific down-drag of an antagonistic world; and if he is to have a real church, it must stand out from the world and challenge it, not be harmonized with it.

In the third place, modernism has even watered down and thinned out the central message and distinctive truth of religion, the reality of God. One does not mean by that, of course, that modernists are atheists. One does mean, however, that the intellectual culture of the late nineteenth and early twentieth centuries, to which modernism adjusted itself, was predominantly man-centered. Man was blowing on his hands and doing such things at such a rate as never had been done or dreamed on earth before. Man was pioneering new truth and building a new social order. You young people who were not here then can hardly imagine with what cheerful and confident trust we confided to man the saving of the world. So the temptation was to relegate God to an advisory capacity, as a kind of chairman of the board of sponsors of our highly successful human enterprise. A poet like Swinburne could even put the prevailing mood into candid words:

Thou art smitten, thou God, thou art smitten; thy death is upon thee, O Lord.

And the love-song of earth as thou diest resounds through the wind of her wings—

Glory to Man in the highest! for Man is the master of things.

Look out on the world today and try, if you can, to repeat those words of Swinburne and still keep your face straight! At any rate, if ever I needed something deeper to go on than Swinburne's sentimental humanism, with man as the master of things, it is now—a philosophy, namely, a profound philosophy about what is ultimately and eternally real in this universe. We modernists were so disgusted with the absurdities of the old supernaturalistic theology that we were commonly tempted to visit our distaste on theology as a whole and throw it away. But theology means thinking about the central problem of existence—what is ultimately and eternally real in this universe. And in the lurid light of days like these it becomes clearer, as an increasing number of atheists are honestly saying, that if the eternally real is merely material, if the cosmos is a physical fortuity and the earth an accident, if there is no profounder reason for mankind's being here than just that at one stage in the planet's cooling the heat happened to be right, and if we ourselves are "the disease of the agglutinated dust," then to stand on this temporary and accidental earth in the face of this vast cosmos and try lyrically to sing,

Glory to Man in the highest! for Man is the master of things,

is an absurd piece of sentimental tomfoolery. And because I have been and am a modernist it is proper that I should confess that often the modernistic movement, adjusting itself to a man-centered culture, has encouraged this mood, watered down the thought of the Divine, and, may we be forgiven for this, left souls standing, like the ancient Athenians, before an altar to an Unknown God!

On that point the church must go beyond modernism. We have been all things to all men long enough. We have adapted and adjusted and accommodated and conceded long enough. We have at times gotten so low down that we talked as though the highest compliment that could be paid Almighty God was that a few scientists believed in him. Yet all the time, by right, we had an independent standing-ground and a message of our own in which alone is there hope for humankind. The eternally real is the spiritual. The highest in us comes from the deepest in the universe. Goodness and truth and beauty are not accidents but revelations of creative reality. God is! On that point come out from among them and be ye separate! As the poet imagined Paul saying:

Whoso has felt the Spirit of the Highest cannot confound nor doubt Him nor deny:

yea with one voice, o world, tho' thou deniest,
Stand thou on that side, for on this am I.

Finally, modernism has too commonly lost its ethical standing-
ground and its power of moral attack. It is a dangerous thing for a great
religion to begin adjusting itself to the culture of a special generation.
Harmonizing slips easily into compromising. To adjust Christian faith to
the new astronomy, the new geology, the new biology, is absolutely
indispensable. But suppose that this modernizing process, well started,
goes on and Christianity adapts itself to contemporary nationalism,
contemporary imperialism, contemporary capitalism, contemporary
racialism—harmonizing itself, that is, with the prevailing social status
quo and the common moral judgments of our time—what then has
become of religion, so sunk and submerged in undifferentiated identity
with this world?

This lamentable end of a modernizing process, starting with
indispensable adaptations and slipping into concession and compromise,
is a familiar phenomenon in religious history. For the word "modernism"
may not be exclusively identified with the adjustment of Christian faith
and practice to the culture of a single era. Modernization is a recurrent
habit in every living religion. Early Protestantism, itself, emerging along
with a new nationalism and a new capitalism, was in its day modernism,
involving itself and us in entanglements and compliances with political
and economic ideas in whose presence we still are tempted to be servile.
Every era with powerful originative factors in it evokes from religion
indispensable adaptations, followed by further concessive acquiescences,
which in time must be superseded and outgrown. Early Christianity went
out from an old Jewish setting into a new Greek culture and never would
have survived if it had not assimilated into its faith the profound insights
of Greek philosophy. So in the classic creeds, like that of Nicaea, we
have a blending of the old faith with the new philosophy, and in that
process John and Paul themselves had already played a part. But, alas,
early Christianity in its adjustment of its faith to Greek culture did not
stop with adaptation to the insights of philosophy. At last it adapted
itself to Constantine, to the licentious court, to war, to the lucrative
enjoyment of imperial favors, to the use of bloody persecutions to coerce
belief. One after another, it threw away the holiest things that had been
entrusted to it by its Lord until, often hardly distinguishable from the
culture it lived in, it nearly modernized itself into moral futility. Lift up
that history, as it were a mirror, in which to see the peril of our
American churches.

It is not in Germany alone that the church stands in danger of
being enslaved by society. There the enslavement is outward, deliberate,
explicit, organized. Here it is secret, quiet, pervasive, insidious. A
powerful culture—social, economic, nationalistic, militaristic—impinging
from every side upon the church, cries with persuasive voices, backed by
all the sanctions and motives most urgent to the self-interest of man,

Adjust yourself, adapt yourself, accommodate yourself!

When Great Britain was as mad about the Boer War as Italy is mad today about the Ethiopian War and all the forces of propaganda had whipped up the frenzy of the people to a fever heat, John Morley one night in Manchester faced an indignant, antagonistic crowd, and pleaded with his countrymen against the war. This in part is what he said: "You may carry fire and sword into the midst of peace and industry; it will be wrong. A war of the strongest government in the world with untold wealth and inexhaustible reserves against this little republic will bring you no glory: it will be wrong. You may make thousands of women widows and thousands of children fatherless: it will be wrong. It may add a new province to your empire: it will still be wrong." John Morley did not call himself a Christian. He called himself an agnostic. But he was far nearer standing where Christ intended his church to stand than the church has often been.

We modernists had better talk to ourselves like this. So had the fundamentalists—but that is not our affair. We have already largely won the battle we started out to win; we have adjusted the Christian faith to the best intelligence of our day and have won the strongest minds and the best abilities of the churches to our side. Fundamentalism is still with us but mostly in the backwaters. The future of the churches, if we will have it so, is in the hands of modernism. Therefore let all modernists lift a new battle cry: We must go beyond modernism! And in that new enterprise the watch-word will be not, Accommodate yourself to the prevailing culture! but, Stand out from it and challenge it! For this unescapable fact, which again and again in Christian history has called modernism to its senses, we face: we cannot harmonize Christ himself with modern culture. What Christ does to modern culture is to challenge it.

"Handling Life's Second-Bests"

Riverside, March 12, 1944; National Vespers, April 30, 1944

Note: Fosdick's orally ad-libbed insertions, taken from his emended 1931 text, are indicated with *italics* (in all instances, his ad-libbed words were not in the National Vespers broadcast); his verbal omissions, with brackets; and the language that was in the Riverside version but excised for time constraints in the National Vespers program, with **bold** (as taken from a transcript of the April 30, 1944, broadcast). Thus, the following text demonstrates how Fosdick orally delivered his speeches and how he slightly condensed his radio broadcasts.

Even in ordinary times few persons have a chance to live their lives on the basis of their first choice. Whistler, the artist, for example, stated out to be a soldier and failed at West Point because he could not pass in chemistry. ["If silicon had been a gas,"] He used to say, "*If silicon had been a gas*, I should have been a major-general." So, failing in his first choice, he half-heartedly tried engineering and then tried painting--with such remarkable results as the whole world knows.

Even ordinary life is full of this problem--having to do the best we can with *our* second and third choices--but in these days who escapes it? This ghastly era is no first choice of ours as an age to live in, and as for our individual fortunes, think of these millions of young men and women whose first choices have been scrapped now and whose task is and will be somehow to make something out of their second and third bests.

A natural starting point for our thought about this matter is found in the Sixteenth Chapter of the book of The Acts, where, in the record of Paul's journeys, we read this: "When they were come over against Mysia, they assayed to go into Bithynia; and the Spirit of Jesus suffered them not; and passing by Mysia, they came down to Troas. And a vision appeared to Paul in the night: There was a man of Macedonia standing, beseeching him, and saying, Come over into Macedonia, and help us. And when he had seen the vision, straightaway we sought to go forth into Macedonia, concluding that God had called us to preach the gospel unto them."

Now, [So] so brief and simple is this narrative one would hardly [suspect] *guess* that it describes one of the most significant events in *all* history. *For* [Here] here, by way of Troas and Macedonia, Christianity passed over from Asia into Europe. That was a tremendous event. But, so the story runs, Paul had not planned *that*. *He had not intended* to go to Europe. That was a second choice. Paul had planned to go to Bithynia, and no wonder, for Bithynia was one of the richest provinces of Asia Minor, and to have carried Christianity there would have been a triumph indeed.

Moreover, we may be sure that if Paul wanted to go to Bithynia he wanted to go very much, for Paul was never a half-way man. [But] *And* he could not go; the way was blocked; his plan was broken. Undoubtedly it seemed to Paul most deplorable. One pictures his arriving *there* on the shores of the Aegean, saying, *Alas*, I wanted to go to Bithynia and here I am in Troas! But lo! through Troas a way opened to the pre-eminent ministry of his career. [So] Paul carried Christianity into Europe, rendering his most significant service with the left-overs of a broken plan.

Well, wanting Bithynia and getting Troas is a familiar experience. But to take Troas, the second best, the broken plan, the remnant of a disappointed expectation, and make of it our greatest opportunity--how much less familiar that is! Yet, powerful living has always involved this victory Paul won in Troas over his own soul and his situation.

When a *great* career has at last been finished and the halo of well-deserved reputation hangs over it so that one cannot think the name without thinking of some high enterprise with which the name is associated, then in the glamour of that retrospect we are tempted to forget that almost always, back there somewhere, the turning point of the career was the experience that Paul had--getting Troas when he wanted Bithynia.

The name of Phillips Brooks means to us a powerful spiritual ministry. **Of all the letters that Phillips Brooks received, it is said that he cherished most this one from a small tailor shop near Copley Square in Boston: "Dear Dr. Brooks: I am a tailor in a little shop near your church. Whenever I have the opportunity I always go to hear you preach. Each time I hear you preach I seem to forget all about you, for you make me think of God."** Nevertheless, remember that Phillips

Brooks did not plan to be a preacher. That was a second choice. He planned to be a teacher. That was his Bithynia. Graduating from college, he plunged into his chosen profession of teaching and he failed. He failed completely. Listen to young Brooks writing about his scholars as he is *in the process of* failing: "They are the most disagreeable set of creatures without exception that I have ever met with. . . . I really am ashamed of it but I am tired, cross and almost dead, so good night." Listen to Phillips Brooks after he had failed and been dropped from his position: "I don't know what will become of me and I don't care much." Listen to Phillips Brooks's father, concerned about his son, so humiliated that he will not even talk with his friends: "Phillips will not see anyone now, but after he is over the feeling of mortification, he will come and see you."

Well, in a sense Phillips Brooks never recovered from the disappointment. In the flower of his career he came down once from the office of President Eliot, of Harvard, *trembling and* white as a sheet [and trembling] because he had declined a professorship at Harvard which he knew was his last opportunity to [become] *be* a teacher. He wanted Bithynia and he got Troas, but through Troas he found an open door into a service that if he had lived a hundred lives he might never have found again.

Who here has not faced or does not face now the need for that kind of spiritual victory? Who *of us* [here] has not upon his heart some young man or woman in whose life everything depends on the ability to make something worth while out of Troas? So, *this morning*, we ask now what it was in Paul that enabled him to turn his *grievous* disappointment into such notable achievement.

Certainly, [For] for one thing, his religion entered in. Whatever else was shaken when he got to Troas, his conviction still was there that God had a purpose for his life, that if God [had] led him to Troas there must be something in Troas worth discovering, that God's purposes [included] *include* Troas just as much as Bithynia, *and* that God never leads any man into any place where all the doors are shut. Paul's religion entered in.

Indeed, [It] it is in just such situations that one can tell how much real religion a man has. We hear a man reciting a familiar creed *like:* "I believe in God the Father Almighty, Maker of heaven and earth," but no matter how serious he may [seem] *be* about it one cannot tell from that alone how real it is to him.

When, however, a man who, wanting Bithynia, gets Troas, and, still certain that there is a purpose for his life, takes a positive attitude toward Troas as [if] *though* to say, If God has led me here then there is something worth while here to do, you know that that man's religion is practically operative. If, therefore, Paul had merely said what he did say, "To them that love God all things work together for good," we might have cocked suspicious eyebrows at him, thinking that that proposition is extraordinarily difficult to prove--as it is. *"To them that love God all things work together for good." My soul! As a matter of theory I'd like to see a man who could prove that to me!* What is impressive about Paul is that whenever he did land in a disappointing Troas, and he landed in a [good many] *lot* of them, he did so effectually love God that he made all things work together for good. *He lived it out.*

That's a vital fact, my friends, endlessly repeated in great biography. Man's religion can mean to him a positive faith about life and a positive attitude toward life so effective that watching his career is again and again like watching the Battle of Marengo--in the morning an obvious defeat, in the afternoon a resounding victory.

Consider a modern counterpart of Paul, Adoniram Judson. When Judson was a young man he gave himself to missionary service and his ambition centered on India. That was his Bithynia. When at last he reached India the East India Company would not let him [stay] *in* and the governor told him to take the first ship back to America. For a year he tried to open the doors of India and they were bolted shut. So he turned to Burma. That was his Troas--unknown, untouched Burma. Now, do you suppose that through all that disappointment Judson could always see the leadership of God? Of course he could not; he was human. Do you suppose *that* during those months he lay in the prison of the Emperor at Ava and Oung-Pen-La he could always see evidences of the divine purpose? Of course he could not. But he did so handle the affair in Burma, *that second choice*, that doors began to open until no well-instructed man today can think of Burma without thinking of Adoniram Judson, and when we read the stirring story of Dr. Gordon Seagrave in Burma in these recent years, we know that he and his fellows are there and will be there after this war is over (Fosdick inserted these words in an impromptu fashion for the National Vespers broadcast) because of the victory Judson won at his Troas. At first he hated the idea of going to Burma; in the end he said, "I would not leave my present situation to be made a king." My friends, to live life through into the conviction that there is no disappointing Troas a man can land in without a divine purpose there with which he can ally himself and make something worth while out of it, is one of the finest achievements of the human spirit.

Indeed, one of the most thrilling stories in the Old Testament is on this very theme. One day in Palestine we stopped our automobile by the roadside and ate our lunch at Dotham where long ago Joseph had been sold into slavery by his brethren. **Still the ancient camel trail goes up from across Jordan, running down to the coast cities and so to Egypt.** Now, that boy Joseph, stolen from his home, betrayed by his brethren, dropped into a pit, sold to Midianite slavedealers, made a manservant in a household in Egypt, lied about by his master's wife and put in prison--do you suppose that during all that humiliation and disgrace he could see where God was taking him? Of course not. But he so kept his faith and handled his life that the doors opened into the biggest business of his career, a service [that] he never could have rendered had he stayed *back* in Canaan, and when at last those penitent and frightened brethren stood before him, you remember what he said *to them*: "I am Joseph your brother, whom ye sold into Egypt. And now be not grieved, nor angry with yourselves, that ye sold me hither: for God did send me before you to preserve life. . . . So now it was not you that sent me hither but God." My word! I suppose that is what Shakespeare meant *when he said*:

"There is some soul of goodness in things evil,
Would men observingly distil it out."

At any rate, Paul felt so as afterward he looked back on [the] *that* day *when* he missed Bithynia and got Troas; at first he called it hard luck, but in the end he said to hard luck, "It was not you that sent me hither, but God," and such may be our judgment some day if in our Troas in any similar fashion we let our religion enter in [this was in the National Vespers and it was also in the text for the Riverside sermon, but for some reason Fosdick did not deliver it at Riverside]."

In the second place, it was not simply Paul's religion that enabled him to win this victory but the fine fruit of his religion, his care about people.

The trouble with *so* many of us when we land in Troas is that we begin to pity ourselves. Paul could have done that *easily*. He could have started the process we indulge in, *that is*, "ifing." If I had not missed Bithynia; if my plans had not been broken, *if I could have had my first choice*, if, if! I have given up everything for [Jesus] Christ, Paul might have said; I could today be one of the great rabbis of Jerusalem saluted in the market place; *and* I have given it all up for Christ; I spent fourteen years in a little, trying, difficult, unrecognized ministry in Cilicia, at odds even with my Christian brethren because once I persecuted them; and now, when I am just beginning to get on a good footing with my fellow Christians, with Barnabas and a few others trusting me, I have come up through Asia Minor on a preaching mission; see what they have done to me--they stoned me and left me for dead in Lystra; even after that, all I asked was that I might have a chance to get into Bithynia and do some good work and now I cannot; I am foiled; my plan is broken. How easy it would have been for Paul in Troas to have felt *exceedingly* sorry for himself!

Upon the contrary, he at once began thinking about other people. Might not someone be better off just because he landed in Troas? He had not been there a night before he saw a man from Macedonia saying, Come over, *come over*, and help us. That was the kind of person Paul was. He would see [that] *the* man from Macedonia. *Most of us wouldn't, he would*. It was Paul's unselfishness, his generosity, his magnanimity that opened the doors for him in Troas.

Once there was a man named William Duncan who gave himself

to the missionary cause and in time was sent by his board to a little Indian village in Alaska called Metlacatla. One thinks of that neck of the woods *just* now because some of our sons are there. It was an unlikely Troas for a young man to land in who had doubtless dreamed of some much more attractive Bithynia, for those Indians were a poor, ignorant, miserable tribe, and their morals [were] vile beyond description. Dean Brown, of Yale, however, who visited Metacatla after William Duncan had been there [about] forty years, makes this report: that you will find every Indian family in a separate house with all the decent appointments of home life, that you will find a bank, a cooperative store, a sawmill, a box factory, and a salmon cannery where Indian boys and girls learn to read and write and think and live, and church where an Indian minister preaches the gospel of eternal life, and [where] an Indian musician, who once was a medicine man playing a tom-tom, now plays a pipe organ, and a congregation of Indians sing the great hymns of the church to the praise of Almighty God. [And] All because a man named William Duncan, landing in Troas, cared enough about people to find there the chance of his life!

My friends, that spirit and its consequence can be transferred to our lives. *It had better be!* **Just as at Sebastopol each heart thought a different name while they all sang Annie Laurie, so when today we say "Troas" each of us thinks . . .** Each of us today thinks of some situation we are in we would not have planned to be in. There is only one way out. Was it not George MacDonald who said, "Nothing makes a man strong like a cry for help"? You walk down the street utterly fatigued, so tired that you would like to lie down on the curb and go to sleep, and suddenly there is a cry; there has been an accident; a child is hurt; and you never remember how tired you are until it is all over. Nothing makes a man strong like a [call] *cry* for help.

A mother is completely fatigued. She has been telling her friends for weeks that there is nothing *more* left [of] *in* her and then a child falls ill and needs her help. Week after week by night and day she stands by, and forgets [being] *she's* tired. Nothing makes one strong like a call for help.

Many of us *now* hate this Troas of a bloody generation we are in, but we are awake too to the dangers of our civilization, to the possibility of losing it, to the critical need of a new world order if this is to be a decent earth for human children to be born into. *And* [That] that is our strength, our man from Macedonia, crying, Come over, *Come over*, and help us.

This, then, is the conclusion of the matter: because Paul had these two elements in his life, a practical working religion and a generous willingness to answer a call for help, as soon as he landed in Troas his imagination was filled not with disappointment and defeat but with victory. Coue was right when he said that it is the imagination that makes or unmakes *most of* us. If you put a thirty foot plank on the ground, anyone can walk it. *But* [If] if you put the same plank as high as a cathedral tower, almost nobody can walk it, [and it is] not because the physical difficulties are greater but because one's imagination keeps picturing [him] *one* falling off. So when we get into a Troas we imagine ourselves defeated, I wanted Bithynia, we say; I have got Troas. So we think defeat, we say defeat, we picture defeat, and we are defeated. But as soon as Paul landed in Troas he saw God opening a *new* door, and *he* heard a man calling for help.

If you were to ask what it was that helped Paul most in that crisis, I suspect that his thought went back, as it so habitually did, to the Cross of his Master. That was a Troas to land on! What a Bithynia it would have been if his people had *welcomed and* accepted Jesus as Messiah! And now, shut out from that Bithynia, he came to his Troas, his Calvary. Take a good look, my friends, at what our Lord did with his Troas:

"All the light of sacred story
Gathers round its head sublime."

Calendar of Sermons

(See Chronology of Speeches for secular addresses.)

The Reverend Harry Emerson Fosdick delivered most of his sermons in four churches that are coded thusly: FPC, First Presbyterian Church, New York City; PABC, Park Avenue Baptist Church, New York City; RC, Riverside Church, New York City; and TBE, Temple Beth-El, New York City (from October 1929 to June 1930, the Park Avenue congregation, having sold its edifice, held services in Temple Beth-El until it could occupy the newly constructed Riverside Church). Radio sermons that were delivered over the National Vespers are coded NV. Other sermons are given with place of deliverance.

 A number of sermons were subsequently published in one or more of Fosdick's numerous books. The title of the book follows the sermonic data (see bibliography for complete publication details for Fosdick's books).

Accepting Responsibility for One's Personality, RC, October 23, 1938; NV, December 11, 1938.
Achieving Personal Integrity, RC, November 2, 1941; NV, November 23, 1941.
The Adequacy of the Gospel, FPC, October 14, 1923.
The Adventure for a Real Religion, TBE, December 15, 1929; RC, February 5, 1933; NV, April 2, 1933; RC, June 2, 1944.
After All, It's Character That Counts, RC, September 21, 1947.
After Forty Years in the Ministry, RC, November 14, 1943; NV, November 21, 1943. *A Great Time To Be Alive.*
The Age of Revolt, PABC, January 15, 1928; Chicago Sunday Evening

Club, Chicago, Illinois, January 29, 1928.

All That Is Within Me, FPC, November 23, 1924.

All Things Come Alike to All, FPC, February 17, 1924; PABC, January 2, 1927; NV, March 4, 1929.

Almost, PABC, September 30, 1928; NV, October 28, 1928; RC [revised and retitled Decision of Character], November 17, 1935; NV [revised and retitled Decision of Character], January 5, 1936; RC, Watch Night Service [revosed and retitled Decision of Character] (broadcast over NBC), December 31, 1939.

Another Christmas--Idealism Confronts Realism, RC, December 19, 1937; NV, December 19, 1937.

The Appeal from Christianity to Christ, RC, December 25, 1932; RC, December 25, 1934.

An Appeal from the Present to the Future, RC, January 3, 1937; NV, February 7, 1937. *Successful Christian Living.*

Appeal of Our Ancestors, FPC, November 27, 1919.

Are Christian Missions in the Far East Worthwhile? FPC, October 16, 1921.

Are Religious People Fooling Themselves? TBE, November 3, 1929; Dartmouth College, December 6, 1929; Harvard University, December 8, 1929; Union Theological Seminary, January 13, 1930.

Are We First-Hand or Second-Hand Christians? RC, January 20, 1952.

Are We Fit to Keep Our Democracy? RC, June 2, 1940; RC, August 4, 1940; NV, October 20, 1940.

Are We Part of the Problem or of the Answer? RC, February 24, 1946; NV, February 24, 1946. *On Being Fit to Live With, Riverside Sermons.*

Aren't You Ashamed of Yourself? RC, Children's Day, May 7, 1939; NV, May 7, 1939.

The Art of Being Good Without Trying, TBE, May 11, 1930; NV, May 11, 1930. *The Hope of the World* (retitled Being Good Without Trying).

As Thy Soul Prospereth, FPC, October 15, 1922.

Banking on Youth, RC, Children's Day, May 7, 1933.

The Basic Conditions of Spiritual Well-Being, RC, February 3, 1935; NV, February 24, 1935. *The Power To See It Through.*

The Basis of Moral Obligation, FPC, October 21, 1928.

Be Still and Know, RC, December 4, 1932; NV, January 22, 1933. *The Secret of Victorious Living.*

Beautiful Ideals and Brutal Facts, RC, December 20, 1931.

Being Christian in New York, PABC, November 7, 1926; PABC, May 12, 1929.

Being Inwardly Quiet in a Noisy World, RC, June 7, 1942; NV, October 4, 1942.

Being Rich Without Knowing It, RC, February 1, 1942; NV, March 1, 1942.

Belief in Christ, FPC, April 6, 1924; City Temple, London, England, May 18, 1924.

Belief in God, FPC, March 30, 1924.

Belief in Immortality, FPC, April 20, 1924.

Belief in the Cross, FPC, April 13, 1924.

Beyond Reason, PABC, March 11, 1928; NV, April 15, 1928.

Big Returns on Small Investments, RC, February 4, 1945.

Blessed Are the Meek, PABC, February 13, 1927; NV, February 12, 1928; RC, July 5, 1931; RC, March 3, 1940; Princeton University, March 10, 1940; University of Chicago, March 31, 1940.

Blessed Are the Peacemakers, PABC, November 11, 1928; radio broadcast from Carnegie Hall, New York, November 13, 1928; NV, November 10, 1929.

Building a Family Church, RC, February 15, 1931.

Can We Build an Abiding Civilization on a Materialistic Basis? FPC, November 6, 1921

Capitalizing Discontent, RC, November 5, 1933; NV, January 21, 1934.

A Challenge to the Riverside Church, RC, January 12, 1941.

Charge to Rev. Jesse Lyons, RC, November 11, 1956.

Choosing a Mountain, PABC, April 14, 1929.

Christ and the Inferiority Complex, TBE, October 20, 1929; NV, December 15, 1929.

Christ, Champion of Personality, PABC, April 8, 1928; NV, April 28, 1928.

Christ Himself Is Christianity, RC, Decamber 16, 1945; NV, December 16, 1945. *On Being Fit To Live With.*

The Christ of History and of Experience, PABC, December 23, 1928; NV, December 23, 1928; RC, December 24, 1930. *What Is Vital in Religion.*

Christian Attitudes in Social Reconstruction, RC, May 17, 1936; RC, August 2, 1936; NV, November 8, 1936. *Successful Christian Living.*

The Christian Church's Message to America Today, RC, October 1, 1939; NV, October 8, 1939.

A Christian Conscience About War, Geneva, Switzerland, September 13, 1925.

A Christian Crusade Against War, FPC, November 11, 1923.

Christian Faith--Fantasy or Reality? RC, March 6, 1938; NV, April 3, 1938 RC, February 2, 1941; NV, April 27, 1941; RC, July 27, 1941; First Baptist Church, Montclair, New Jersey, October 19, 1947; Balboa Union Church, April 16, 1948. *Living Under Tension, Riverside Sermons.*

The Christian Interpretation of Life as a Terrific Fact, RC, October 9, 1932; NV, November 20, 1932. *The Secret of Victorious Living.*

The Christian Outlook on Life, PABC, April 21, 1929; Smith College, April 28, 1929; NV, May 19, 1929; RC, November 29, 1933. *What*

Is Vital in Religion.

The Christian Refusal to be Emotionally Regimented, RC, February 18, 1945; NV, February 18, 1945.

Christianity: A Challenge or a Compromise? PABC, October 2, 1927; NV, October 30, 1927; TBE, June 15, 1930; NV, November 2, 1930; RC, July 22, 1934.

Christianity, a Religion Not of Clergymen but of Laymen, RC, October 24, 1943; NV, October 24, 1943.

Christianity and Freedom, PABC, January 20, 1929; Chicago Sunday Evening Club, Chicago, Illinois, January 27, 1929; NV, February 10, 1929; RC, May 23, 1934.

Christianity and Unemployment, RC, November 16, 1930.

Christianity as a Deed, FPC, November 2, 1924.

Christianity at Home in Chaos, RC, March 12, 1933; NV, March 12, 1933. *The Hope of the World.*

Christianity More Than Duty--Not Weight but Wings, RC, January 15, 1933; NV, February 12, 1933. *The Hope of the World.*

Christianity Not a Form But a Force, RC, October 31, 1943; NV, January 4, 1944. *A Great Time To Be Alive.*

Christianity's Stake in Internationalism, PABC, November 13, 1928; RC, May 29, 1938.

Christianity's Stake in the Social Situation, RC, November 20, 1932. *The Hope of the World.*

Christianity's Supreme Rival, PABC, November 13, 1927. *The Hope of the World.*

Christians and the World-Wide Epidemic of Hatred, RC, January 15, 1939; NV, February 19, 1939.

Christians Face World Revolution, RC, February 8, 1942; NV, March 15, 1942.

Christians in Spite of Everything, RC, January 20, 1935; NV, February 17, 1935; RC, April 28, 1940; NV, October 6, 1940; NV, October 10, 1943. *The Power to See It Through, Riverside Sermons.*

Christians and the World-Wide Epidemic of Hatred, RC, January 15, 1939; NV, February 19, 1939.

Christmas Eve Sermon, RC, December 24, 1942.

Christmas Eve Sermon, RC, December 24, 1943.

Christmas Eve Sermon, RC, December 24, 1944.

Christmas Eve Sermon, RC, December 24, 1945.

The Christmass Message Girds Us for the New Year, RC, December 28, 1941; NV, January 4, 1942; RC, July 19, 1942.

Christmas Sermon, FPC, December 21, 1924.

Christmas, The Festival of Triumphant Personality, RC, December 25, 1938; NV, December 25, 1938; RC, December 24, 1940.

Christmas This Year Means Something Special, RC, December 20, 1942; NV, December 20, 1942.

The Church--Friend or Foe of Christianity? RC, March 17, 1935.

The Church Is Dead! Long Live the Church!, RC, April 11, 1937.

The Church Must Go Beyond Modernism, RC, November 3, 1935; NV, January 12, 1936. *Successful Christian Living, Riverside Sermons.*

Church Night Address, RC, February 25, 1942.

Church Night Address, RC, May 31, 1944.

Church Night Address, RC, September 27, 1944.

Church Night Address, RC, November 29, 1944.

Church Night Address, RC, May 31, 1945.

The Church of Christ in a Warring World, RC, December 14, 1941; NV, December 14, 1941; NV, December 21, 1941.

Civilization Needs a Soul, RC, May 11, 1941; NV, May 11, 1941.

A Clean Life in a Soiled World, RC, October 27, 1940; NV, December 1, 1940.

The Common Sense Wisdom of Christianity, RC, May 9, 1943; NV, October 17, 1943; RC, August 13, 1944.

A Confession of Faith in a Democracy, PABC, February 12, 1928.

A Confused Generation Wants Religious Certainty, RC, May 11, 1947.

Conquering Fear, RC, October 5, 1941; NV, October 26, 1941.

Conquering the Sense of Humiliation, RC, May 14, 1933; RC, October 31, 1934; NV, May 31, 1936.

The Conquest of Fear, RC, March 5, 1933; NV, March 5, 1933; NV, April 21, 1940. *The Hope of the World.*

The Conservative and Liberal Temperaments in Religion, PABC, January 22, 1927; NV, October 21, 1928. *What Is Vital in Religion.*

The Constructive Uses of Fear, RC, April 7, 1946; NV, May 19, 1946. *On Being Fit to Live With.*

Contemporary Meaning in an Old World--Salvation, RC, December 5, 1937; NV, January 9, 1938.

The Contemporary Movement Back to Religion, RC, January 8, 1939; NV, February 5, 1939.

The Contemporary Prevalence of Polytheism, RC, November 15, 1936; Harvard University, November 29, 1936; NV, January 10, 1937. *Successful Christian Living.*

Conventiality Versus Heroism, RC, March 20, 1932; NV, March 20, 1932; RC, April 13, 1938.

Conversion, place unknown, October 10, 1920.

Courage, FPC, January 14, 1923; RC, November 29, 1931; NV, January 10, 1932; RC, March 28, 1934.

Courage for Tough Times, RC, November 19, 1950.

The Crazy World and the Sane Individual, RC, February 18, 1934; NV, March 18, 1934; RC, September 29, 1937.

Crisis and Surprise, FPC, March 11, 1923; RC, October 1, 1933; NV, December 3, 1933; RC, July 29, 1934.

The Cross, An Amazing Paradox, RC, April 10, 1938; NV, April 10, 1938; RC, February 26, 1941; First Baptist Church, Montclair, New Jersey, October 5, 1947. *Living Under Tension.*

The Cross and the Ordinary Man, RC, March 21, 1937; NV, May 9, 1937. *Successful Christian Living.*

The Cross Confronts Our Easy-Going Christianity, RC, April 2, 1939; NV, April 2, 1939.

The Cross Confronts Our Modern Moods, RC, April 5, 1936; NV, April 5, 1936; RC, April 1, 1942.

The Cross Is a Fact, RC, November 7, 1943.

The Cross, Symbol of Life's Costliness, RC, March 29, 1931; NV, March 29, 1931; RC, March 24, 1937; RC, November 1, 1942; RC, April 17, 1946.

Crucified by Stupidity, RC, April 9, 1933; University of Chicago, April 23, 1933. *The Hope of the World.*

Crying Peace, Peace, When There Is No Peace, RC, November 8, 1942; NV, November 8, 1942.

The Cure of Cynicism, PABC, April 24, 1927.

The Cure of Disillusionment, RC, October 8, 1933; NV, October 15, 1934.

The Danger of an Overextended Life, FPC, November 20, 1921.

The Danger of Going to Church, RC, November 22, 1953. *What Is Vital in Religion.*

The Dangers of Spiritual Privilege, PABC, March 24, 1929; NV, March 24, 1929; RC, February 25, 1942.

Death Swallowed Up in Victory, RC, April 1, 1945; NV, April 1, 1945.

The Deathless Hope That Man Cannot Escape, RC, April 5, 1942; NV, April 5, 1942. *A Great Time to be Alive.*

The Decisive Babies of the World, RC, December 22, 1940; NV, December 22, 1940; television broadcast, December 28, 1941. *Living Under Tension.*

Decisive Battles Behind Closed Doors, RC, October 18, 1942; NV, December 6, 1942; RC, August 6, 1944. *A Great Time To Be Alive.*

Dedication Sermon, Pullen Memorial Baptist Church, Raleigh, North Carolina, October 29, 1950.

The Deep Sources of Eternal Hope, RC, April 17, 1938; NV, April 17, 1938.

The Deepening of Faith, FPC, December 2, 1923.

The Deepest Experience in Christian Living, RC, June 3, 1945.

Despise Ye the Church of God? FPC, March 14, 1920; RC, February 8, 1931; NV, March 8, 1931; dedication of Christ Church (place unknown), November 23, 1933; First Baptist Church, Middletown, New York, October 18, 1940. *What Is Vital In Religion.*

The Dignity of Being Up-to-Date, RC, November 8, 1936; RC, July 18, 1937; NV, October 24, 1937. *Successful Christian Living.*

The Dilemma of Herod, PABC, January 13, 1929; NV, February 24, 1929.

Discovering What We Can Do with Ourselves, RC, October 27, 1935; NV, December 15, 1935; RC, August 1, 1937. *Successful Christian*

Living.

The Divinity of Jesus, FPC, February 11, 1923.

Do We Really Want Jesus? RC, February 11, 1934; NV, March 11, 1934. *The Secret of Victorious Living.*

Do We Want War in the Far East? FPC, October 9, 1921.

Does Our Western Christianity Need Reformation? FPC, October 23, 1921.

Does the Present World Situation Refute or Confirm Christian Faith? RC, October 22, 1939; NV, October 22, 1939.

Don't Be Discouraged About Human Nature, RC, March 15, 1942; NV, May 10, 1942; RC, July 26, 1942.

Don't Let This Grim Generation Get You Down, RC, April 24, 1949.

Don't Lose Faith in Human Possibilities, RC, October 8, 1939; NV, October 15, 1939; Teachers College Chapel, Columbia University, December 6, 1939; Protestant Teacher's Association, New York City, February 18, 1940; RC, July 14, 1940; RC, July 20, 1941; RC, December 31, 1943. *Living Under Tension.*

Easter's Message to This Present Time, RC, April 25, 1943; NV, April 25, 1943.

Encountering God in Unlikely Places, RC, November 10, 1940; NV, December 15, 1940.

Escaping from Loneliness into Fellowship, RC, October 19, 1941; NV; November 9, 1941.

The Essence of Christmas, TBE, December 22, 1929; NV, December 22, 1929; RC, May 31, 1933; RC, December 25, 1936; RC, December 24, 1941.

The Essence of Great Religion, RC, March 4, 1945.

The Essence of Personal Christianity, RC, April 18, 1937; NV, October 30, 1938; NV, March 26, 1944.

The Essential Elements in a Vital Christian Experience, RC, March 5, 1939; RC, July 16, 1939; NV, October 22, 1939. *Living Under Tension, Riverside Sermons.*

The Eternal Victorious Over the Temporal, RC, April 21, 1946; NV, April 21, 1946. *On Being Fit To Live With, Riverside Sermons.*

The Ethical Foundations of Prosperity, RC, January 13, 1935; NV, February 10, 1935; RC, December 8, 1940; NV, January 12, 1941. *The Power To See It Through.*

The Ethical Problems of Neutrality, RC, October 15, 1939; NV, November 12, 1939.

Every Man a Gambler, RC, December 30, 1934; NV, December30, 1934. *The Power To See It Through.*

Every Man's Religion His Own, RC, March 3, 1935; NV, March 10, 1935. *The Power To See It Through.*

Facing an Uncertain Year, RC, December 31, 1944.

Facing Life's Central Test, RC, April 2, 1944; NV, April 2, 1944. *A Great Time To Be Alive.*

Facing the Challenge of Change, RC, March 19, 1933; NV, November 4, 1934. *The Hope of the World.*

Facing Toward the New Year, RC, December 26, 1943; NV, December 26, 1943.

Faith and Immortality, Union Theological Seminary, January 26, 1953. *What Is Vital In Religion.*

Faith in Life Confronts Cynicism at New Year's Time, RC, January 4, 1942; NV, January 11, 1942.

Faith Thrives on Difficulty, RC, January 2, 1944.

Family Religion, PABC, October 16, 1927, NV, November 13, 1927; NV, November 24, 1929. *The Power To See It Through, Riverside Sermons.*

Fares Please: A Budget Sermon, RC, April 17, 1932.

Farewell, FPC, March 1, 1925.

The Festival of Beauty, PABC, December 25, 1927; NV, December 5, 1927; NV, December 24, 1928.

The Field Is the World, RC, May 14, 1944; NV, May 28, 1944. *A Great Time To Be Alive.*

Financial Chivalry, RC, April 19, 1931.

Finding God in Unlikely Places, RC, November 30, 1952; Chicago Sunday Evening Club, Chicago, Illinois, February 1, 1953; Pomona College, Claremont, California, March 8, 1953. *What Is Vital In Religion.*

Finding Unfailing Resources, RC, November 9, 1941; NV, February 1, 1942; NV, January 6, 1946. *On Being Fit To Live With, Riverside Sermons.*

The Fine Art of Keeping Young, RC, December 27, 1931; RC, December 31, 1934.

The Fine Art of Letting Yourself Go, RC, February 28, 1943; NV, March 14, 1943.

The Fine Art of Making Goodness Attractive, RC, October 16, 1932; NV, November 27, 1932. *The Hope of the World.*

The Five Sectors of the Peace Movement, Carnegie Hall, New York, April 22, 1936; RC, July 19, 1936; RC, January 10, 1937; NV, February 21, 1937.

Foresight: A Sermon for Boys and Girls, RC, May 1, 1932.

The Forgiveness of Sins, FPC, November 18, 1923. *The Secret of Victorious Living, Riverside Sermons.*

The Foundations of a Sustaining Philosophy, RC, October 10, 1937; NV, December 5, 1937.

The Free Spirit Confronts the World's Coercion, RC, October 29, 1939; Harvard University, November 26, 1939; NV, December 3, 1939. *Living Under Tension.*

Freeing Religion from Supernaturalism, RC, December 7, 1930; Harvard University, December 14, 1931.

Fresh Light on an Old Beatitude, NV, October 29, 1944.

Fundamental Christianity, RC, November 8, 1931; NV, December 6, 1931; RC, July 23, 1933.

A Fundamentalist Sermon by a Modernist Preacher, RC, January 17, 1932; NV, April 3, 1932. *The Power To See It Through*.

The Futility of Borrowed Religion, FPC, February 5, 1922; NV, March 1, 1931; TBE, December 31, 1931.

Getting Out of Us the Best That's In Us, RC, February 12, 1933; NV, April 30, 1933; RC, June 1, 1941; NV, October 5, 1941. *The Hope of the World*.

Getting Ready to Keep Christiams, RC, December 12, 1943; NV, December 12, 1943.

Getting the Best Out of the Worst, RC, April 30, 1944; NV, October 15, 1944. *A Great Time To Be Alive*.

The Ghost of a Chance, RC, December 28, 1930; NV, December 28, 1930. *The Power To See It Through*.

The Gist of the Christmas Message, RC, December 26, 1937; NV, December 26, 1937.

Giving the Highest a Hearing, RC, September 25, 1935; RC, November 23, 1941. *Successful Christian Living*.

Glorifying the Commonplace, RC, October 6, 1935.

God Talks to a Dictator, RC, October 13, 1940; NV, November 10, 1940. *Living Under Tension, Riverside Sermons*.

The God Who Made Us and the Gods We Make, RC, May 28, 1939; NV, November 5, 1939. *Living Under Tension*.

A God Who Really Matters Morally, RC, December 16, 1934; NV, January 13, 1935.

God's Call to Christian Laymen, RC, October 21, 1945; NV, October 21, 1945.

The Golden Rule, FPC, November 2, 1919.

Good and Bad Religion, FPC, November 30, 1924.

Good News About Human Nature, RC, January 31, 1932; NV, February 28, 1932; RC, August 13, 1933.

Good Sportsmanship, FPC, February 24, 1924.

Good Taste, PABC, January 16, 1927.

Goodness, a Matter of Quantity as Well as Quality, RC, February 27, 1938; NV, March 27, 1938.

The Gospel of Hope, RC, April 5, 1931

The Great Christ and the Little Churches, RC, September 29, 1946. *What Is Vital in Religion*.

A Great Faith for 1947, RC, December 29, 1946.

A Great Hour, City Temple, London, April 18, 1918.

The Great Hours of a Man's Life, RC, February 3, 1946

A Great Memory, PABC, January 8, 1928.

A Great Message for Christmas: Vitality Is Mightier than Size, RC, December 22, 1946; Little Forum, Bronxville, New York, December 29, 1947.

A Great Year for Easter, RC, April 13, 1941; NV, April 13, 1941. *Living Under Tension.*

The Greatness of God, PABC, January 6, 1929; NV, February 3, 1929. *The Secret of Victorious Living, Riverside Sermons.*

Handicapped Lives, TBE, January 19, 1930; TBE, February 16, 1930; RC, August 7, 1932. *The Power To See It Through, Riverside Sermons.*

Handling Life's Second-Bests, FPC, October 29, 1922; RC, January 18, 1931; NV, February 8, 1931; RC, November 2, 1938; RC, March 12, 1944; NV, April 30, 1944. *The Hope Of The World, Riverside Sermons.*

Handling Our Emotions in a Stormy Time, RC, May 19, 1940; NV, May 19, 1940.

Handling Our Primitive Instincts, FPC, March 18, 1923; RC, June 5, 1932.

Handling Our Sense of Responsibility, RC, October 4, 1942; NV, November 1, 1942; RC, July 11, 1943.

A Happy New Year, FPC, December 30, 1923.

Have Faith in God, PABC, October 24, 1925.

Having a Faith That Really Works, RC, April 19, 1942; NV, October 18, 1942. *What Is Vital in Religion.*

Having a Good Excuse and Not Using It, RC, June 8, 1947.

Hearers and Doers, FPC, October 26, 1919; PABC, June 2, 1929.

The High Road to Self-Respect, RC, May 22, 1938; NV, May 28, 1939.

The High Use of Memory, RC, May 31, 1931; NV, May 31, 1931.

The High Uses of Serenity, RC, November 4, 1934; NV, December 2, 1934; RC, January 3, 1940. *The Power To See It Through, Riverside Sermons.*

The High Uses of Trouble, RC, February 4, 1934; NV, March 4, 1934; NV, February 25, 1940; RC, December 31, 1941; NV, December 31, 1941. *The Secret of Victorious Lliving.*

Highways to Science That Lead to Truth, RC, April 25, 1937; RC, July 25, 1937; NV, October 17, 1937.

The Holy Spirit, RC, March 15, 1931.

Honesty in the Pulpit, FPC, June 3, 1923

The Hope of the World in Its Minorities, RC, May 3, 1931; NV, November 1, 1931; RC, July 2, 1932. *The Hope of the World.*

Horses and Riders, PABC, March 25, 1928.

Hospitality to the Highest, RC, December 23, 1934; NV, December 23, 1934. *The Power To See It Through, Riverside Sermons.*

How Believe in a Good God in a World Like This? RC, April 21, 1940; RC, August 11, 1940,; NV, October 13, 1940. *Living Under Tension, Riverside Sermons.*

How Fares Goodness without God? RC, May 8, 1938; NV, October 16, 1938.

How Much Do We Care About Our Children? RC, October 2, 1938; NV, November 15, 1938; RC, March 20, 1949.

How Much Do We Really Care For the Church? RC, November 16, 1946.

How Much Do We Want Democracy? RC, February 23, 1936; NV, March 1, 1936; RC, November 25, 1937; NV, February 20, 1938.

How Much Do We Want Liberty? RC, February 24, 1935; NV, October 27, 1935. *The Power To See It Through.*

How Much Do We Want Peace? RC, November 11, 1934; NV, October 27, 1935. *The Power To See It Through.*

How to Stand Up and Take It, RC, December 29, 1940; NV, December 29, 1940. *Living Under Tension.*

How We All Miss the Bus, RC, January 5, 1941; NV, January 5, 1941.

Humanizing Religion, TBE, February 9, 1930; NV, March 9, 1930.

I Believe in Man, FPC, October 28, 1923; PABC, February 24, 1929; PABC, May 5, 1929.

I Want My Own Way, RC, May 5, 1940; NV, May 5, 1940.

The Ideas That Use Us, RC, October 14, 1934; NV, November 18, 1934; RC, November 29, 1939; NV, April 28, 1940; NV, November 4, 1945. *The Power To See It Through, Riverside Sermons.*

If Foresight Equalled Hindsight, RC, March 2, 1941; NV, March 16, 1941.

If I Were a Businessman, RC, February 26, 1933; NV, March 26, 1933.

If Jesus Were a Modernist, PABC, March 3, 1929; NV, April 7, 1929.

Immortality and Eternal Life, PABC, March 31, 1929; NV, March 31, 1929.

The Importance of Being Young, RC, May 3, 1942; NV, May 3, 1942.

The Importance of Doubting Our Doubts, RC, April 12, 1953; live radio broadcast, Chicago Sunday Evening Club, February 28, 1954. *What Is Vital in Religion.*

The Importance of Our Incidental Living, RC, March 29, 1936; NV, April 26, 1936.

The Importance of the Consumer, RC, July 30, 1933.

The Importance of the Individual, FPC, December 17, 1922; PABC, December 19, 1926; NV, April 14, 1929.

The Importance of the Ordinary Man, PABC, December 16, 1928; NV, January 13, 1929, RC, May 31, 1936; NV, October 11, 1936.

The Impossibility of Being Irreligious, RC, October 1, 1944; NV, November 5, 1944. *On Being Fit To Live With.*

The Impossibility of Living on a Physical Basis Alone, FPC, March 30, 1919; TBE, February 23, 1930; Yale University, March 16, 1930; Smith College, April 27, 1930; NV, May 4, 1930.

In a Day of Confused Moral Standards, RC, December 3, 1933; NV, May 6, 1934.

In the Day of Adversity, RC, October 4. 1931.

An Inclusive Church, first sermon preached in PABC, May 31, 1925.

The Inescapable Judgment, RC, December 1, 1940; NV, February 2, 1941. *Living Under Tensions, Riverside Sermons.*

An Inexpensive Church, RC, April 2, 1933.
The Inheritance of Our Father, FPC, May 29, 1921; RC, January 14, 1934.
The Inner Road to God, TBE, October 6, 1929.
The Innermost Problem of Human Nature: Desire, RC, May 8, 1932.
Intelligent Prayer, TBE, January 12, 1930; NV, February 9, 1930.
The Interpretation of Life, FPC, October 25, 1920; Madison Avenue Presbyterian Church, March 6, 1921; TBE, June 22, 1930; NV, October 26, 1930; RC, May 9, 1937; NV, October 3, 1937; RC, December 28, 1938.
An Interpretation of Pacificism, RC, May 20, 1934. *The Secret of Victorious Living.*
The Intimations of Immortality, RC, April 1, 1934; NV, April 1, 1934. *The Secret of Victorious Living.*
Inward Demands of Outward Reforms, RC, October 15, 1933.
Is Our Christianity Appealing to Our Softness or Our Strength? RC, January 22, 1933; NV, February 19, 1933. *The Hope of the World.*
Jesus and the Individual, FPC, December 17, 1922.
Jesus Christ, the Abiding Center of Christianity, RC, May 22, 1932.
Jesus, Our Contemporary, RC, December 24, 1933; NV, December 24, 1933.
Jesus's Appeal to the Irreligious, PABC, April 29, 1928.
Jesus's Ethical Message Confronts the World, RC, February 19, 1939; NV, March 26, 1939. *Living Under Tension.*
Jesus's Insistence of Moral Reality, FPC, February 25, 1923; TBE, February 2, 1930; NV, March 2, 1930.
Jesus, the Revelation of God, FPC, October 8, 1922.
Judas Not Iscariot, FPC, May 11, 1919; PABC, April 28, 1928; NV, March 25, 1928; RC, April 8, 1936.
Keeping Faith in Persuasion in a World of Coercion, RC, October 25, 1942; NV, December 13, 1942. *A Great Time To Be Alive.*
Keeping One's Faith in a Changing Time, RC, November 2, 1930; NV, January 4, 1931; RC, July 24, 1932; RC, June 7, 1936; NV, April 25, 1937.
Keeping One's Footing in a Slippery Time, RC, April 30, 1933; RC, June 4, 1939; NV, December 10, 1939; RC, February 3, 1943. *The Hope of the World.*
Keeping Our Enthusiasm, TBE, January 5, 1930; NV, January 18, 1931; Chicago Sunday Evening Club, April 12, 1931; RC, July 16, 1933.
Keeping Our Morale as Christians, RC, November 16, 1941; NV, February 8, 1942; RC, July 11, 1943; NV, October 3, 1943.
The Kind of Penitence That Does Some Good, RC, October 11, 1942; NV, November 15, 1942. *A Great Time To Be Alive.*
The Kind of Prayer These Times Call For, RC, November 18, 1945; NV, November 18, 1945.
Knowing How to Abound, PABC, November 21, 1926; NV, February 17,

1927; Thanksgiving Address, Hotel Plaza, New York City, November 29, 1928.

Lawlessness, FPC, January 7, 1923.

Lest We Forget, FPC, April 6, 1919.

Let's All Be Realistic, RC, November 18, 1934; Harvard University, December 9, 1934; NV, October 20, 1935. *The Power To See It Through.*

Let's All Give In to Temptation (Children's Day sermon), RC, May 6, 1934; NV, December 1, 1935.

Let Us Be Thankful for the Enemies of Christianity, RC, December 18, 1932; NV, January 15, 1933.

Life Is What We Make It (Children's Day sermon), RC, May 4, 1941; NV, May 4, 1941.

The Life of the Spirit, FPC, November 7, 1919; RC, March 15, 1931; NV, April 19, 1931; RC, June 3, 1936.

Life That Keeps It Savor, RC, January 7, 1940; NV, February 18, 1940; RC, December 30, 1945; NV, December 30, 1945.

Life Victorious over Death, RC, March 28, 1937; NV, March 28, 1937.

Life's Central Demand: Be a Real Person, RC, October 16, 1938; NV, December 4, 1938.

The Light of the World, PABC, December 26, 1926.

The Light That No Darkness Can Put Out, RC, December 19, 1943; NV, December 19, 1943. *A Great Time To Be Alive.*

The Limitations of Anxiety, PABC, May 6, 1928; NV, May 27, 1928; RC, February 3, 1935.

The Limitations of the Law, PABC, November 28, 1926.

A Little Morality Is a Dangerous Thing, TBE, October 27, 1929; NV, January 12, 1930.

Living at Our Best, TBE, November 17, 1929; NV, January 5, 1930; RC, November 26, 1935.

Living Under Tension, RC, October 6, 1940; NV, December 8, 1940. *Living Under Tension.*

The Lord Speaks to the Preacher, FPC, November 14, 1920; RC, April 3, 1932.

Loyalty, the Basic Condition of Liberty, RC, December 7, 1941; NV, February 22, 1942. *A Great Time To Be Alive.*

Magnifying God, PABC, December 18, 1927.

The Mainsprings of Human Motive, RC, February 17, 1935; NV, March 17, 1935; RC, November 1, 1939. *The Power To See It Through.*

Maintaining the Sprirtual Front (budget sermon), RC, January 10, 1943; NV, Red Cross appeal, February 28, 1943.

The Major Fault of Religious Liberalism, RC, November 19, 1939.

Making a Practical Success of Christian Living, RC, February 7, 1937; NV, March 14, 1937. *Successful Christian Living.*

Making Conscience Behave Itself, RC, April 14, 1940; NV, October 27, 1940.

Making Exceptions of Ourselves, FPC, October 21, 1923.

Making the Best of a Bad Mess, TBE, March 2, 1930; NV, March 23, 1930; RC, July 13, 1941; NV, October 19, 1941. *The Hope of the World*.

Making the Most of Friendship, RC, September 27, 1936; NV, November 1, 1936; RC, May 1, 1940; RC, January 6, 1946.

Making the New Year Happy, RC, January 3, 1932; NV, January 17, 1932; RC, August 6, 1933; RC, May 31, 1939.

A Man Is What He Proves to Be in an Emergency, RC, January 14, 1945; NV, February 11, 1945. *On Being Fit To Live With*.

Manhood and Money (budget sermon), RC, April 15, 1934; RC, March 1, 1939.

Mankind's Deepest Need: The Sense of Community, RC, February 25, 1940; NV, April 7, 1940; RC, July 21, 1940. *Living Under Tension, Riverside Sermons*.

Man's Critical Need of Interior Stability, RC, October 3, 1937; NV, October 31, 1937; NV, December 2, 1945.

Mary and Martha, PABC, October 9, 1927; NV, November 6, 1927.

Mastering Depression, RC, October 12, 1941; NV, November 2, 1941.

Master's Dislike of Sentimentality, FPC, January, 1924.

The Meaning and Use of Change, FPC, April 2, 1922; PABC, June 30, 1929; NV, November 17, 1929.

The Meaning of Crisis in Human Life, RC, October 1, 1933.

The Meaning of Freedom, PABC, October 17, 1926; Yale University, March 20, 1927; Wellesley College, June 19, 1927; Princeton University, October 30, 1927; University of Chicago, January 30, 1928; Wentworth Institute, Boston, June 12, 1929; Chicago Sunday Evening Club, May 25, 1930; Riverside Guild, January 14, 1951.

The Meaning of Grace, RC, May 10, 1931; NV, May 10, 1931.

The Meaning of the Incarnation, RC, December 21, 1930; NV, December 21, 1930; RC, December 25, 1935.

The Meaning of Trouble, Chapel Service, Medical Center, place unknown, December 2, 1956.

The Meaning of Trust in God, FPC, November 21, 1920; RC, November 23, 1930; NV, February 1, 1931; RC, September 30, 1936.

The Meaning of Worship, PABC, May 12, 1929; NV, May 26, 1929; National Association of Organists, April 21, 1929; National Organization of Organists, May 31, 1931.

The Means Determine the End, RC, January 2, 1938; NV, January 2, 1938. *Living Under Tension*.

A Message for a Confused Time, RC, February 7, 1932; NV, February 26, 1933.

The Message of Advent, Union Theological Seminary, December 6, 1950.

The Miracle of Changed Lives, RC, October 4, 1936; NV, October 15, 1936; RC, November 27, 1940.

Miracles of Character Possible for All, RC, October 9, 1938; NV,

November 20, 1938; RC, April 3, 1940. *What Is Vital In Religion.*

A Miss Is as Bad as a Mile, RC, January 7, 1934; NV, February 18, 1934.

Modern Civilization's Crucial Problem, RC, November 9, 1930; NV, December 7, 1930, RC, July 17, 1932. *The Hope Of The World, Riveside Sermons.*

A Modern Preacher's Problem in His Use of the Scripture, inaugural address as professor of Practical Thelogy, Union Theological Seminary, New York City, September 30, 1915.

The Modern World Gets Back to the Need for Salvation, RC, November 6, 1932; RC, September 27, 1939; RC, May 29, 1940.

The Modern World's Discovery of Sin, RC, December 18, 1938; NV, February 26, 1939; RC, August 13, 1939; RC, July 28, 1940. *Living Under Tension.*

The Moral Demands of the Machine Age, TBE, October 13, 1929; NV, December 1, 1929.

Moral Experimentation, TBE, April 6, 1930; NV, April 6, 1930.

The Moral Gain from Material Disaster, RC, April 25, 1932; NV, November 6, 1932.

Moral Independence, RC, October 19, 1930; NV, November 30, 1930; RC, July 31, 1932.

Moral Reality in Religion, RC, October 26, 1930; NV, November 22, 1932.

Morals Secede from the Union, RC, October 18, 1931.

The Most Disturbing Factor in the Christian Faith, RC, March 17, 1940; NV, March 17, 1940; RC, October 29, 1941.

The Most Durable Power in the World, RC, November 24, 1935; NV, January 19, 1936; RC, August 15, 1937. *Successful Christian Living.*

The Most Neglected Real Estate in the World, FPC, December 31, 1922; PABC, January 1, 1928; RC, May 23, 1936.

The Most Satisfying Happiness Known to Man, RC, February 26, 1939; NV, April 23, 1939; RC, May 28, 1941.

The Most Thrilling Rescue Story in the World, RC, March 25, 1945; NV, March 25, 1945. *On Being Fit To Live With.*

My Account with the Unknown Soldier (see The Unknown Soldier).

The Mystery of Life, TBE, May 4, 1930; RC, May 21, 1939. *The Secret of Victorious Living, Riverside Sermons.*

The Narrow Gate, FPC, January 11, 1925; RC, February 21, 1932.

The Narrow Limits of Death's Dominion, RC, March 24, 1940; NV, March 24, 1940.

The Need of Brains In Religion, RC, February 22, 1931; Princeton University, March 22, 1931; University of Chicago, April 12, 1931; Chi Alpha, place unknown, April 18, 1931; Smith College, May 24, 1931; NV, October 25, 1931.

The Need of a New Patriotism, TBE, November 10, 1929.

The Need of Dependable Character, RC, January 10, 1932; NV, March

6, 1932.

The New Demand for Personal Religion, RC, March 22, 1942; NV, May 17, 1942.

A New Kind of Epidemic, RC, May 3, 1936; NV, May 10, 1936.

New Knowledge and the Christian Faith, see Shall the Fundamentalists Win?

A New Year When Almost Anything May Happen, RC, December 27, 1942; NV, December 27, 1942.

No Dry-as-Dust Religion Will Do Now, RC, May 28, 1944; NV, October 1, 1944. *A Great Time To Be Alive.*

No Fair Weather Religion Will Do Now, RC, January 17, 1943; NV, February 14, 1943.

No Man Need Stay the Way He Is, RC, November 25, 1934; NV, January 20, 1935. *The Power To See it Through, Riverside Sermons.*

Not For Sale! RC, November 26, 1944; NV, November 26, 1944.

The Old Religion in the New World, FPC, November 5, 1922; RC, May 17, 1931.

On Being Adequate for Life, RC, March 1, 1936; NV, March 29, 1936; RC, December 29, 1937.

On Being a Realistic Pacifist, RC, November 10, 1935; NV, November 10, 1935.

On Being a Rugged Individual, RC, December 15, 1935; NV, February 16, 1936; NV, October 8, 1944.

On Being Christians Unashamed, RC, November 1, 1936; NV, December 13, 1936. *Successful Christian Living.*

On Being Civilized to Death, RC, October 13, 1935; NV, February 23, 1936; Johns Hopkins University, June 7, 1937. *Successful Christian Living.*

On Being Discouraged About the World, RC, December 11, 1938; NV, March 19, 1939.

On Being Fit to Live Together, RC, May 6, 1945.

On Being Fit to Live With, RC, February 17, 1946; NV, February 17, 1946. *On Being Fit To Live With.*

On Being Indifferent to Religion, RC, January 17, 1937; NV, February 28, 1937; RC, April 12, 1942; NV, October 11, 1942. *Successful Christian Living.*

On Being Level-Headed, RC, October 28, 1934; NV, November 25, 1934.

On Being Only a Drop in the Bucket, RC, November 12, 1944; NV, February 4, 1945. *On Being Fit To Live With.*

On Being Realistic, RC, April 26, 1942; RC, August 9, 1942; NV, October 25, 1942.

On Being Strongly Tempted to Be Christian, RC, January 16, 1944; NV, February 13, 1944. *A Great Time To Be Alive.*

On Believing in Miracles, RC, February 6, 1944; NV, March 5, 1944. *A Great Time To Be Alive.*

On Catching the Wrong Bus, RC, February 25, 1945; NV, February 25,

1945. *On Being Fit To Live With, Riverside Sermons.*

On Escaping from This World, RC, December 31, 1933; NV, February 4, 1934. *The Secret of Victorious Living.*

On Feeling That God Is Real, RC, February 14, 1943; NV, April 4, 1943.

On Finding It Hard to Believe in God, RC, May 10, 1936; RC, July 26, 1936; NV, October 18, 1936; RC, April 29, 1945; NV, April 29, 1945. *Successful Christian Living.*

On Gaining a Clear Sense of Right and Wrong, RC, Janaury 16, 1938; NV, February 13, 1938.

On Getting Christianity Out of Its Pigeonholes, RC, October 2, 1944; NV, October 22, 1944. *On Being Fit To Live With.*

On Having an Aim in Life, RC, May 7, 1944; NV, May 7, 1944.

On Having an Independent Character, RC, February 16, 1936; NV, March 22, 1936.

On Learning How to Hope, RC, December 31, 1944; NV, December 31, 1944.

On Learning How to Pray, RC, March 11, 1934; RC, December 4, 1938; NV, March 5, 1939; NV, March 19, 1944. *The Secret of Victorious Living, Riverside Sermons.*

On Making Christianity Too Easy, RC, March 25, 1934; NV, March 25, 1934. *The Secret of Victorious Living.*

On Managing One's Own Life, RC, May 5, 1946; NV, May 5, 1946.

On Not Being Able to Escape God, RC, February 9, 1936; NV, March 15, 1936.

On Not Being Too Good for This World, RC, March 18, 1945; NV, March 18, 1945.

On Running Away from Home, RC, May 2, 1937; NV, May 2, 1937.

On Seeming as Christian as We Are, RC, October 7, 1934; NV, October 28, 1934; RC, February 5, 1939; NV, March 12, 1939. *The Power To See It Through.*

On Shouldering One's Own Responsibility, RC, December 2, 1934; NV, January 6, 1935. *The Power To See It Through.*

On Worshiping Things We Manufacture, RC, October 8, 1944; NV, November 12, 1944. *On Being Fit To Live With.*

The One Calm Person in Pilate's Court, RC, April 18, 1943; NV, April 18, 1943.

One Kingdom That Cannot Be Shaken, RC, March 1, 1942; NV, April 26, 1942.

One World for Religion, annual meeting of the Protestant Council, New York City, January 31, 1946.

Open Doors, FPC, January 13, 1924.

Our Commonest Hindrance to Great Living, RC, January 19, 1947.

Our Deep Desire to Feel Important, RC, April 7, 1940; NV, February 16, 1941.

Our Desperate Need of Humility, RC, December 1, 1935; NV, February 9, 1936.

Our Difficulty in Forgiving Our Enemies, RC, May 27, 1945. *On Being Fit To Live With*.

Our Generation Tempted, Not by Its Weakness, but by Its Power, RC, December 6, 1942; NV, March 7, 1943.

Our Goodly Heritage, RC, November 29, 1934.

Our Greatest Single Resource for Living, RC, October 11, 1936; RC, December 20, 1936.

Our Moral Muddle, RC, March 8, 1931; NV, April 26, 1931.

Our Perennial Use of Alibis, RC, December 31, 1939; NV, December 31, 1939.

Our Souls Need a Balanced Budget, Too, RC, January 22, 1950.

Our Strange Capacity for Self-Deception, RC, May 12, 1940; NV, May 12, 1940.

Our World Confronts a Child, RC, March 21, 1943; NV, April 11, 1943. *A Great Time To Be Alive*.

Overcoming the World, PABC, November 18, 1928; Harvard University, December 9, 1928; NV, December 16, 1928; Chicago, January 27, 1929; Mt. Holyoke College, April 28, 1929; Booth Bay Harbor Congregational Church, Booth Bay, Maine, July 25, 1929; Columbia University, August 7, 1929; Seal Harbor, Maine, August 25, 1929; RC, December 31, 1935.

The Overcrowded Life, PABC, November 25, 1928; NV, December 30, 1928; RC, December 3, 1939; Union Theological Seminary, December 13, 1939; NV, January 14, 1940.

The Past Speaks to the Present, Riverside Church Centennial sermon, RC, February 9, 1941.

People Who Suppose They Have No Personal Relationships with God, RC, May 12, 1946; NV, May 12, 1946. *On Being Fit To Live With*.

The Peril of Privilege, RC, February 21, 1937. *Successful Christian Living*.

The Peril of Resignation, FPC, January 8, 1922; FPC, January 18, 1925; PABC, December 30, 1928; RC, August 9, 1931.

The Peril of Worshiping Jesus, RC, October 26, 1930; NV, March 15, 1931. *The Hope of the World*.

The Perils of Abundance, FPC, November 23, 1919.

The Perils of Pettiness in Religion, RC, January 11, 1931; NV, February 22, 1931.

Personal Friendship: The Key to the Master's Last Week, RC, March 29, 1942; NV, March 29, 1942; RC, April 4, 1945.

Personal Responsibility in the Present Crisis, RC, November 15, 1931; NV, November 15, 1931.

Personality Changes the World, RC, December 22, 1935; RC, December 24, 1937.

The Personality of Jesus, the Soul of Christianity, TBE, April 13, 1930; NV, April 13, 1930.

Pilate's Wife, RC, February 7, 1943.

A Plea for Fellowship (budget sermon), RC, March 22, 1936; RC, April 29, 1942.

A Plea for Goodwill, RC, April 20, 1934; NV, May 20, 1934; RC, November 5, 1939; NV, December 17, 1939. *The Secret of Victorious Living.*

A Plea for True Individualism, RC, October 22, 1933; NV, December 17, 1933; RC, November 3, 1940; NV, November 3, 1940. *The Secret of Victorious Living.*

The Possiblity of Transformed Personality, RC, November 13, 1938; Harvard University, November 27, 1938; NV, May 14, 1939; RC, July 30, 1939.

The Power of a Disciplined Life: A Sermon for George Washington's Birthday, February 21, 1932; NV, February 21, 1932.

The Power of a Great Tradition, RC, January 14, 1934; NV, February 11, 1934; NV, May 30, 1937; RC, November 23, 1939; First Baptist Church, Montclair, New Jersey, November 23, 1947. *The Secret of Victorious Living.*

The Power of Imagination, RC, February 14, 1932; NV, March 13, 1932; RC, December 17, 1939; NV, February 4, 1940.

The Power of Steadiness, RC, April 26, 1931; NV, May 17, 1931; RC, December 30, 1936.

The Power of the Tongue, PABC, April 3, 1927; NV, October 9, 1927.

The Power of Willingness, PABC, May 15, 1927; NV, December 18, 1927.

The Power to Become, FPC, March 12, 1924.

The Power to See It Through, RC, January 6, 1935; NV, February 3, 1935. *The Power To See It Through, Riverside Sermons.*

The Power to Turn Evil into Good, RC, October 3, 1943; NV, November 7, 1943.

The Practical Use of Faith, RC, November 19, 1933; Harvard University, December 10, 1933; NV, January 7, 1934. *The Secret Of Victorious Living, Riverside Sermons.*

A Practical Working Faith, RC, March 13, 1932; NV, April 24, 1932.

A Prelude to Thanksgiving in a Difficult Year, RC, November 17, 1940; NV, November 17, 1940.

The Present State of the World as an Argument for Christian Faith, RC, September 26, 1937.

The Prevalence of Unrecognized Religion, RC, April 2, 1934.

Preventive Religion, PABC, October 23, 1927; NV, January 8, 1928; RC, July 9, 1933; RC, February 4, 1940; NV, March 3, 1940. *The Power To See It Through, Riverside Sermons.*

The Principle of Released Power, RC, November 20, 1938; NV, January 15, 1939.

Procrastination, FPC, May 15, 1921; RC, December 31, 1938.

The Prodigal Son Comes to Himself, FPC, June 6, 1920.

Progress: The Illusion and the Reality, RC, November 26, 1933; NV,

December 31, 1933; RC, May 24, 1942; NV, January 17, 1943. *The Secret of Victorious Living.*

Progressive Christianity, FPC, May 8, 1921. *Science and Religion.*

The Prohibition Question, PABC, October 14, 1929.

A Prophet's Summons to Modern America, RC, February 10, 1946; NV, February 10, 1946.

A Protestant Service for the United Nations, RC, November 10, 1946.

Pull Yourself Together, TBE, November 24, 1929; NV, January 19, 1930; RC, November 12, 1939.

Putting Christ into Uniform, RC, November 12, 1939.

Putting Great Horizons Around Our Christianity, RC, February 14, 1937; NV, February 21, 1937. *Successful Christian Living.*

Putting Manhood First, RC, January 12, 1936; NV, May 17, 1936.

Putting Religion into the Thick of Daily Life, RC, February 11, 1940; NV, February 11, 1940.

Queens Baptist Church Anniversary, Queens, New York, October 29, 1947.

Radiant Life, PABC, April 14, 1929.

Reaching Tomorrow By Way of Yesterday, RC, May 30, 1943; NV, May 30, 1943.

Real Issues and Great Choices, FPC, November 12, 1922.

The Real Point of Conflict Between Science and Religion, RC, February 18, 1940; NV, March 10, 1940; RC, August 3, 1941. *Living Under Tension.*

Real Versus Formal Religion, PABC, January 9, 1929; NV, October 23, 1929; RC, April 29, 1936.

Reality in Religion, PABC, February 19, 1928; NV, March 11, 1928.

Recovering Our Angels, RC, December 24, 1942.

The Recovery of a Powerful Religion, RC, October 25, 1936; NV, December 6, 1936.

Redigging Old Wells, PABC, May 29, 1927; RC, June 1, 1930. *What Is Vital in Religion.*

Regaining Faith in the Worth of Life, RC, October 20, 1935; NV, November 24, 1935.

The Reign of Moral Law, PABC, December 4, 1927; NV, January 22, 1928.

Reinforcement for a Time of Sacrifice, RC, November 15, 1942; NV, January 3, 1943.

Religion: A Bore or a Blessing? PABC, May 22, 1927.

Religion and Play, PABC, May 5, 1929; RC, July 26, 1931; University Club, Norfolk, Connecticut, June 7, 1929; Vassar College, June 9, 1929; Lehigh University, June 11, 1929; Walnut High School, Natick, Massachusetts, June 13, 1929; Boston University, June 18, 1929; Pratt Institute, June 20, 1929; RC, April 26, 1936; NV, May 3, 1936; RC, April 4, 1948.

Religion: Dispensable or Indispensable? PABC, October 7, 1928; NV,

November 4, 1928.

A Religion of Action, PABC, March 27, 1927.

A Religion That Really Gets Us, RC, March 14, 1943; NV, October 31, 1943. *What Is Vital In Religion.*

A Religion That Really Works, RC, November 5, 1944.

A Religion to Support Democracy, RC, February 12, 1939; NV, February 12, 1939. *What Is Vital In Religion.*

A Religion Where Something Actually Happens, RC, February 20, 1930; NV, March 20, 1938.

A Religion with Its Feet on the Ground, RC, March 27, 1938.

Religion's Indebtedness to Science, PABC, February 27, 1927; NV, October 16, 1927.

A Religious Faith for a Discouraging Year, RC, February 28, 1932; NV, April 17, 1932.

Religious Faith: Privilege or Problem? RC, March 1, 1931; NV, March 22, 1931; RC, July 10, 1932. *The Hope of the World.*

Religious Living as a Fine Art, TBE, March 30, 1930; NV, March 30, 1930.

Reproducible Experiences, FPC, October 12, 1924; PABC, January 22, 1928; NV, February 19, 1928.

Resources for a Courageous Life, RC, October 31, 1937; NV, November 21, 1937.

Resources for the Mastery of Life, RC, May 19, 1946; NV, May 26, 1946. *On Being Fit To Live With.*

The Restoration of the Soul, FPC, January 15, 1922; PABC, April 15, 1928; NV, May 20, 1928.

Rethinking the Problem of World-Wide Christianity, PABC, March 13, 1927.

The Return to Discipline, RC, December 15, 1940; NV, February 9, 1941. *Living Under Tension.*

The Return to Religion, RC, February 28, 1937; NV, May 16, 1937.

Reverence, FPC, November 4, 1923; RC, May 16, 1937; NV, May 23, 1937.

The Revival of Religious Interest, St. Martin's in the Field, London, England, summer, 1924.

The Revolt against Irreligion, RC, February 25, 1934; NV, April 22, 1934. *The Secret Of Victorious Living.*

The Revolt against Paganism, RC, December 3, 1944; NV, January 14, 1945.

Righteousness First! RC, February 20, 1944; NV, February 20, 1944. *A Great Time To Be Alive.*

The Roots of Dependable Character, RC, October 24, 1937; NV, May 22, 1938.

Ruling the Spirit, FPC, October 26, 1924; NV, November 23, 1924; NV, May 12, 1929.

The Sacred and the Secular Are Inseparable, RC, February 13, 1938;

NV, March 13, 1938.

Saints in Caesar's Household, RC, November 4, 1945.

A Saving Religion, PABC, June 3, 1928; NV, November 25, 1928.

Science Demands Religion, RC, October 14, 1945; NV, October 28, 1945. *On Being Fit To Live With*.

The Secret of Dynamic Religion, RC, December 6, 1931; Harvard University, December 13, 1931; RC, June 3, 1934; RC, June 2, 1937.

The Secret of Victorious Living, RC, March 4, 1934; NV, April 29, 1934. *The Secret of Victorious Living*.

The Security of the Divine Fellowship, RC, November 21, 1937; NV, February 6, 1938.

Self-Sacrifice an Absurdity--And Yet! RC, April 6, 1941; NV, April 6, 1941; RC, April 21, 1943.

The Sense of God's Reality, FPC, date unknown.

The Sense of Honor, PABC, March 10, 1929; Yale University, March 17, 1929; NV, October 20, 1929; RC, November 24, 1932.

A Serious Thanksgiving, RC, November 30, 1933; RC, November 21, 1940.

A Sermon for the Older Generation, RC, October 17, 1943; NV, January 16, 1944.

The Sermon on the Mount, NV, March 17, 1926; PABC, October 31, 1926. *The Hope of the World*.

The Service of Religious Faith to Mental Health, RC, October 23, 1932. *The Hope of the World, Riverside Sermons*.

Shall the Fundamentalists Win, FPC, May 21, 1922.

Shall We End War? FPC, June 5, 1921.

The Sin of Prejudice, PABC, June 5, 1927; NV, November 20, 1927.

Sins of Conservatism: A Washington's Birthday Sermon, RC, February 21, 1943; NV, February 21, 1943.

Six Paradoxes Concerning Trouble, RC, December 13, 1936; NV, January 17, 1937. *Successful Christian Living*.

Six Ways in Which Modern Man Can Pray, RC, May 24, 1936; RC, August 5, 1936; NV, October 25, 1936. *Successful Christian Living*.

Six Ways to Tell Right from Wrong, RC, October 30, 1932; NV, January 8, 1933. *The Hope of the World, Riverside Sermons*.

Some Cannot Find God, Others Cannot Escape Him, RC, November 13, 1932; NV, December 18, 1932.

The Soul's Invincible Surmise, RC, April 16, 1933; NV, April 16, 1933. *The Hope of the World*.

The Spiritual Basis of Material Prosperity, RC, December 8, 1940; NV, January 12, 1941.

The Spiritual Foundations for a Better World, RC, April 23, 1944; NV, May 14, 1944. *A Great Time To Be Alive*.

Spiritual Priorities, 1942, RC, January 11, 1942; NV, April 19, 1942.

The Spiritual Problems of a Machine Age, PABC, February 20, 1927;

NV, February 23, 1930.

The Springs of Surplus Power, RC, October 17, 1937; NV, November 7, 1937.

Stand By the Church, RC, March 19, 1939.

Standing By the Best in an Evil Time, RC, October 7, 1945; NV, October 7, 1945. *On Being Fit To Live With.*

Standing in the Need of Prayer, RC, December 13, 1942; NV, February 7, 1943.

Starting with Trouble and Ending with Hope, RC, March 7, 1943; NV, May 9, 1943. *A Great Time To Be Alive.*

Steadfastness Under the Highest Leadership, RC, November 7, 1937; NV, November 14, 1937.

The Strange Mystery of Trouble in God's World, RC, April 15, 1945; NV, April 15, 1945.

A Strange Time to See God, RC, March 26, 1944; NV, April 23, 1944.

A Strange World in Which to Be a Christian, RC, September 25, 1938; NV, October 2, 1938.

The Strangest Anticlimax in the Bible, RC, December 2, 1945; NV, January 13, 1946.

Strength for the New Year, RC, January 5, 1947.

The Strong Comfort of Christmas, RC, December 24, 1944; NV, December 24, 1944.

Superficial Optimists: The Peril of a Serious Time, RC, January 8, 1933; NV, February 5, 1933. *The Hope of the World.*

Sustained By an Exciting Faith, RC, October 26, 1941; NV, November 16, 1941; RC, August 2, 1942.

Take Care and Don't Lose It, RC, May 1, 1938; NV, May 1, 1938.

Take What You Want and Pay for It, RC, March 31, 1946; NV, April 7, 1946. *On Being Fit To Live With.*

Taking God Seriously, RC, February 15, 1942; NV, March 22, 1942.

Taking Jesus Seriously, RC, February 27, 1944; NV, February 27, 1944. *A Great Time To Be Alive, Riverside Sermons.*

Taking Life Seriously, PABC, February 26, 1928; NV, March 18, 1928.

Taking the Offensive Toward Life, RC, February 22, 1942; NV, April 12, 1942.

Technique in Religion, PABC, May 26, 1929; NV, October 27, 1929.

The Temporal and the Eternal, FPC, March 27, 1921; RC, March 27, 1932; NV, March 27, 1932.

The Temptations of Maturity, PABC, May 22, 1929; RC, February 19, 1933; NV, March 19, 1933; RC, June 6, 1937. *What Is Vital in Religion.*

Thanksgiving Day Sermon, RC, November 26, 1936.

Thanksgiving Day Sermon, RC, November 24, 1938.

That Appalling Sense of Inferiority, RC, October 30, 1938; NV, December 18, 1938.

That Fascinating Man on the Cross, RC, March 3, 1946.

That Strange Realist from Bethlehem, RC, December 21, 1941; NV, December 28, 1941.

That Unescapable Future Tense, RC, April 9, 1939; NV, April 9, 1939.

There Really Is a God, Institute for Religious and Social Studies, New York City, January, 1952.

There Is No Death, RC, March 12, 1936; NV, March 12, 1936. *Successful Christian Living.*

Things That Money Cannot Buy, RC, April 3, 1938; Chicago Sunday Evening Club, Chicago, April 24, 1938; NV, May 8, 1938. *What Is Vital in Religion.*

Things That Never Wear Out, RC, December 29, 1935; NV, December 29, 1935; RC, December 31, 1937.

Things Unshaken in a Shaken Time, RC, November 22, 1931; NV, November 29, 1931; Knights Templar Service, June 5, 1932; RC, December 31, 1936.

This Is a Grand Year for Christmas, RC, December 24, 1939; NV, December 24, 1939; RC, Ministry of Music Service, December 21, 1941.

This Is a Great Time to Be Alive, RC, April 11, 1943; RC, July 25, 1943; NV, December 5, 1943; RC, July 30, 1944. *A Great Time to Be Alive.*

This Is a Miraculous World, RC, December 12, 1937; NV, January 16, 1938.

This Is the Time to Believe in the Church, RC, January 9, 1944; NV, February 6, 1944.

This Nation Needs a Rebirth of Honorable Character, RC, November 11, 1951; Pomona College, March, 1953.

This Year We Need Easter, RC, April 9, 1944; NV, April 9, 1944.

The Three Crosses, FPC, April 9, 1922.

Three Crosses on One Hill, RC, March 5, 1944.

Thrills, PABC, November 6, 1927; NV, November 27, 1927; RC, November 28, 1935.

Through the Social Gospel into Personal Religion, RC, November 27, 1932. *The Hope of the World.*

Tightening the Nation's Moral Fiber, TBE, February 16, 1930; NV, March 16, 1930.

A Time to Stress Unity, RC, February 13, 1944; NV, March 12, 1944. *A Great Time To Be Alive.* Holding the record for the National Vespers, Fosdick received over eight thousand requests for this sermon.

Titus in Crete, FPC, October 19, 1924.

The Towering Question: Is Christianity Possible? RC, October 29, 1933; NV, January 14, 1934; RC, April 30, 1939; NV, October 1, 1939; NV, March 10, 1946. *The Secret Of Victorious Living, Riverside Sermons.*

The Tragedy of Misused Power, PABC, April 1, 1928; NV, April 1, 1928.

The Transient and the Abiding, PABC, November 14, 1926; NV, April 29, 1928.

The Triumph of Rejected Things, RC, November 29, 1942; NV, January 10, 1943; RC, Address to Midshipmen, May 30, 1943.

Truth Through Personality, RC, December 20, 1936; NV, December 27, 1936.

Two Kinds of Lives: The Pushed and the Pulled, TBE, May 18, 1930; NV, May 18, 1930; NV, March 30, 1941.

The Two Prayers of the Prodigal, FPC, February 27, 1921; RC, February 1, 1931; NV, February 15, 1931; RC, April 27, 1938.

An Unavoidable Choice Faces Our Jerusalem, Too, RC, April 14, 1946; NV, April 14, 1946.

Unclaimed Heritage, FPC, January 4, 1925.

The Unknown Soldier, RC, November 12, 1933; My Account with the Unknown Soldier, Broadway Tabernacle, May 4, 1934; Brown University, March 16, 1934; Yale University, March 18, 1934. *The Secret of Victorious Living, Riverside Sermons.*

The Universality of Religion, PABC, February 5, 1928; PABC, February 26, 1928; NV, March 3, 1935.

Unprejudiced Goodwill, PABC, November 4, 1928; NV, December 2, 1928.

The Unrecognized God, FPC, January 30, 1921; RC, October 12, 1930; NV, November 23, 1930; RC, June 5, 1938; NV, October 23, 1938; RC, July 23, 1939.

The Unshaken Christ, FPC, March 2, 1919. This was Fosdick's first sermon at First Presbyterian Church.

Unshaken in a Shaken Time, RC, April 1, 1951.

Unto a Full-Grown Man, FPC, December 7, 1924.

Urgency of Ethical as well as Economic Reconversion, RC, September 30, 1945; NV, October 14, 1945. *On Being Fit To Live With.*

The Use and Misuse of Power, RC, January 21, 1934; NV, February 25, 1934. *The Secret of Victorious Living.*

The Use and Misuse of Religion, PABC, October 10, 1926; NV, October 2, 1927; RC, March 10, 1934; NV, October 13, 1935; RC, May 25, 1941; NV, May 25, 1941; NV, October 12, 1941.

The Use of Faith, PABC, September 25, 1927; NV, December 4, 1927; RC, March 13, 1938; NV, May 15, 1938; RC, October 2, 1940; NV, February 23, 1941.

The Use of Freedom, PABC, June 10, 1928.

V-E Day Address, RC, May 8, 1945.

The Validity of Abiding Experiences, RC, November 14, 1937; NV, December 12, 1937.

The Veracity of Our Religious Experience, RC, May 15, 1938; NV, November 6, 1938.

Victims of Fate or Masters of Destiny? RC, October 11, 1931; NV, November 8, 1931.

The Victorious Nations in Pilate's Shoes, RC, May 20, 1945; NV, May 20, 1945.

The Victory of Faith, FPC, October 5, 1924. Also delivered over a radio station, before National Vespers, on October 19, 1924.

Vitality Is Mightier than Size, RC, December 22, 1946; RC, October 29, 1947.

Wanted: A Saving Minority, RC, May 21, 1933.

Wartime's Effect on Our Personal Religion, RC, December 17, 1944; NV, January 7, 1945.

Watch Night Sermon, RC, December 31, 1940; NV, December 31, 1940.

Watch Night Sermon, RC, December 31, 1942.

Watch Night Service, RC, December 31, 1946.

The Way Out from Dry-as-Dust Religion, RC, November 1, 1931; NV, January 3, 1932.

We Can Choose Our Ancestors, RC, May 31, 1942; NV, May 31, 1942.

We Need Faith in Immortality, RC, November 25, 1945; NV, November 25, 1945.

What About the Church? PABC, November 20, 1927 (for the laying of the cornerstone for the Riverside Church); RC, December 17, 1933.

What About God? RC, December 14, 1933; NV, May 13, 1934. *The Secret of Victorious Living.*

What About Our Social Pessimism? RC, February 10, 1935; NV, March 10, 1935. *The Power To See It Through.*

What an Armistice Day! RC, November 11, 1945; NV, November 11, 1945.

What Are You Doing with Your Imagination? RC, December 17, 1939.

What Are You Standing For?, FPC, February 10, 1924; PABC, May 28, 1928; RC, November 30, 1930; NV, January 11, 1931; RC, December 31, 1933; Riverside Guild Service, RC, October 9, 1938. *The Secret of Victorious Living, Riverside Sermons.*

What Christians Have Done to Christ, RC, December 27, 1936; NV, March 21, 1937. *Successful Christian Living.*

What Do We Protestants Really Stand For? Council of Churches of Buffalo and Erie County, Buffalo, New York, October 26, 1952; St. Louis, Missouri, November 1, 1953.

What Do Ye More Than Others? PABC, April 22, 1928; NV, May 6, 1928; RC, May 10, 1942; NV, May 24, 1942.

What Does It Really Mean to Be Great? RC, October 29, 1944; NV, November 19, 1944. *On Being Fit To Live With.*

What Does the Divinity of Jesus Mean? RC, March 26, 1939; NV, May 21, 1939. *Living Under Tension, Riverside Sermons.*

What Is Christian Prayer? PABC, December 5, 1926.

What Is Life Doing to Your Self-Esteem? RC, October 2, 1932; NV, November 13, 1932; RC, July 15, 1934.

What Is Right? PABC, February 10, 1929; NV, March 10, 1929.

What Is Vital in Religion? PABC, February 17, 1929; NV, April 21, 1929. [This sermon is not related to Fosdick's book entitled *What Is Vital In Religion.*]

What It Means to Grow Up, RC, November 6, 1938; NV, January 8, 1939; RC, May 16, 1943; NV, May 16, 1943.

What Keeps Religion Going? RC, February 16, 1941; NV, May 18, 1941; RC, August 10, 1941; NV, March 4, 1945. *Living Under Tension, Riverside Sermons.*

What the Law Cannot Do, RC, November 22, 1936; NV, January 3, 1937; RC, March 17, 1946; NV, March 31, 1946. *On Being Fit To Live With.*

What Matters in Religion? RC, October 5, 1930. This was Fosdick's first sermon delivered in the newly constructed Riverside Church.

What Shall We Do with Jesus? FPC, November 26, 1922.

When Christ Is Born in Us, RC, December 23, 1945; NV, December 23, 1945.

When Christianity Gets Us Into Trouble, RC, October 21, 1934; NV, December 16, 1934. *The Power To See It Through.*

When Conscience Outruns Religion, RC, January 5, 1936; University of Chicago, April 19, 1936; RC, July 12, 1936; NV, February 14, 1937. *Successful Christian Living.*

When Each Man Cleans Up His Own Life, RC, March 8, 1936; Princeton University, March 15, 1936; Chicago Sunday Evening Club, April 19, 1936; NV, May 4, 1936. *Successful Christian Living.*

When Evil Wins Its Victories, What Must Christians Do? RC, January 9, 1938; University of Chicago, April 24, 1938; NV, May 29, 1938; RC, July 9, 1939.

When Faith in God Costs a Struggle, RC, November 28, 1943; NV, January 2, 1944.

When God Lets Us Down, RC, March 7, 1937; NV, April 11, 1937. *Successful Christian Living.*

When Great Events Make Common Tasks Seem Trivial, RC, March 23, 1941; NV, March 30, 1941. *Living Under Tension.*

When Life Gets Us Down, RC, December 10, 1939; NV, January 7, 1940; Chicago Sunday Evening Club, March 31, 1940; RC, June 4, 1944.

When Life Goes All to Pieces, RC, May 13, 1934; NV, October 21, 1934; RC, May 3, 1939; RC, May 26, 1940; NV, May 26, 1940. *The Power To See It Through.*

When Life Reaches Its Depths, RC, May 14, 1939; NV, November 19, 1939; RC, May 21, 1944; NV, May 21, 1944. *A Great Time To Be Alive, Riverside Sermons.*

When Man Grows Tired of Freedom, RC, April 23, 1939; NV, April 30, 1939; RC, August 6, 1939.

When Noah Got Drunk, RC, April 22, 1945; NV, April 22, 1945.

When Prayer Means Power, RC, March 30, 1941; NV, March 25, 1941; First Baptist Church, Montclair, New Jersey, November 2, 1947.

Living Under Tension, Riverside Sermons.

When Spiritual Forces Confront a Brutal World, RC, October 20, 1940.

When the Devil Looks Like an Angel, RC, April 27, 1941.

When We Are Alone We Are Not Alone, RC, June 6, 1943.

When We Are at Our Wit's End, RC, April 4, 1943; NV, May 23, 1943.

Who Do You Think You Are? RC, April 25, 1944. *What Is Vital In Religion.*

Who Killed Jesus? PABC, April 10, 1927; NV, April 12, 1933. *What Is Vital In Religion.*

Why Be Religious Anyway, RC, March 6, 1932; NV, April 10, 1932.

Why Is God Silent While Evil Rages? RC, October 10, 1943; NV, November 14, 1943. *A Great Time To Be Alive.*

Why Is Religion Indispensable? RC, January 4, 1941; NV, May 31, 1931.

Why Not Live the Good Life Without Religion? RC, January 19, 1936; NV, March 8, 1936.

Why We Believe in God, RC, March 10, 1946; NV, March 17, 1946. *On Being Fit To Live With.*

Why Worship? RC, December 6, 1936; NV, April 18, 1937. *Successful Christian Living.*

Will the New Year Be Really New, RC, January 7, 1945.

Winning the War of Ideas, RC, March 16, 1941; NV, March 23, 1941; RC, July 20, 1941. *Living Under Tension.*

Winning the War of Nerves, RC, February 23, 1941; NV, March 2, 1941. *Living Under Tension.*

With a Troubled Foreground, What About Your Background? RC, January 25, 1948.

Works Without Faith Are Dead, NV, December 3, 1944; Vesper Service, USNR Midshipmen's School, RC, April 22, 1945.

The World at the Crossroads: A Special Service of Worship in View of the San Francisco Conference, RC, April 25, 1945.

The World Tries to Get Rid of Religion: A New Year's Sermon, RC, January 1, 1939; NV, January 1, 1939.

Worshiping the Gods of a Beaten Enemy, RC, November 21, 1943; NV, November 28, 1943. *A Great Time To Be Alive.*

The Wrong Way to Build a Church, FPC, March 13, 1921; TBE, March 23, 1930.

Ye Must Be Born from Above, PABC, February 3, 1929; NV, March 3, 1929.

The Younger Generation, PABC, January 16, 1927; Layman's League of Weston, Massachusetts, June 19, 1927; Wellesley College, June 19, 1927; Smith College Commencement, June 20, 1927.

Your Money or Your Life, RC, January 14, 1940.

Your Present Is the Past of Your Future, RC, May 26, 1946. This was Fosdick's farewell and last sermon as a full-time minister in the Riverside Church.

Chronology of Speeches

(See Calendar of Sermons for alphabetical listing of homilies.)

Handicapped Men, Fifty-Fourth Anniversary Exercises, The Packard
    Commercial School, New York City, 1912.
Modern Preacher's Problems in His Use of the Scriptures, inaugural
    address as Morris K. Jessup Professor of Practical Theology,
    Union Theological Seminary, New York City, September 30, 1915.
The Value of a Great Heritage, Washington Association of New Jersey,
    Morristown, New Jersey, February 22, 1921.
Landing of the Pilgrims, New England Society of New York, New York
    City, December 18, 1921.
The Foundations of Character, Sixty-fourth Anniversary Exercises, The
    Packard Commercial School, Mew York City, May 25, 1922.
Prayer for the Spiritual Union of Mankind, Religious Activities
    Committee of The League of Nations' Non-Partisan Committee,
    radio station WJZ, November 9, 1924.
Address, Thirty-ninth Annual Dinner of New York Southern Society,
    New York City, December 10, 1924.
The Challenge of International Relations to North America, Empire
    Club of Canada, Toronto, Canada, April 27, 1925.
The Need of Modern Religious Leadership, convocation, University of
    Wisconsin, Madison, Wisconsin, March 27, 1925.
Inaugural Dinner Address, President Henry Sloane Coffin, Union
    Theological Serminary, New York City, November 4, 1926.
A Clergyman's View of Mental Hygiene, Eighteenth Annual Meeting of
    National Committe for Mental Hygiene, New York City,
    November 10, 1927.
Tribute to Dr. Cornelius Woelfkin, New York City, January 9, 1928.
Limitations of Humanism, Union Theological Seminary, New York City,
    September 25, 1929.
A Widening Outlook, National Institute of Social Science, New York
    City, December 31, 1929.
Neighbors, International House, New York City, September 28, 1930.
Freeing Religion from Supernaturalism, Harvard University, December
    14, 1931. See also Calendar of Sermons.
Social Reform and Personal Character, Chicago Sunday Evening Club,
    April 23, 1933.
Teacher and Friend, Memoriam to Arthur Cushman McGiffert, Union
    Theological Seminary, New York City, May 23, 1933.
The Five Sectors of the Peace Movement, Emergency Peace Campaign,
    Academy of Music, Philadelphia, Pennsylvania, January 7, 1937.
    See also Calendar of Sermons.
We Were Unmercifully Gypped, Emergency Peace Campaign,
    Washington, D.C., April 6, 1937.

Fifteenth Anniversary of National Religious Radio, New York City, May 23, 1938.

The Free Spirit Confronts the World's Coercion, Harvard University, November 26, 1939. See also Calendar of Sermons.

Conscription, radio address on Columbia Broadcasting Company, New York City, September 1, 1940.

Religious Faith, Stimulus Not Escape, Columbia University Conference on Religion in the Modern World, New York City, February 4, 1942.

The Truth of the Gospel, graduation exercises, Union Theological Seminary, New York City, May 19, 1942.

One World for Religion, Annual Meeting of Protestant Council of the City of New York, New York City, January 31, 1946.

Address at Protestant Service for the United Nations, New York City, November 10, 1946.

Something More in Education, Haverford College, Haverford, Pennsylvania, May 15, 1951.

There Really Is a God, Institute for Religious and Social Studies, Jewish Theological Seminary, New York City, January 1952.

Address, Illinois Executive's Club, Chicago, January 25, 1952.

Adequate Power is Available, the Eternal Is Real, and Vitality Is Mightier than Size, Earl Lecture, Pacific School of Religion, February 1952.

Have We Lost Our Moral Heritage? Economic Club, Detroit, Michigan, May 19, 1952. (*Vital Speeches of the Day*, August 1, 1952, pp. 628-31.)

Idea of God as Affected by Modern Knowledge, Garvin Lecture, Lancaster, Pennsylvania, November 13, 1952.

The Most Critical Problem in Our American Universities, Pitcairn-Crabbe Foundation Lecture, April 14, 1953.

Faith in Man as Affected by Modern Life, Northwestern University, March 11, 1954.

Bibliography

A student of the Reverend Harry Emerson Fosdick's rhetoric has a rich repository of original materials in which to conduct research. Fosdick gave his papers to Union Theological Seminary, New York City, where they are gathered in the Harry Emerson Fosdick Collection. The Riverside Church, New York City, also has sermon materials on Fosdick that duplicates Union's holdings. Particularly useful is that church's publication, *The Church Monthly*, which reprinted most of Fosdick's sermons from the time of Park Avenue Baptist Church through Temple Beth-El to Riverside.

THE FOSDICK COLLECTION, UNION THEOLOGICAL SEMINARY

His homilies are arranged by title in folders that are collected in the Sermon Boxes of Harry Emerson Fosdick. Although the material in a sermon folder varies, a rhetorical researcher may usually expect one or more drafts of a given sermon, handwritten emendations for further revisions, a program of the church service, and reprints of the sermon as collected from a variety of publications. Fosdick's sermons were taken stenographically by Margaret Renton. See the Calendar of Sermons for a listing of Fosdick's sermons, where they were delivered, and the titles of books in which he reprinted important ones.

Newspaper clippings are collected in several boxes indexed by that title. The fundamentalist controversy figures prominently in these boxes. Of special note is the fact that many of the documents are underlined in pencil. Either Fosdick closely read them or someone wanted him to read the underlined materials, which presumably he did. In most cases, unfortunately, the publication data was inadvertently deleted when Fosdick or someone else clipped columns from newspapers and magazines.

There are several boxes of miscellaneous materials that Dorothy Noyes, Fosdick's secretary for years, collected. Some documents are labeled in folders; other sources are included in no discernible fashion or order. Important listings for speeches and sermons are as follows:

"Charge to Rev. Lyons, November 11, 1956"

The Christian Scotsman, no. 6 [pamphlet with no publication details]

"Harry Emerson Fosdick"

"Lectures to the Missionaries in the Orient, I: Christianity and the Social Movement"

"Methods of Sermon Preparation"

"Odd Items about Dr. Fosdick's Broadcasting"

"On Preaching"

Straton, John Roach, "Shall the FunnyMonkeyists Win?" [pamphlet with no publication details]

AUDIO AND VIDEO COLLECTIONS

Union Theological Seminary has some early voice recordings of Fosdick's sermons, but these are so rare and fragile that until they are re-recorded on modern equipment the researcher cannot listen to them. The Reigner Recording Library, Union Seminary, Richmond, Virginia, contains voice recordings for some of Fosdick's sermons that he delivered at Riverside and some video tapes of early television shows on which Fosdick appeared. These materials are available for loan from the Reigner Recording Library and include the following categories as catalogued by the library:

Audio Recordings

Are We Part of the Problem or the Answer, February 24, 1946, F-748-2

Christian Faith: Fantasy or Truth, July 27, 1941, F-748-3

Facing Life's Central Test, April 2, 1944, F-748-7

The Field is the World, May 14, 1944, F-748-9

The Great Christ and Little Churches, September 29, 1946, F-748-4

A Great Time to Be Alive, April 11, 1943, F-748-8

Handling Life's Second-Bests, March 12, 1944, F-748-5

The Importance of Doubting Our Doubts, April 12, 1953, F-748-1

Living Under Tension, October 6, 1940, F-748-6

The Most Thrilling Rescue Story in the World, March 25, 1946, F-748-13

On Being Fit to Live With, February 17, 1946, F-748-11

When Life Reaches its Depths, May 24, 1944, F-748-10

Why We Believe in God, March 10, 1946, F-748-12

Video Recordings

"What Christmas Means to Me," Movie 184
"People at Home: Harry Emerson Fosdick," Biography for Eye and
  Ear Television Program, 1956, Movie 112

The bibliography is divided into six sections: (1) books by Fosdick, which lists, where appropriate, the titles of anthologized sermons; (2) front matter by Fosdick, which lists other authors' or editors' books for which Fosdick wrote parts or all of the front matter; (3) articles by Fosdick, which details Fosdick's own essays on speech and sermonic subject matter; (4) books and major essays about Fosdick, which lists studies of Fosdick's ministry and sermonizing; (5) articles about Fosdick, which includes signed and unsigned works; and (6) dissertations about Fosdick.

BOOKS BY HARRY EMERSON FOSDICK

Fosdick's books are listed chronologically. Since many of his books are collections of his sermons, the sermon titles are listed (see Calendar of Sermons for complete data on individual sermons).

The Assurance of Immortality. New York: Macmillan Company, 1913.
The Manhood of the Master. New York: Association Press, 1913.
The Meaning of Prayer. New York: Association Press, 1915.
The Meaning of Faith. New York: Association Press, 1917.
The Challenge of the Present Crisis. New York: Association Press, 1917.
The Church's Message to the Nation. (Pamphlet.) New York: Association
  Press, 1919.
Finishing the War. (Pamphlet.) New York: Association Press, 1919.
The Meaning of Service. New York: Association Press, 1920.
Christianity and Progress. (Cole Lectures, Vanderbilt University.) New
  York: Fleming H. Revell Company, 1922. Sermons: The Idea of
  Progress, The Need for Religion, The Gospel and Social Progress,
  Progressive Christianity, The Perils of Progress, Progress and God.
The Second Mile. New York: Association Press, 1922.
Twelve Tests of Character. New York: Association Press, 1923. Sermons:
  First Things First, Long Ropes and Strong Stakes, A High Opinion
  of Oneself, Seeing the Invisible, The Privilege of Living, Minding
  Ones Own Business, Obedience, Above the Average, Harnessing
  the Caveman, Magnanimity, Possessing a Past Tense, The Power
  to See It Through.
The Modern Use of the Bible. (Yale University Lyman Beecher Lectures.)
  New York: Macmillan Company, 1924.
Science and Religion. (Co-authored with Sherwood Edd.) New York:
  George Doran, 1924.

Adventurous Religion. New York: Harper and Brothers, 1926. Sermons: Adventurous Religion, Moral Autonomy or Downfall, I Believe in Man, On Being a Real Skeptic, How Shall We Think of God?, Concerning Prayer, Science and Religion, Evolution and Religion, Will Science Displace God?, Science and Mystery, The Desire for Immortality, Limitation or Liberty, Tolerance, What Christian Liberals are Driving At, The Dangers of Modernism, The Need of Modern Religious Leadership, The New Religious Reformation.

Spiritual Values and Eternal Life. (Ingersoll Lecture.) Cambridge: Harvard University Press, 1927.

A Pilgrimage to Palestine. New York: Macmillan Company, 1927.

What Religion Means to Me. (Co-authored with A. Bruce Curry and Ernest Fremont.) Garden City: Doubleday, Doran, and Co., Inc., 1929.

As I See Religion. New York: Harper and Brothers, 1932.

The Hope of the World. New York: Harper and Brothers, 1933. Sermons: The Hope of the World in Its Minorities, Christianity at Home in Chaos, Christianity's Stake in the Social Situation, Through the Social Gospel into Personal Religion, Modern Civilization's Crucial Problem, The Service of Religious Faith to Mental Health, The Conquest of Fear, Handling Life's Second-Bests, Keeping One's Footing in a Slippery Time, Is Our Christianity Appealing to Our Softness or Our Strength?, The Peril of Worshiping Jesus, Facing the Challenge of Change, Making the Best of a Bad Mess, Six Ways to Tell Right from Wrong, Superficial Optimists: The Peril of a Serious Time, The Sermon on the Mount, Christianity's Supreme Rival, Christianity More Than Duty--Not Weight but Wings, Religious Faith: Privilege or Problem?, Getting Out of Us the Best That Is in Us, The Fine Art of Making Goodness Attractive, Being Good Without Trying, Beautiful Ideas and Brutal Facts, Crucified by Stupidity, The Soul's Invincible Surmise.

The Secret of Victorious Living. New York: Harper and Brothers, 1934. Sermons: The Secret of Victorious Living, The High Uses of Trouble, The Cure of Disillusionment, On Making Christianity Too Easy, Progress: The Illusion and the Reality, The Towering Question: Is Christianity Possible?, A Plea for True Individualism, The Use and Misuse of Power, A Plea for Goodwill, The Unknown Soldier, An Interpretation of Pacifism, Forgiveness of Sins, The Practical Use of Faith, The Mystery of Life, The Revolt Against Irreligion, What About God?, The Greatness of God, Do We Really Want God?, On Escaping from This World, On Learning How to Pray, Be Still and Know, The Power of a Great Tradition, What Are You Standing For?, The Christian Interpretation of Life--A Terrific Fact, The Intimations of Immortality.

The Power To See It Through. New York: Harper and Brothers, 1935.
Sermons: The Power to See It Through, Christians in Spite of
Everything, When Christianity Gets Us into Trouble, When Life
Goes All to Pieces, Handicapped Lives, No Man Need Stay the
Way He Is, Preventive Religion, Let's All Be Realistic, The Ghost
of a Chance, How Much Do We Want Liberty?, The Ethical
Foundations of Prosperity, How Much Do We Want Peace?, The
High Uses of Serenity, Basic Conditions of Spiritual Well-Being,
Every Man's Religion His Own, Every Man a Gambler, On
Seeming as Christian as We Are, The Ideas That Use Us, What
Is Our Religion Doing to Our Character?, A Fundamentalist
Sermon by a Modernist Preacher, Family Religion, The
Mainsprings of Human Motive, What About Our Social
Pessimism?, On Shouldering One's Own Responsibility, Hospitality
to the Highest.
Successful Christian Living. New York: Harper and Brothers, 1937.
Sermons: Successful Christian Living, Six Ways in Which Modern
Man Can Pray, Discovering What We Can Do with Ourselves, On
Finding It Hard to Believe in God, When God Lets Us Down,
The Contemporary Prevalence of Polytheism, On Being Civilized
to Death, On Being Christians Unashamed, The Most Durable
Power in the World, When Conscience Outruns Religion, Christian
Attitudes in Social Reconstruction, The Peril of Privilege, When
Each Man Cleans Up His Own Life, What Christians Have Done
to Christ, The Church Must Go Beyond Modernism, Why
Worship?, Putting Great Horizons Around Our Christianity, On
Being Indifferent to Religion, Six Paradoxes Concerning Trouble,
The Cross and the Ordinary Man, An Appeal from the Present
to the Future, The Dignity of Being Up to Date, Giving the
Highest a Hearing, Decision of Character, There Is No Death.
A Guide to Understanding the Bible. New York: Harper and Brothers,
1938.
Living Under Tension. New York: Harper and Brothers, 1941. Sermons:
Living Under Tension, Don't Lose Faith in Human Possibilitites,
Winning the War of Nerves, Christian Faith--Fantasy or Truth?,
Winning the War of Ideas, What Keeps Religion Going?, The
Inescapable Judgment, When Prayer Means Power, Mankind's
Deep Need--The Sense of Community, How to Stand Up and
Take It, The Means Determine the End, The Modern World's
Rediscovery of Sin, The God Who Made Us and the Gods We
Make, The Free Spirit Confronts the World's Coercion, The Real
Point of Conflict Between Science and Religion, What Does the
Divinity of Jesus Mean?, Jesus's Ethical Message Confronts the
World, God Talks to a Dictator, The Essential Elements in a Vital
Christian Experience, When Great Events Make Common Tasks
Seem Trivial, The Return to Discipline, How Believe in a Good

God in a World Like This? The Decisive Babies of the World,
The Cross: An Amazing Paradox, A Great Year for Easter.

On Being a Real Person. New York: Harper and Brothers, 1943.

A Great Time To Be Alive. New York: Harper and Brothers, 1944.
Sermons: A Great Time To Be Alive, Decisive Battles Behind
Closed Doors, Righteousness First!, The Field Is the World,
Spiritual Foundations for a Better World, Getting the Best Out of
the Worst, The Common Sense Wisdon of Christianity, Taking
Jesus Seriously, A Kind of Penitence that Does Some Good,
Christianity Not a Form but a Force, Our World Confronts a
Child, On Being Strongly Tempted to be Christian, Starting with
Trouble and Ending with Hope, On Believing in Miracles, Loyalty-
-the Basic Condition of Liberty, A Time to Stress Unity,
Worshiping the Gods of a Beaten Enemy, Why Is God Silent while
Evil Rages?, No Dry-as-Dust Religion Will Do Now, Keeping
Faith in Persuasion in a World of Coercion, When Life Reaches
Its Depths, After Forty Years in the Ministry, The Light that No
Darkness Can Put Out, Facing Life's Central Test, The Deathless
Hope that Man Cannot Escape.

On Being Fit To Live With. New York: Harper and Brothers, 1946.
Sermons: On Being Fit To Live With, Are We Part Of The
Problem or of the Answer?, Science Demands Religion, On
Getting Christianity Out of Its Pigeonholes, What The Law Cannot
Do, What Does It Really Mean To Be Great, Take What You
Want And Pay For It, The Urgency Of Ethical As Well As
Economic Reconversion, Our Difficulty in Forgiving Our Enemies,
The Impossibility of Being Irreligious, Why We Believe in God,
Finding Unfailing Resources, Standing By the Best in an Evil
Time, On Worshiping Things We Manufacture, The Constructive
Uses of Fear, On Catching the Wrong Bus, The Great Hours of
a Man's Life, A Man Is What He Proves to Be in an Emergency,
Resources for Life's Mastery, People Who Suppose They Have No
Personal Relationships with God, On Being Only a Drop in the
Bucket, Christ Himself Is Christianity, The Most Thrilling Rescue
Story in the World, An Unavoidable Choice Faces Our Jerusalem
Too, The Eternal Victorious over the Temporal.

The Man From Nazareth: As His Contemporaries Saw Him. New York:
Harper and Brothers, 1949.

The Three Meanings: Prayer, Faith, and Service. Garden City: Garden City
Books, 1951.

Rufus Jones Speaks to Our Time. New York: Macmillan Company, 1951.

Great Voices of the Reformation. New York: Random House, 1952.

A Faith for Tough Times. (See Earl Foundation Lectures, Chronology of
Speeches.) New York: Harper and Brothers, 1952.

What Is Vital in Religion. New York: Harper and Brothers, 1955.
Sermons: Finding God in Unlikely Places, Having a Faith That

Really Works, The Great Christ and the Little Churches, The Christ of History and the Christ Of Experience, Miracles of Character Possible for All, A Religion That Really Gets Us, When God Becomes Real, Conservative And Liberal Temperaments in Religion, The Importance of Doubting Our Doubts, The Christian Outlook on Life, Life's Forced Decisions, Despise Ye the Church of God?, The Danger of Going to Church, Things That Never Wear Out, Redigging Old Wells, Things That Money Cannot Buy, Who Do You Think You Are?, Who Killed Jesus?, A Religion to Support Democracy, The Temptations of Maturity, Faith and Immortality.

Martin Luther. (World Landmark Book.) New York: Random House, 1956.

The Living of These Days: An Autobiography. New York: Harper and Brothers, 1956.

Riverside Sermons. New York: Harper and Brothers, 1958. Sermons: The Ideas That Use Us, The Great Hours of a Man's Life, The Mystery of Life, The Power to See It Through, On Catching the Wrong Bus, When Life Reaches Its Depths, Handling Life's Second-Bests, Handicapped Lives, No Man Need Stay the Way He Is, Preventive Religion, The Service of Religious Faith to Mental Health, Christian Faith--Fantasy Or Truth?, On Learning How to Pray, When Prayer Means Power, Finding Unfailing Resources, The High Uses of Serenity, What Keeps Religion Going?, The Towering Question: Is Christianity Possible?, The Essential Elements in a Vital Christian Experience, Christians in Spite of Everything, What Are You Standing For?, Are We Part of the Problem or of the Answer?, Six Ways to Tell Right from Wrong, The Practical Use of Faith, Family Religion, Mankind's Deepest Need: The Sense Of Community, Modern Civilization's Crucial Problem, How Believe in a Good God in a World Like This?, The Greatness of God, What Does the Divinity of Jesus Mean?, Hospitality in the Highest, Taking Jesus Seriously, Forgiveness of Sins, The Inescapble Judgment, An Unavoidable Choice Faces Our Jerusalem Too, The Cross: An Amazing Paradox, The Eternal Victorious over the Temporal, God Talks to a Dictator, The Unknown Soldier, The Church Must Go Beyond Modernism.

Jesus of Nazareth. (World Landmark Book.) New York: Random House, 1959.

A Book Of Public Prayers. New York: Harper and Brothers, 1959.

Dear Mr. Brown: Letters to a Person Perplexed About Religion. New York: Harper and Brothers, 1961.

The Life Of St. Paul. (World Landmark Book.) New York: Random House, 1962.

The Meaning of Being a Christian. New York: Association Press, 1964.

Meditations from the Manhood of the Master. New York: Association

Press, 1966.

INTRODUCTION, FOREWORD, OR PREFACE BY HARRY EMERSON FOSDICK

Fosdick was often asked to compose front matter for books on preaching, anthologies of sermons, religious topics, and so forth.

Ashworth, Robert A., ed. *Religion: Thirteen Sermons by Cornelius Woelfkin.* Garden City: Doubleday, Doran, and Company, 1928.

Brittain, Vera. *Humiliation with Honor.* New York: Fellowship Publications, 1943.

Brown, Eleanor G. *Corridors of Light.* Yellow Springs: Antioch Press, 1958.

Burton, Margaret E., ed. *Assurances of Life Eternal.* New York: Thomas Y. Crowell, 1959.

Butzer, Albert George. *You and Yourself.* New York: Harper and Brothers, 1933.

Cornell, Julian. *Conscientious Objection and the Law.* New York: John Day, 1941.

Daskam, Max F. *Sermons from an Ecumenical Pulpit.* Boston: Starr King Press, 1956.

Guhse, Herman Paul, ed. *A Book of Invocations.* New York: Fleming Revell Company, 1928.

Hinds, Arthur. *Complete Sayings of Jesus.* Philadephia: John C. Winston Company, 1942.

Hunter, Allan A. *Youth's Adventure.* New York: D. Appleton and Company, 1925.

Jackson, Edgar N. *A Pyschology of Preaching,* Great Neck: Channell Press, 1961.

Landis, Benson Y., ed. *The Walter Rauschenbusch Reader.* New York: Harper and Brothers, 1947.

Lazaron, Morris S. *Bridges not Walls.* New York: The Citadel Press, 1959.

McCauley, Leon and Elfrieda, eds. *The Book of Prayers.* New York: Crown Publishers, 1954.

McComb, Samuel. *Preaching in Theory and Practice.* New York: Oxford University Press, 1926.

Miller, Joseph Hillis. *The Practice of Public Prayer.* New York: Columbia University Press, 1934.

Morrison, Christine, ed. *Prayers for Women Workers.* New York: Doran, 1924.

Motter, Alton M., ed. *Great Preaching Today.* New York: Harper and Brothers, 1955.

_____. *Sunday Evening Sermons*. New York: Harper and Brothers, 1932.

Page, Kirby. *War, Its Causes, Consequences and Cure*. New York: George E. Doran Company, 1923.

Payne, Elizabeth. *Daughter of the Euphrates*. New York: Harper and Brothers, 1939.

Phillips, Harold Cooke. *Seeing the Invisible*. New York: Harper and Brothers, 1932.

Reventlow, Graf E. *Where is God?* London: Friends of Europe, 1937.

Rolofson, Robert H. *Christian Cooperation at the World's Crossroads*. Union Church of the Canal Zone, 1950.

Schilling, Alma. *Living Stone*. St. Louis: Bethany Press, 1936.

Sharpe, Dores Robinson. *Walter Rauschenbusch*. New York: Macmillan Company, 1942.

Sheldon, Charles M. *In His Steps*. New York: Grosset and Dunlap, 1947.

Stifler, James Madison. *The Religion of Benjamin Franklin*. New York: D. Appleton and Comapny, 1925.

Thomas, Wendell M., Jr. *Hinduism Invades America*. Boston: Beacon Press, 1930.

ARTICLES BY HARRY EMERSON FOSDICK

"America's Biggest Problem." *American Mercury*, May 1929, pp. 11-13.

"Are Religious People Fooliong Themselves." *Harper's*, June, 1930, pp. 59-70.

"Are We Fit for Democracy?" *Scribner's Commentary*, January 1941, pp. 89-92.

"Are We Part of the Problem or of the Answer?" *National Education Association Journal*, December 1947, pp. 621-22.

"Are We Producing Character?" *Delinquency*, July 1925, p. 2.

"Best Years of Our Lives." *Reader's Digest*, January 1947, pp. 117-18.

"Blessed Be Biography." *Ladies' Home Journal, April 1924, p. 18.*

"Building a Personality." Reader's Digest, May, 1937 pp. 79-81.

"Can the Church Stop War?" *World Tomorrow*, June 1931, pp. 187-88.

"Christian Ministry." *Atlantic*, January 1929, pp. 24-30.

"Christmas and the Family." *Pictorial Review*, January 1931, p. 1.

"Church and Social Revolution." *Literary Digest*, June 18, 1921, pp. 30-31.

"Civilized to Death." *Reader's Digest*, February 1938, pp. 73-75.

"Conscripts for Conquest?" *Christian Century*, August 21, 1940, p. 1030.

"Democracy Begins at Home." *Scholastic*, April 25, 1951, p. 3.

"Doctor Fosdick's Closing Prayer." *National Council*, November, 1958, p. 7.

"Does Anything Come After Death?" *American Mercury*, March 1923, pp.

5-7.

"Ethical Problems of Neutrality." *Reference Shelf* 14 (1940): 427-37.

"Evolution and Religion." *Ladies' Home Journal*, September 1925, p. 12.

"Faith for Tough Times." *Reader's Digest*, December 1952, pp. 86-88.

"First Things First." *Library Journal*, October 15, 1939, p. 780.

"God of Grace and God of Glory." *Christian Century*, May 21, 1958, p. 611.

"God, an Idea that Never Stops Growing." *Good Housekeeping*, May 1929, p. 59.

"Hope of the World in Its Minorities." *World Tomorrow*, October 1931, p. 320.

"How to Handle Retirement with Zest." *Lifetime Living Magazine*, October 1953, p. 4.

"How to Keep Out of the Psychiatrist's Hands." *Reader's Digest*, July 1947, pp. 9-13.

"I Dare You to Be a Pessimist." *Reader's Digest*, April 1962, pp. 49-52.

"If America Is Drawn Into War, Can You, as a Christian, Participate in It or Support It?: Harry Emerson Fosdick." *Christian Century*, January 22, 1941, pp. 115-18.

"If This Be Heresy." *New York Survey*, April 1, 1925, p. 29.

"If You Have a Good Excuse, Don't Use It!" *Reader's Digest*, June 1948, pp. 19-21.

"Inner Peace and How to Find It." *Reader's Digest*, July 1963, pp. 110-13.

"International Prayer Meeting." *Christian Century*, March 11, 1942, p. 319.

"Jesus's Ethical Message Confronts the World." *Reference Shelf* 13 (1939): 223-33.

"Judas, not Iscariot." *Bible World*, September 1919, p. 451-58.

"Life Without God." *Reader's Digest*, November 1961, pp. 139-41.

"Living for the Fun of It." *American Mercury*, April 1930, p. 57.

"Living for the Fun of It." *Ladies Home Journal*, November 1949, p. 192.

"Modern Child Should Guide Himself." *World's Work*, January 1929, pp. 54-58.

"Moral Laxity or Moral Law?" *Delinquency*, November 1925, p. 10.

"Morals Secede from the Union." *Harper's*, May 1932, pp. 682-92.

"My Account With the Unknown Soldier." *Christian Century*, June 6, 1934, pp. 754-56.

"Need of Modern Religious Leadership." *Ladies' Home Journal*, October 1925, p. 16.

"New Religious Reformation." *Ladies' Home Journal*, April 1926, p. 16.

"No Room in the Inn." *Reader's Digest*, December 1958, pp. 33-34.

"On Being a Real Person." *Reader's Digest*, March 1943, pp. 121-37; March, 1959, pp. 117-29.

"One Unfailing Resource." *Reader's Digest*, June 1946, pp. 51-54.

"One World for Religion Too." *Reader's Digest*, May 1946, pp. 72-74.

"Opportunity for the Churches." *Ladies' Home Journal*, October 1924, p.

16.

Pacifism Means Peace." *Review of Reviews*, May 1937, pp. 54-55.

"Personality that Christmas Celebrates." *Life*, December 24, 1945, pp. 74-76.

"Power of Faith." *American Mercury*, May 1926, pp. 18-19.

"Prince of Peace: Hymn." *Christian Century*, November 5, 1930, p. 1337.

"A Prayer." *Christian Century*, August 12, 1959, pp. 919-20.

"Prayer for Graduates." *Good Housekeeping*, June 1919, p. 19.

"Putting Christ into Uniform." *Christian Century*, November 12, 1939, pp. 1539-42.

"Religion and Birth Control." *Outlook*, June 19, 1929, p. 301.

"Religion without God." *Harper's*, December 1929, pp. 50-60.

"Religion's Debt to Science." *Good Housekeeping*, March 1928, p. 21.

"Revolt Against Paganism." *Ladies' Home Journal*, February 1946, p. 6.

"Second Mile." *Reader's Digest*, March 1944, pp. 63-64.

"Shall American School Children Be Religious Illiterate?" *School and Society*, November 29, 1947, pp. 401-06.

"Shall We Be Mad?" *Nation*, November 9, 1921, pp. 523-24.

"Should Legal Barriers Against Birth Control Be Removed?" *Congressional Digest*, April 1931, pp. 110-12.

"Should Your Child Be Allowed to Choose His Own Religion?" *Reader's Digest*, May 1947, pp. 59-62.

"Stay Neutral, Says Fosdick." *New York Times*, September 5, 1939, p. 14.

"A Step Toward Fascism." *Parent's Magazine*, November 1944, p. 17.

"Teaching Your Child Religion." *World's Work*, February 1929, pp. 52-56.

"Time for Great Faiths." *Ladies' Home Journal*, October 1947, p. 42.

"Tomorrow's Religion." *United Nations World*, December 1951, pp. 40-43.

"Trenches and the Church at Home." *Atlantic*, January 1919, pp. 22-23.

"Union and Liberty in the Churches." *Outlook*, November 13, 1929, p. 423.

"Vitality is Mightier than Size." *Ladies' Home Journal*, December 1950, p. 11.

"Wages of Hate." *American Mercury*, May 1928, pp. 16-17.

"War Against Unemployment." *American City*, December 1930, p. 153.

"What Are We Standing For?" *Delinquency*, February 1926, p. 2.

"What Christian Liberals Are Driving At." *Ladies' Home Journal*, January 1925, p. 18.

"What Do You Say to Yourself?" *American Mercury*, October 1929, p. 35.

"What Force Is Stronger than the Atomic Bomb?" *Ladies' Home Journal*, April 1946, p. 48.

"What Great Britain Thinks About War." *Ladies' Home Journal*, December 1924, p. 30.

"What Is Christianity?" *Harper's*, April 1929, pp. 551-61.

"What Is Happening to the American Family?" *American Mercury*,

October 1928, pp. 20-21.
"What Is the Matter with Preaching?" *Harper's*, July 1928, pp. 133-41.
"What is Religion?" *Harper's*, March 1929, pp. 424-34.
"Whose God is Dead?" *Reader's Digest*, October 1966, pp. 67-71.
"Why Religion Helps Mess Up the World." *Ladies' Home Journal*, April 1947, p. 40.
"The Years of Adventure." *Guideposts*, November 1959, pp. 2-4.
"Yes, But Religion is an Art!" *Harper's*, January 1931, pp. 129-40.
"You Own the Most Neglected Piece of Real Estate in the World." *American Mercury*, January 1924, pp. 32-33.
"You're More Important than You Think." *Ladies' Home Journal*, March 1946, p. 45.
"What Is the Matter with Preaching?" *Harper's*, July 1928, pp. 133-41.
"What the War Did to My Mind." *Christian Century*, January 5, 1928, pp. 10-11.

BOOKS AND MAJOR ESSAYS ABOUT FOSDICK

Brack, Harold. "Neo-Orthodoxy and the American Pulpit." In *Sermons in American History*. Edited by DeWitte Holland. Nashville: Abingdon Press, 1971.

Clark, Robert D. "Harry Emerson Fosdick." In *History and Criticism of American Public Address*. Edited by Marie Kathryn Hochmuth. New York: Russell and Russell, 1955.

Coffin, Henry Sloane. *A Half Century of Union Theological Seminary: An Informal History*. New York: Charles Scribners, 1954.

Crocker, Lionel. *Harry Emerson Fosdick's Art of Preaching: An Anthology*. Springfield, Ill.: Charles C. Thomas, 1971.

Exman, Eugene. "Fosdick as Author." *Christian Century*, May 21, 1958, pp. 617-19.

Fosdick, Harry Emerson. *The Living of These Days: An Autobiography*. New York: Harper and Brothers, 1956.

Furniss, Norman F. *The Fundamentalist Controversy, 1918-1931*. New Haven: Yale University Press, 1954.

Hudnut, William H., Jr. "Fosdick as Teacher." *Christian Century*, May 21, 1958, pp. 615-16.

Hutchison, William R. *Errand to the World: American Protestant Thought and Foreign Missions*. Chicago: University of Chicago Press, 1987.

_____. *The Modernist Impulse in American Protestantism*. Cambridge: Harvard University Press, 1986.

Linn, Edmund Holt. *Preaching as Counseling*. Valley Forge: The Judson Press, 1966.

MacVaugh, Gilbert Stillman. "Structural Analysis of the Sermons of Dr. Harry Emerson Fosdick." *Quarterly Journal of Speech* 18 (1932):

531-46.

Marsden, George. *Reforming Fundamentalism: Fuller Seminary and the New Evangelicanism*. Grand Rapids: William B. Eerdmans Publishing Company, 1987.

Marsden, George M. *Fundamentalism and American Culture*. New York: Oxford University Press, 1980.

McCall, Roy C. "Harry Emerson Fosdick: A Study in Sources of Effectiveness." In *American Public Address: Studies in Honor of A. Craig Baird*. Edited by Loren Reid. Columbia: University of Missouri Press, 1961.

Miller, Robert Moats. *American Protestantism and Social Issues 1919-1939*. Chapel Hill: University of North Carolina Press, 1958.

_____. *Harry Emerson Fosdick: Preacher, Pastor, Prophet*. New York: Oxford University Press, 1985.

Moody, Larry A. "A Bibliography of Works by and about Harry Emerson Fosdick." *American Baptist Quarterly* 1 (1982): 81-98; 2 (1983): 65-88

Russell, C. Allyn. *Voices of American Fundamentalism: Seven Biographical Studies*. Philadelphia: The Westminster Press, 1976.

Ryan, Halford Ross. "Harry Emerson Fosdick." In *American Orators of the Twentieth Century: Critical Studies and Sources*. Edited by Bernard K. Duffy and Halford R. Ryan. Westport: Greenwood Press, 1987.

Sager, Allan. "The Fundamentalist-Modernist Controversy, 1918-1930." In *Preaching in American History*. Edited by DeWitte Holland. Nashville: Abingdon Press, 1969.

Sandeen, Ernest R. *The Roots of Fundamentalism: British and American Millenarianism 1800-1930*. Chicago: University of Chicago Press, 1970.

ARTICLES ABOUT FOSDICK

"Anti-War Pledge Given by Fosdick." *New York Times*, May 8, 1934, p. 1.

"Ave atque Vale." *Time*, April 8, 1946, p. 66.

Ban, Joseph D. "Two Views of the Age: Fosdick and Straton." *Foundations* 14 (1971): 153-71.

"The Best Is Yet to Be." *Christian Century*, May 21, 1958, pp. 621-22.

"The 'Best' Protestant Preachers." *Literary Digest*, March 21, 1925, pp. 32-33.

"Beyond Modernism." *Christian Century*, December 4, 1935, pp. 1549-52.

Bliven, B. "Mr. Rockefeller's Pastor." *New Republic*, December 31, 1956, p. 20.

Bryan, William Jennings. "The Fosdick Case." *Presbyterian Advance*,

June 5, 1924, p. 5.

_____. "The Fundamentals." *The Forum*, July 23, 1923, pp. 1665-80.

"Can One Live Agnostically?" *Catholic World*, October 1931, pp. 98-106.

"Centennial of Worship: 10th Year in Riverside Church." *Newsweek*, February 24, 1941, pp. 66-67.

Chandler, Daniel Ross. "Harry Emerson Fosdick." *Harvard Divinity Review*, February 1979, p. 5.

_____. "Harry Emerson Fosdick: Spokesman for the Modernist Movement." *Religious Communication Today* 5 (1982): 1-4.

Clampett, Dr. Frederick W. "Radio Changes Style of Oratory." San Francisco *Examiner*, September 12, 1927.

"Clergymen Score U.S. Aid to Diem." *New York Times*, August 15, 1963, p. 3.

Crocker, Lionel. "The Rhetorical Theory of Harry Emerson Fosdick." *Quarterly Journal of Speech* 22 (1936): 207-13.

"Crowd Turned Away at Riverside Church." *New York Times*, October 6, 1930, p. 11.

Diffenbach, A. C. "Lost Leaders of Protestantism." *Independent*, September 17, 1927, pp. 270-71.

"Dr. Fosdick Accepts the Challenge." *Christian Century*, October 15, 1930, pp. 1239-41.

"Dr. Fosdick Attacked by Conservative Presbyterians." *Current Opinion*, January 1923, pp. 85-86.

"Dr. Fosdick and the 'Auburn' Affirmation." *Presbyterian*, May 8, 1924, p. 20.

"Dr. Fosdick at Eighty." *Newsweek*, May 5, 1958, p. 76.

"Dr. Fosdick at Geneva." *Review of REviews*, November, 1925, p. 538.

"Dr. Fosdick Opposes Haste in Draft Bill; Radio Talk Suggest Alternative Plans." *New York Times*, August 8, 1940, p. 2.

"Dr. Fosdick Shifts the Emphasis." *Christian Century*, November 20, 1935, pp. 1480-82.

"Dr. Fosdick Will Retire Next May." *Christian Century*, June 20, 1945, p. 725.

"Dr. Fosdick's Farewell." *New Republic*, March 18, 1925, p. 91.

"Dr. Fosdick's Hail and Farewell." *Literary Digest*, March 21, 1925, pp. 31-32.

"Dr. Fosdick's New Church." *World's Work*, July 1929, pp. 56-58.

"Dr. Fosdick's New Kind of Church." *Literary Digest*, June 20, 1925, pp. 33-34.

"Dr. Fosdick's Refusal to be a Presbyterian." *Literary Digest*, October 25, 1924, pp. 32-33.

"Dr. Fosdick's Religion." *Outlook*, March 11, 1925, p. 364.

"Dr. Fosdick's Resignation." *Outlook*, October 15, 1924, p. 235.

"Dr. Fosdick's Sermon." *Christian Century*, December 4, 1935, pp. 1539-40.

"Dr. Woelfkin Hails Fosdick as Prophet." *New York Times*, September 21,

1925, p. 22.

"Driving Out the Fundamentals." *Christianity Today*, November 21, 1969, p. 16.

Dugan, George. "Fosdick, 80 Today, Is Still Writing." *New York Times*, May 24, 1958, p. 14.

Duffield, Howard. Letter to the Editor. *Presbyterian*, April 2, 1925, p. 20.

Editorial. *Christian Work*, January 20, 1923, p. 74.

Editorial. *Contintent*, November 30, 1922, p. 1518.

Editorial. *Nation*, November 1, 1922, p. 452.

Ferm, Deane William. "Living of These Days: A Tribute to Harry Emerson Fosdick." *Christian Century*, May 3, 1978, pp. 472-74.

"Fight on Pacifism Asked." *New York Times*, May 8, 1934, p. 7.

"For Finland." *Time*, December 25, 1939, p. 25.

"Fosdick and the Philadelphia Presbyterians." *Christian Work*, May 19, 1923, p. 614.

"Fosdick at Seventy-five, Still a Rebel." *New York Times Magazine*, May 24, 1953, pp. 14ff.

"Fosdick Forsees Pacifist Martyrs." *New York Times*, May 21, 1934, p. 13.

"Fosdick Summons Church to End War in Geneva Session." *New York Times*, September 14, 1925, pp. 1, 4.

"Fosdick Versus the Fundamentalists." *Current Opinion*, December 1924, p. 756-57.

"Fosdick's Challenge for Peace." *Literary Digest*, October 3, 1925, pp. 31-32.

"Fosdick's Last Year." *Time*, June 18, 1945, p. 56.

Gordon, James Craig. "One Heaven of a Fellow." *Coronet Magazine*, December 1947, pp. 35-41.

"Great Crowd Hears Dr. Fosdick Preach." *New York Times*, January 14, 1924, p. 14.

"Harry Emerson Fosdick." *Christian Century*, June 6, 1934, pp. 746-47.

"Harry Emerson Fosdick." *Christian Century*, May 21, 1958, pp. 611-12.

"Harry Emerson Fosdick." *Christianity Today*, October 24, 1969, p. 31.

Hawley, L. J. "I Was a Stranger." *Pictorial Review*, September 1932, p. 4.

Hill, Edward Yates. "Why They Protested." *The Continent*, November 2, 1922, p. 4.

Hodges, Graham. "Fosdick at 90." *Christian Century*, May 22, 1968, p. 684.

"Honor to Dr. Fosdick." *Christian Century*, May 20, 1953, p. 595.

"Hymns for 8,000,000." *Time*, October 14, 1935, p. 32.

"In Calvin's Stead." *New York Times*, September 15, 1925, p. 24.

"Inside Story: Preacher and Church." *Christian Century*, November 7, 1956, pp. 1294-95.

"Law and Order in the Church." *New Republic*, October 29, 1924, pp. 215-16.

"The Liberal." *Time*, May 25, 1953, pp. 62-64.

MacVaugh, Gilbert Stillman. "Structural Analysis of the Sermons of Harry Emerson Fosdick." *Quarterly Journal of Speech* 18 (1932): 531-46.

McAfee, Cleland. "The Presbyterian Church Facing the Future." *Christian Century*, November 9, 1922, pp. 1385-88.

McCall, Roy C. "Harry Emerson Fosdick: Paragon and Paradox." *Quarterly Journal of Speech* 39 (1953): 283-90.

McKinney, William W. "The Center of the Controversy." *Presbyterian*, June 12, 1924, p. 6.

McLaughlin, Raymond W. "Intentional-Extensional Language as a Measure of Semantic Orientation." *Bulletin of Evangelical Theological Society*, 10 (1967): 145-51.

Merrill, William Pierson. "Protestantism at the Crossroads." *Christian Century*, February 1924, p. 423.

Mingos, H. "Fosdick, Liberal Preacher." *World's Work*, October, 1925, pp. 645-53.

"Modernism in Confusion." *New Republic*, September 1, 1926, pp. 33-34.

"Mr. Fosdick and the Presbyterians." *Nation*, October 22, 1924, p. 433.

"My Account with the Unknown Soldier." *Christian Century*, June 6, 1934, pp. 754-56.

Neibuhr, Reinhold. "Fosdick: Theologian and Preacher." *Christian Century*, June 3, 1953, pp. 657-58.

Newton, Joseph Fort. "The New Preaching." *Christian Century*, December 21, 1922, p. 1590.

"New York Presbytery Before the Assembly." *Presbyterian*, May 14, 1925, p. 5.

"New York's Riverside." *Christian Century*, November 28, 1951, p. 1371.

"Non-Sectarian Christian." *Independent*, October 18, 1924, p. 270.

Obituary. *Christian Century*, October 15, 1969, p. 1306; *Time*, October 17, 1969, p. 90.

"Olive Branch for Fosdick." *Literary Digest*, June 21, 1924, p. 33.

"Open Shop Parson." *Time*, March 15, 1943, p. 54.

"Opportunity for the Churches." *Ladies' Home Journal*, October, 1924, p. 16.

Osborn, Ronald E. "In the Fight to Set Men Free: Harry Emerson Fosdick (1878-1969)." *Encounter* 31 (1970): 177-81.

Phillips, Robert A., Jr. "Fosdick and the People's Concerns." *Foundations* 13 (1970): 262-76.

Portrait. *Literary Digest*, May 26, 1934, p. 20.

Portrait. *Review of Reviews*, February, 1929, p. 132.

Portrait. *Saturday Review of Literature*, January 21, 1952. p.

"The Presbyterian Attack on Dr. Fosdick." *Literary Digest*, November 18, 1922, p. 36-37.

Reiland, Karl. "The Gist of Modernism." *Religious Weekly Review*, February 9, 1924, p. 180.

"Respectable Heretic." *Outlook*, October 9, 1929, pp. 208-10.
"Riverside Church." *Time*, October 6, 1930, pp. 70-72.
Sihlhide, G. E. "The Presbytery of New York Not All Untrue to the Standards of Our Church." *Presbyterian*, April 3, 1924, p. 8.
Sleeth, Ronald E. "What Is the Matter with Preaching? A Fosdick Retrospective." *Perkins School of Theology Journal* 32 (Summer 1979): 28-30.
Skinner, S. K. "Master Preacher." *Christian Century*, June 6, 1956, p. 695.
"Stay Neutral, Says Fosdick." *New York Times*, September 5, 1939, p. 14.
Sweet, Leonard I. "Liberalism's Lost Days: A Re-evaluation of Fosdick." *Christian Century*, December 18, 1985, pp. 1176-79.
"This Liberal Christian." *Newsweek*, October 8, 1956, p. 60.
Toohey, William and William D. Thompson, eds. *Recent Homiletical Thought: A Bibliography, 1935-1965*. Nashville: Abingdon Press, 1967.
"Two Men and Two Churches." *Newsweek*, April 8, 1946, pp. 76-77.
"Unforgetable Harry Emerson Fosdick." *Reader's Digest*, January 1971, pp. 69-73.
Villard, Oswald Garrison. "Dr. Fosdick Renounces War." *Nation*, May 23, 1934, p. 581.
Warlick, Harold C. "Fosdick's Preaching Method." *Religion in Life* 41 (1972): 509-23.
"What 20,000 Clergymen Think." *Nation*, May 9, 1934, p. 524.
"What Can the Minister Do?" *Review of Reviews*, December 1932, p. 15.
"What Price the Baptist Cathedral." *Literary Digest*, November 1, 1930, pp. 20-21.
Woolf, S. J. "A Religion to Fit the Life of Today." *New York Times Magazine*, October 5, 1930, p. 5.

DISSERTATIONS ABOUT FOSDICK

Bonney, Katharine Alice. "Harry Emerson Fosdick's Doctrine of Man." Ph.D. dissertation, Boston University, 1958.
Bowyer, Ralph A., III. "Interrelatedness of Pastoral Counseling and Preaching with Special Emphasis upon the Ministries of the Reverend Dr. Harry Emerson Fosdick and the Reverend Dr. Leslie Dixon Weatherhead." Ph.D. dissertation, Temple University, 1960.
Brees, Paul. "A Comparative Study of the Devices of Persuasion Used in Ten Sermons by Harry Emerson Fosdick and Eight Sermons by William Ashley Sunday." Ph.D. dissertation, University of Southern California, 1948.
Brister, C. W. "The Ethical Thought of Harry Emerson Fosdick--A Critical Interpretation." Ph.D. dissertation, Southwestern Baptist

Theological Seminary, 1957.

Burtner, Elmer Edwin. "The Use of Biblical Materials in the Sermons of Harry Emerson Fosdick." Th.D. dissertation, Boston University, 1959.

Clemons, Hardy. "The Key Theological Ideas of Harry Emerson Fosdick." Ph.D. dissertation, Southwestern Baptist Theological Seminary, 1966.

Hall, Joseph Calvin. "Basic Theological and Ethical Concepts of Harry Emerson Fosdick." Ph.D. dissertation, The Southern Baptist Theological Seminary, 1958.

Harbour, Brian Lee. "The Christology of Harry Emerson Fosdick." Ph.D. dissertation, Baylor University, 1973.

Landry, Fabaus. "The Preaching of Harry Emerson Fosdick: An Analysis of It's Intent, Style, and Language." D. Div. dissertation, Vanderbilt University Divinity School, 1972.

Lawson, Douglas Miller. "The Idea of Progress in the Theology of Harry Emerson Fosdick." Ph.D. dissertation, Duke University, 1963.

Leininger, Charles Earl. "The Christian Apologetic of Harry Emerson Fosdick." Th.D. dissertation, The Southern Baptist Theological Seminary, 1967.

Linn, Edmund Holt. "The Rhetorical Theory and Practice of Harry Emerson Fosdick." Ph.D. dissertation, The University of Iowa, 1952.

McDiarmid, Allan B. "A Critique of Harry Emerson Fosdick's Concept of Preaching as Personal Counseling on a Group Scale." Ph.D. dissertation, Pacific School of Religion, 1961.

McLaughlin, Raymond William. "A Comparison of the Language Structures of the Sermons of Harry Emerson Fosdick and Oral Roberts to Determine Their Intensional-Extensional Orientation." Ph.D. dissertation, University of Denver, 1959.

Miller, Philip V. "Fosdick and Scherer: Their Sermons Judged by Their Theories and the Speeches in the Acts of the Apostles." D. of Min. dissertation, Southern Methodist University, 1974.

Moody, Larry Alan. "The Anthropology of Harry Emerson Fosdick: Becoming a Real Person." Ph.D. dissertation, Aquinas Institute of Theology, 1980.

Ross, Calvin Wayne. "Homecoming as a Metaphor for Understanding the Preaching of Harry Emerson Fosdick." Ph.D. dissertation, Southern Baptist Theological Seminary, 1986.

Scruggs, Julius Richard. "A Comparative Study of the Social Consciousness of Harry Emerson Fosdick and Martin Luther King, Jr." D. Min. dissertation, Vanderbilt University Divinity School, 1975.

Shelton, Robert McElroy. "The Relationship Between Reason and Revelation in the Preaching of Harry Emerson Fosdick." Th.D. dissertation, Princeton Theological Seminary, 1965.

Spear, Ted C. "A Comparative and Critical Analysis of the Preaching of Harry Emerson Fosdick and Clarence Edward Macartney on the Issue of War and Peace." Ph.D. dissertation, Southwestern Baptist Theological Seminary, 1987.

Weaver, Samuel Robert. "The Theology and Times of Harry Emerson Fosdick." Th.D. dissertation, Princeton Theological Seminary, 1961.

Index

ABOUT THE AUTHOR

Halford R. Ryan is professor of public speaking and director of forensics at Washington and Lee University, Lexington, Virginia. He received the B.A. in 1966 from Wabash College; attended Princeton Theological Seminary on a Rockefeller Theological Fellowship, 1966-67; and received the M.A. in 1968 and the Ph.D. in 1972 from the University of Illinois.

He is the author of *Persuasive Advocacy: Cases for Argumentation and Debate* and *Franklin D. Roosevelt's Rhetorical Presidency*; editor and contributor for *American Rhetoric from Roosevelt to Reagan* and *Oratorical Encounters: Selected Studies and Sources in Twentieth-Century Political Accusations and Apologies*; and co-editor, with Bernard K. Duffy, of *American Orators Before 1900: Critical Studies and Sources* and *American Orators of the Twentieth Century: Critical Studies and Sources*. He is presently at work on a book about the Reverend Henry Ward Beecher.

Great American Orators

Defender of the Union: The Oratory of Daniel Webster
Craig R. Smith

Eugene Talmadge: Rhetoric and Response
Calvin McLeod Logue